MW01067567

A HALO FO... ... .
The Life of Ernie Davis
The Elmira Express
#44

One Hero Who Didn't Disappoint Us
First Black to Win the Heisman Trophy

Adapted from book written and copyrighted
by K. Coralee Burch 1982
and film script written and copyrighted
by K. Coralee Burch 1988 and 1990

by K. Coralee Burch, Ph. D.
Copyright September 10, 2008

"A Halo for a Helmet: The Complete Story of Ernie Davis"

www.erniedavis.info

Please check our website for more information about Ernie, photographs, stories and comments of readers and friends, reviews and information about educational use of this book, along with book club and classroom related questions.

Also find information there about buying additional copies of this book, buying signed copies from author and about the parallels to President Obama's story of road to the 44th presidency.
"The Legacy of # 44".

This book is dedicated to my three husbands, who through the years encouraged me, put up with the time and expense of this endeavor and enabled me to follow my lifelong commitment to this story so that it can be of encouragement to young people of today and tomorrow.

Ernesto Michelucci

David E. Hannie

Jonathan G Adams

In addition, a special thanks to **John Brown**, who never gave up on my long lasting endeavor and continued to encourage me through the years.

4

What a great book! You have truly captured the Ernie Davis Era. Toward the ending I could not put the manuscript down. Coralee, you have done a tremendous, thoughtful, accurate writing of an American Icon. I just want people to know that Ernie Davis was a gentle man who was a gentleman.

John Brown, S.U. 1962

Cleveland Browns

Pittsburgh Steelers

5

January 20, 2009, Special Inaugural Dedication to 44th President Barack Obama

It was a surprise to realize that Barack Obama would be the 44th President of the United States. Already to many of us who knew Ernie Davis and his story, the number 44 was special, often referred to as the Legacy of 44. 44 is the number that Ernie Davis wore at Syracuse University, previously made famous by Jim Brown. At the end of Ernie Davis' career it meant something even more significant; it identified, a young man who had shown all the qualities of a true hero who did not disappoint us and overcame incredible obstacles, mostly relating to race, in order to break open acceptance for African Americans as full fledged athletes in college and national football. Now it is more common than not to see an African American win the Heisman Trophy.

The legacy of this number, however, is much more significant than breaking down a racial barrier. It is about winning against difficult odds with an integrity of a level rarely observed before or since.

Let me note here that we have not yet observed the entire career of our new President, but I would still like to indicate the most apparent similarities.

- Ernie treated everyone of every race with the same love and sensitivity. Barack has shown equal concern for diverse race, culture, religion, and gender.

- Ernie was a tough and unconquerable fighter, against tremendous odds. Barack surprised us all by coming almost out of nowhere and forging an amazing battle for the Presidency.

- In spite of his toughness as a competitor, Ernie was the gentlest and kindest of men, showing his compassion for all around him, even when they appeared not to deserve it. Barack is a soft spoken thoughtful gentleman under extremely tense situations; unflappable and congenial under pressure and when attacked.

- Ernie understood the value of teamwork and the importance of every player's role in the outcome of the game. Barack has put together a team of players who will not just put a rubber stamp on his ideas, and he is expected to request and listen to their diverse points of view.

- Ernie was not afraid of any opponent, nor is Barack, so much so that he invited many of them into his inner circle.

For these reasons, I dedicate this book to our new President Barack Obama in hopes that he retains his fine character and continues the legacy of 44 in its greatest tradition. I hope he will read the story of Ernie and perceive that his most outstanding quality, as identified by all who knew him well, was his humility. The lack of that is probably what has caused the most errors in any Presidency. Confidence, courage, strength and compassion are not counter to humility.

*In October 2008 Universal Pictures and Davis Entertainment released "The Express," a film about Ernie Davis, mostly set during his time at Syracuse University during which he was the first African American to win the Heisman Trophy. Ernie lived an exemplary life and died an extremely premature death from acute leukemia. This book tells the rest of the story as the entire and complete biography of Ernie Davis, approved by Marie Fleming, his mother. It tracks his life from early childhood to the moment of his last breath. It is the story about the lives, influences and character that went into making a superstar who was the best at sports and the best at life itself. It is a heart warming yet heartbreaking story about **a hero who didn't disappoint us**.*

Ernie wore #44 through his college football career a Syracuse University, a number that has become a legend.

Author's personal notes:

We were terribly proud of our high school, EFA, Elmira Free Academy. We knew from the beginning we were really special, but it was Ernie Davis who brought it home to us. I was of the class of 1960 and Ernie was of the class of 1958. His was the only class that didn't have a Burch in it the year I was a freshman. My sisters and I always attracted a crowd that year, three girls in high school all together, freshman, sophomore and senior. The boys (and girls) knew they could come to our house and always find a welcome, not just from us, but from our Mom and Dad who had brought us up with as much love and as little prejudice as was possible in that post World War II era. My older sister and brother were both married with children at the time.

My sophomore year I made cheerleader, one of the few sports available to girls. That was the year that Ernie led EFA to the regional basketball championship. When I went to practice in our small school gymnasium, Ernie was always there, before all the others, shooting baskets. He would call me over and teach me to shoot baskets. There was no one in that school or that city who did not believe that Ernie was their special friend just as I had. And it was this quality about Ernie, not the fact that he was one of the greatest athletes to live, nor the fact that he was the first Black to win the Heisman Trophy, nor the sad fact that he died shortly afterward of acute leukemia, that he remained in the hearts and minds of all who had experienced that one moment of contact with him. That moment left a burning vibrant impression, bringing tears to their eyes 15 years after his death in 1963.

I was at Syracuse University the year Ernie died. He drove by in his Thunderbird, given to him by Elmira well wishers. I waved at him, just another admiring young woman. He pulled the car over, got out, came over and shook hands asking about my family. Ernie, who barely knew me, had taken his time and made a special effort to speak with me. Ernie was sick then, his cheeks and neck were swollen. My Dad, the local radiologist, had told me why. Ernie did not live long after that.

It was in the late 1970s that I decided to be his biographer. In that year I began a lifelong endeavor of research and interviews to try to sort out why this young African American man, with the perfect body, who died too young, left such an impact on White and Black alike as to change their lives. I can give you quotes from dozens of well known people who acknowledge Ernie's impact on their lives. Some say that they kept a picture of Ernie in their desk drawer or on their wall and... when they got confused or frustrated, looked to it for guidance, thinking of Ernie and what he would have done. Yes, hard to believe, but that is what guided me to this costly and exhausting endeavor.

Now, more than 35 years since that day, the book is published. It first took the form of a book, then a film treatment, then a complete film script and now I have blended it all into a book saying what needs to be said about a life that should go on impacting other lives, just as it did when he was living. Ernie's mother gave me full rights for film and book in 1982, so that his story would be told. The movie, "The Express," has set the ball rolling; now his full and complete story is available in this book, "A Halo for a Helmet." It is not in the form of a documentary but a very enticing and entertaining story of a young man who turned even the staunchest adversary into a friend and admirer. The book is taken from hundreds of interviews of those who lived this story with Ernie. The basic facts are absolutely accurate, but the dialog, although often taken directly from an interview, may be somewhat elaborated on for smoothness and clarity. The film created by a different group is primarily based on his college football career. It is a fine entertaining Hollywood film. I applaud the work and talent that went into this production. I must clarify, however, that the details and characters of the individuals portrayed in the movie have been somewhat embellished and altered to fit their storyline and concept. That is why, if you love the story of Ernie, it is equally important to read the book that tells more of his gentle and loving spirit. For better or for worse Ernie never wanted to hurt anyone's feelings. This book covers the entire life of Ernie and the true spirit of him, so those interested can understand even more about that period, the racism and the ability of a modest and sensitive young man to impact so many livs in such a short time, turning around attitudes in minutes that might normally have required lifetimes.

For this book, I interviewed coaches, friends, co-players, physicians, lawyers, and family members extensively about Ernie, his life and that period of racial and sports history. I sat for hours in private interviews with the famous Ben Schwartzwalder, coach at Syracuse University, enjoying his personal commentary, watching him put plays on the blackboard to illustrate what he was trying to do with Ernie and the winning team, viewing with him films of Ernie playing football, seeing various plays he drew for me on the blackboard, including his famous scissors play developed specifically for Ernie. Then he shared with me his most personal stories and his tears at the loss of his friend and famous athlete. The name of the book, "A Halo for a Helmet" came directly from Ben Schwartzwalder who through his tears said that now Ernie wears a "halo for a helmet." Many of the coaches and many of Ernie's friends and companions are gone now, but they were able to document every detail of his story through our interviews and now, finally in this book.

The Ernie Davis story goes way beyond that of "Brian's Song". It should stand also at the top of significant racial firsts in the media, such as "Ragtime" set in the 20s, then "A Soldier's Story" set in the 40s. Now there are "The Express" (the movie) and "A Halo for a Helmet" (the book) set in the North in the 60s. This was one of the most important times in our racial history. Most of all, this is a book about a Superhero who didn't disappoint us.

Special note: In faithfulness to the story and the period in which it took place, the author asks for understanding in the use of politically incorrect language. Since race issues are an intrinsic part of Ernie's story, I often use black and white to determine racial differences, along with African American in the story. In addition, other terminology, including "Members," "Negroes," "Niggers" and "Colored people" are used as necessary for understanding the time, mood or attitude. This story is told in the language of the many people interviewed over a period of 35 years and is set in the time in which the author shared those people and with Ernie Davis.

This book is a life told in the form of a story. It is the author's intent to be as faithful to the actual people, circumstances, incidents and conversations as possible. For accuracy and smoothness, readability and understanding many conversations are created from hearsay and interviews involving many different individuals' memories. I apologize for the creative license used without which no biographical story would be possible, but I assure the reader that the accuracy in this lovely tale of a beautiful and heroic life is of the highest level.

Prologue

1962 Cleveland Stadium, Nighttime

It was between games during the first double header ever to be played in NFL. The lights flickered at the Cleveland Stadium while the 80,000 person crowd became noisier than ever, fighting for bathrooms and food and drinks. Within a few minutes however they began to return to their seats and settle in, thinking that between the games there would surely be a fabulous show.

All the tickets had been sold out and so people squeezed in together in excellent spirits awaiting the show. As the lights now began to dim, a hush of anticipation came over the crowd. But the lights did not stop at a low level, they went to total darkness. First there was a hush of surprise, then low noises of wonder, as confusion and excitement began to emerge. Suddenly the stadium went silent as the crowd focused on distinguishing what was happening. In the dark of the night two figures appeared out of nowhere walking on to the playing field. They walked slowly, but decisively to the very center of the field. The hush was almost noisy in its silence as one of the figures left the other one there and walked back off the field.

The lights began to shine again, very slowly starting with dim. And as one at a time they reached viewable intensity, the crowd began to whisper in awe. "Ernie", "it's Ernie Davis", "what's Ernie doing down there?". Then the word passed on down the row, now only one word... "Ernie" growing in volume, "Ernie" the discovery had become universal and no one needed to ask, "who is Ernie?". The volume increased to a repetitive beat, "Ernie, Ernie, Ernie"... louder and louder; and as it finally became a roar, the crowd, almost as one, rose in their seats, shouting his name and applauding: "ERNIE DAVIS" .

And then just slightly above the clamor came the music. First the cheerleaders appeared at one end of the stadium, then the majorettes, throwing their batons in the air, leading the marching band down the field toward Ernie. The fans settled back into their seats to enjoy the performance with all its formations, stretching a bit to be sure they could still see Ernie. The music rose in volume to the top seats in the stadium.

Art Modell arrived in the center of the field beside Ernie just as the first batons were thrown in front of him. Into the microphone Modell raised his voice above the din.

"You are experiencing a historic moment in the NFL today. This is the first double header ever to be played. And it is only right that an immense moment like this in pro ball should be dedicated to Ernie Davis, who shows the courage every athlete should nurture and who still displays the dedication to excellence in a sport that is played by the finest of men. I can speak for myself when I say that I personally admire Ernie Davis and strive to be like him in attitude and dedication to my every endeavor." Ernie, dressed in spiffy suit and tie, who had sat on the bench through the first game; once in a while jumping up and running to the coach or to the other players, cheering them on, giving them advice and giving them support; bowed his head as tears seeped from his usually shining brave eyes. He was unable to control the immense emotion he was feeling.

Ernie returned to the bench and pretended that nothing had happened. Low voices whispered in a subdued, but intense massive murmur…

"I heard he can't play."

"I heard he's been practicing anyway."

"They say he's better than ever."

"Brown won't play him…. A darn shame."

"My buddy says that Modell and Brown fought over it."

"Ernie'll be all right, won't he?"

"I'll never forget this night."

And they never did.

Chapter 1

"Every persecuted individual and race should get consolation out of the great human law, which is universal and eternal, that merit, no matter under what skin found, is in the long run recognized and rewarded."

Booker T. Washington

December 14, 1939, Footedale, PA.

In the year 1939 the great gospel singer, Marian Anderson, was denied the use of the Continental Hall in Washington, DC by the Daughters of the American Revolution. Not to be daunted, she went on to give her Easter concert before 75,000 people right outside at the Lincoln Memorial.

It was into this world that a very beautiful healthy "Negro" boy baby was born to Marie Davis, on December 14, 1939 in Footedale, a small town in the southwest part of Pennsylvania. Not too long after his birth, Ernie's father was murdered in the street. Although a tragedy, the Davis family, used to working together for each other, embraced Ernie, son of their eldest daughter, Marie, into the home as one of their own. Their youngest child, Chuck, was just barely 2 years old and shortly after there was another on the way, Walter. That made thirteen of their own and a fourteenth made little difference. Besides Ernie was immediately a lovely baby and child to have around, with a pleasant and docile disposition.

Dad moved the family to Uniontown, Pennsylvania where he took a job in the local coal mine. The town was a mix of Polish and Negro families. The Polish lived up on the hillside and the Negroes lived in the valley. Although they all worked together in the mines, the two groups didn't associate much, except for attending the same school and occasional forays down to the valley by the Polish kids for a pickup game of basketball.

The Davis family established itself in a rambling white house with a big old-fashioned porch and a yard for the children.. Across the street from the house was a housing development with no shortage of children to join the Davis kids on the street for sports and other games.

Ernie was already used to calling his grandmother and grandfather Mom and Dad like the other children and so, there was no point in clarifying to the neighborhood that Ernie was any different than the others. Marie, who was working age, couldn't find a reasonable job in the area so moved to the big city for work, but being part of a close family and having her own son there, returned frequently.

Although Ernie called his uncles and aunts sisters and brothers and didn't really pay much attention to his different status, somewhere in the back of his mind, he realized he was different. He didn't mind the special attention that only he got from Marie, who often brought him gifts, but being already shy in a big family, Ernie clung to his grandmother more than the other children. This increased as Ernie began to talk and started to develop a very severe stutter. He was more than happy to have others talk for him, especially Chuck, who loved to be the boss of Ernie and manipulate him into all kinds of antics. Ernie began to learn how to silently hold his own and so a pattern was established, of camaraderie and tricks and games.

"Com'on, Chuck," for the third time, Ernie calls Chuck. They have to clean out the basement before Dad gets home at three. He runs a tight ship and the chores have to be done by then. The girls are already in the living room dusting and cleaning. It is a constant battle to keep the coal dust in the mines and out of their lives. Elizabeth Davis (Mom) wages the war with coal dust more successfully than most and makes sure the children know what their individual tasks are. Finally Chuck arrives in the basement, just in time to stack some canned food on shelves. The girls have already finished the dusting and are in the kitchen helping Mom with the baking of the weekly bread. It is hard to feed such a large family on a coal miner's wages, but Mom is good at making most everything from scratch. One of the girls is delegated to watch little Walter, while another shoos Chuck and Ernie out into the garden to do some more weeding.

This summer has been very hot, only occasionally relieved by rain coming from the mountains. No one wants to stay in the house any longer than necessary, so now, chores finished the children empty into the street to play ball or find their friends. Five o'clock sharp Mom sticks her head out the door and everyone knows to tumble in as quickly as possible fighting for the sink to wash up and then rushing to the table before Dad gets impatient.

Ernie and Chuck get to sit closest to Mom's end of the table cause they are still little, while Walter, the baby sits on her lap. Angie, Will and others sit in order of age, with girls on one side of table and boys on the other side. The oldest are closest to Dad.

Dad starts grace and then passes to the oldest for a Bible verse. It goes right down the table in order of age. When it's Chuck's turn, as usual, he begins to falter and looks at Ernie nudging him. Ernie whispers in his ear, while the others at the table pretend not to notice. Chuck bows his head piously and speaks up as though he has been ready with it all along. Now it's Ernie's turn. "Mica 6:6" he says in a load clear voice. Angie, as usual, proud of her little adopted brother, grins at how easily he speaks. No one can get over how badly he stutters when talking and how clear he is when he recites his verse. ".. to be fair and just and merciful, and to walk humbly with your God." 'That's not easy,' he thinks with his head bowed as the last verse is said by little Walter with the coaching of Mom. 'I hope I can be that good,' Ernie is still thinking about his own verse.

Freshly baked bread and rolls are already making their way down the table, starting with Dad. Mom fains a blind eye when Ernie grabs two instead of one. She has a soft spot for this particular child, hers and not hers, so gentle yet quietly determined, growing so fast he seems to need more food than the rest,. What a very sweet boy. She loves him so much.

Now that the chicken and dumplings arrive, the table is alive with laughter and talk. Ernie, however doesn't talk very much. It is too hard to try to compete with the others in conversation, plus he's much too busy stuffing his face to talk. After all, which is more important? Chuck, on the other hand, older, but not any bigger than Ernie, sits staring at his half eaten food, already feeling full.

"You're unbelievable, Ernie. You're a bottomless pit."

Ernie just laughs and leaves Chuck at the table to worry over his plate still half full of food.

The children clean off the table quickly and race outdoors as the evening shadows lengthen and the warm breeze begins to cool things off a bit. The children from the projects across the street are already out and happy to see the very athletic Davis boys available for games. They are in great demand on the pick up teams.

As the light fads, the children hurry back home. The family always spends time on the rambling porch together before their 9PM bedtimes, watching dusk fall on the neighborhood like a thin layer of coal dust. Dad enjoys this time most, surrounded by his lovely large family, satisfied with a good meal, a lovely clean home to come too after the dark and dirty depths of the coal mine. It's a difficult life in the mines, but well worth it for a dependable income.

Chapter 2

Uniontown, PA Spring 1945

The river running through Uniontown is full to the edges and racing at high speeds. Six year old Ernie is playing too close to the raging river with Jimmy, large for his age like Ernie, and known as the local bully. Ernie hasn't paid much attention to that, since Jimmy has never really picked on him. They are throwing sticks into the river and watching in glee as it races away with them. Then unexpectedly Jimmy slips down the muddy side of the bank and tumbles down into the water. Not only is it very cold, but it is deeper than it looks and Jimmy can't get his feet under him. He grabs for some weeds at the side, but they slip through his hands and he slides further in. Jimmy struggles with the slippery mud under him, trying to stand. Instead he slips further into the river as the current picks him up and starts dragging him off. Ernie watches for a moment horrified as the screaming Jimmy is being pulled forward along the edge of the river.

"Help," they both call in unison as Ernie follows along the bank, stumbling over weeds and branches. But there is no one near to hear. Ernie runs ahead and finds a fallen tree that stretches out at the river's edge and comes to rest in the mud below. Before he thinks about what he is doing, Ernie climbs on the log and edges out over the water. Jimmy reaches the point where the tree passes over the water and reaches up trying to grasp a branch. But the current at this point picks up speed and starts to pull him under. Ernie falls flat on his stomach wrapping his legs around the trunk and stretching out his free arm. He yells for Jimmy to grab his hand. Jimmy does, almost pulling Ernie in with him, and they struggle to pull him up on the tree. He keeps slipping down, so Ernie backs up very carefully until Jimmy can get a good foothold in the shallow edge of the water and he scrambles ashore.

"Gee, Ernie," Jimmy says, between tears, "I was so scared. I thought I was going to drown. Thank you." He sputters, shivering and holding on to himself.

"It's okay," says Ernie. "You ssshould go home and dddry off. You seem so ccold."

"No I can't," answers Jimmy, grabbing onto Ernie's shirt. "My Dad'll kill me for playing near the water. Please don't tell anyone, Ernie. I mean it. My Dad'll beat me real bad."

"Nnno ppproblem," responds Ernie plopping down on a sunny strip of grass. Jimmy lies on his back feeling the warmth of the heated grass work its way through his wet shirt and his shivering begins to recede. Ernie lies back too, and they watch the clouds pass mostly in silence. Jimmy is almost dry by the time Ernie pops up and says he has to get home.

"Remember, you promised." Jimmy almost seems in tears again.

"It's okay," says Ernie. "I won't tttell."

They start up the pathway back to town, together, with a common understanding, knowing that they are bonded together in their life threatening experience. The only one Ernie tells is Chuck. Chuck admires Ernie for his bravery, but keeps his admiration to himself.

Chapter 3

Winter arrives early this year, and with Thanksgiving barely over, it is easy to fall into the preparations for Christmas. Now housework actually turns into fun.

For two or three weeks the girls work with their mother, cleaning the house for the festivities and cooking in the kitchen. Nothing is spared to make these moments special and exciting. Ice cream, never available at other times, is now permissible. All kinds of goodies are being prepared in the kitchen. The house is full of warmth, laughter and the wonderful smells of good things baking. The kitchen counter slowly fills up with apple and sweet potato pies and cakes, lots of cakes. Chuck, Ernie and Walter, as the little ones, get contraband passed on to them regularly by the sisters. The boys help make the cookies and decorate them. There are Christmas trees with green sugar and cinnamon ornaments and stars that they cover with sparkling golden sugar. The pitch of excitement rises day by day. Ernie and Chuck share a small room, while Walter still has a bed in his grandparent's room. On Christmas Eve the two go to bed but can't sleep. They talk and giggle late into the night, trying to guess what Santa will bring them making sure, however, that their whispers are so quiet they won't end up with a stocking full of coal.

Morning arrives and as soon as the sun appears over the hill, they scramble out of bed and head downstairs, followed by a house full of eager siblings. Their eyes widen as they descend the stairs and catch a glimpse of what is under the tree. There are sleds all lined up, one for each of the boys. The girls have special new scarves and mittens, while all of them have a set of new clothes for church and lots of Christmas candy. Fortunately Santa has seen to the accessories too, and the ground is laden with fresh snow to accommodate. The girls put on their new scarves and mittens and follow the boys out the door running to the nearby hill. They climb on shared sleds and slide down the white hillside until they are nearly frost-bitten.

When they regretfully return inside, they are rewarded with the warmth that tingles their toes and fingers and the delicious smells of the roasting fresh turkey that has been bought live and plucked and prepared by Mom and the girls. Sitting together around their Christmas table, they are more thankful than ever for the good things that they share together.

When dinner is done, they can barely lift themselves from the table to clear the plates away, their bodies pleasantly warmed now and lethargically saturated from the good food. Almost as soon as Dad sits down in his favorite chair to enjoy his pipe, there is a knock at the door. For the rest of the day, friends flow in, young and old, in an on-going parade. Everyone loves to congregate at the Davis home with its warmth and welcome fun.

Christmas is over and the New Year just around the corner, so Mom lines them all up in a row and gives them their dose of Castor Oil and Black Strap Molasses, to clean them out of the sugar and junk. Again in the Spring Mom will line them up for their cod liver oil. In between she faithfully follows tried and true remedies such as sassafras tea for colds and sulphur poultrice for burns. The children are rarely sick except for childhood diseases and they can't afford to go to a doctor. Elizabeth has been lucky with her fourteen children, that not one of them has ever been hospitalized or seriously ill. They haven't even needed to see a dentist.

Even though Easter is still a ways off, Ernie loves going to church on Sundays. It is his favorite day of the week. The family wakes early for a big breakfast and then dresses for church. This is the day he gets to wear his Christmas clothes so he dresses in his white shirt, tie and lovely new suit, then looks in the mirror. "Not bad," he thinks. He doesn't have many clothes, but he really likes to look his best all the time. He is growing so fast that often his daily clothes are outgrown before he can grow into the older children's clothes that they are still wearing. He has long since passed up Chuck, and left Walter behind. He is glad that his church clothes fit him so well. He loves to see the women all dressed up too. The girls wear pretty pastel organdy dresses even in the early spring days, while the older ones have on their circle skirts, ballerina shoes and dozens of crinkling petticoats that they starch and stand up on the basement floor to dry. Mom too wears light colors and always her gloves and hat.

It isn't just the Davises that look their best this Sunday. The church is a garden, long before the spring flowers have begun to brighten up the yard, everyone decked out. It is a needed change from the weekday drabness of coal sooted work clothes. The tiny redbrick Baptist church is not just a place of worship but the primary social center. Ernie who is naturally shy loves the warmth and feeling that Mom is never very far. The children run ahead to their Sunday School classes in the basement, then join their families upstairs in the sanctuary for the service. Even the service is fun. You never have to worry about falling asleep. The choir marches in wearing their matching white blouses and black skirts or pants, swaying down the aisle as they made their way up front. The singing is vibrant; the pastor is shouting his message.

As the choir settles in, the pastor speaks in his strong rich voice:

"Are you with Him?"

"We're with Him." The congregation responds.

"Are you WITH Him." Repeats the preacher. "I can't hear you."

"Yes, we're with Him." They chant louder.

"Then tell Him so...." Admonishes the preacher.

"We're with You." They shout fervently.

"That's better." Smiles the preacher.

Ernie responds with the others. He is moved by the feeling of the Spirit among them. He is moved by the music, the motion, the chanting, and the enthusiasm. He can feel his heart fill up with gladness and joy and knows that the world is good and he has a place in it. Here by Mom, he feels secure, surrounded by his large family, safe with Dad, who is strong and good. Ernie speaks up loud and clear, no sign of the stutter that usually torments him in school.

In spite of the wonderful home life and small Black community life, prejudice surrounds the Davis family. Almost everyone in Uniontown works in the coal mines. The miners themselves are mostly Black and Polish. They work together, side by side, but when they go home, they go to their separate neighborhoods.

In the schools the Black children make up only 15-20% of the population. All the children sit together and play sports together, but in the 1940's they don't socialize with each other or intermix after school, except for the occasional pickup game and then the sides are clearly drawn.

There are many restrictions about where the Blacks can go and what activities they can participate in. They attend public functions, mostly outdoors, but many indoor activities are off limits to them. In the movie theater they are allowed only in the balcony. Although the boys play sports together, the African American girls are not allowed to be cheerleaders or baton twirlers.

In some respects southern Pennsylvania isn't that different from the deep South. The Blacks can't sit at the lunch counter in Woolworths and they have to ride in the back of the buses. They can't stay at the local hotel, so they have to be put up in someone's home when they come to visit Uniontown.

The children, busy with school, sports and home obligations don't always pay attention to these slights, but internally they have a big impact on their feelings. They will never forget the humiliation of the limitations and years later the memory of it never fails to produce anger and resentment. But, as is often the case with children, they go on with their lives within the confines of these boundaries and make the best of their current environment.

Chapter 4

The Davis children take advantage of all the sports activities available to them. They not only enjoy every one of the seasonal sports, football, basketball, baseball, and Lacrosse but they excel in all of them. The older boys passing on their experience and expertise to the younger ones.

Almost as soon as Ernie can talk he has trouble with his stutter. Maybe it is the cause of his innate shyness, or perhaps a result of it. Whatever the reason, speech is so difficult for Ernie that he tries to avoid it at any cost. As a result school is painfully uncomfortable. Out on the street it is easier, because he can speak with his body. Growing stronger and quite large for his age, Ernie throws himself into sports, playing every street game there is often with kids many years older than himself. They are always happy to see Ernie come bounding out of the white house. He is an asset to any team and easy to deal with. Never starts fights or picks on the kids smaller than him. That is "almost never".

Fortunately, or maybe unfortunately Ernie has lots of help, so he doesn't have to speak often. His siblings always step in for him, especially Angie who is just old enough to be his protector.

Not yet dusk, the youngest boys are playing outside. Chuck and Walter can't help themselves; they start laughing and teasing Ernie every time he tries to speak. Angie, watching over the younger ones scolds them severely. And since family IS family, as soon as the other kids on the street arrive for games, they happily jump in with words for Ernie, speaking on his behalf.

"Ernie wants it this way." Chuck assures the others.

"Ernie wants it that way." He says with confidence, never bothering to find out what Ernie REALLY wants.

Ernie doesn't say anything right away, but it is a different story when they are headed home in the evening.

"I didn't say that!" He protests.

"Yes, but you would have if you could have talked," Chuck chides him.

He and Chuck start up to their shared room at bedtime. As they head upstairs Ernie falls back, procrastinating, ready for some retaliation for the days antics. It seems that no matter how many times he does this, Chuck always falls for it.

"Com'on," calls Chuck who is halfway up the stairs and scared to go up alone.

"I'm coming," shouts Ernie. "you go ahead. I'm right behind you."

Chuck knows better, but Ernie seems so sincere this time. As soon as Chuck is halfway down the hallway, Ernie switches the light off from below.

"Hey, turn the light on!" screams Chuck, frightened to death of the dark. Ernie is too busy rolling with laughter to get to the light switch again.

"Hey, com'on," now Chuck is begging as he stands frozen unable to move.

So Ernie gives in... turns the light back on and takes the stairs two at a time. Once in bed, Ernie laughs with Chuck about the day's escapades and is amused at Chuck's antics and how they fool others by working as a team and letting Chuck speak for him. Chuck and Walter actually depend on Ernie more and more to win friendships, battles and victories, something Ernie seems to do with great ease. Ernie reports back to Chuck all the things he has heard during the day. Because he spends more time listening then talking, other kids often forget he is there and say things they might otherwise have kept to themselves. Then the two boys plan what to do about the things the others have said about Chuck, the habitual trouble-maker. The next day, they will put it all into action.

"Cut out that noise," shouts Mom from the other room, never able to understand how they can talk so long at night when Ernie won't say a word during the day. Much of the time in these evening planning sessions, Ernie is able to talk without a stutter,

Finally in the dark, Ernie pulls out the little penlight he got for Christmas. Chuck had long ago lost his. So Ernie drags out a comic from under his pillow, pulls the covers over his head and starts reading. Then, just for the fun of it, he pulls the light out for a moment and shines it into Chuck's eyes.

"Hey," protests Chuck. "Gimme that. I'm scared."

"Here it is!" And he pretends to throw it to him.

Now Chuck is mad, but Ernie, oblivious to Chuck's complaints and begging, just returns to under the covers with his comic book.

"Hey," Chuck says, "I'll tell Mom."

Ernie shines the light in his eyes again and then retreats under the covers. He's been in this scenario before and knows just what to do.

"Mom...," Chuck screams. His Mom comes running up the stairs, afraid someone is hurt. She opens the door.

"He got the light on again. I can see it." He exclaims to his poor tired mother.

In she comes and looks around.

"What're you saying, Chuck. Don't tell stories. He's sound asleep. He doesn't have the light on." She whispers as she peers down at Ernie's angelic sleeping face.

As soon as the door shuts, the penlight comes back on under the covers. That's it! Chuck will just have to get even in the morning.

Next morning as soon as Ernie goes into the bathroom, Chuck rampages through all of Ernie's stuff looking for the penlight. Just like always... he doesn't find it. Ernie must always carry it with him, he thinks.

A nearby orchard has the most wonderful apples and as fall arrives, they turn bright red. The neighborhood kids can't resist. Just as it's getting dark they sneak into the field and Chuck climbs a nearby tree and starts shooting apples down to the other kids. Suddenly they hear a yell from the field and the farmer who has caught eye of them is quickly approaching. All the kids scatter except Ernie and Chuck, who is caught up in the tree. It is too late for him to get down.

"Don't worry," says Ernie, just stay cool and stay quiet. So Ernie stands right under the tree and puts on his most innocent look. The farmer approaches Ernie and asks him about the kids stealing his apples.

"Aw, I don't know," says Ernie, "they were just passing by, I think." Meanwhile, Chuck is beginning to slip a little, but hangs on for dear life, hoping the farmer doesn't look up.

"Well, they better leave those apples alone," he comments under his breath, "or else." Ernie nods agreement as the farmer walks off.

"Com'on down, Chuck and let's get out of here." Ernie yells. He doesn't want to wait until the farmer comes back.

"Gee thanks, Ernie. Weren't you scared?" asks Chuck.

"Naw," says Ernie, "I wasn't stealing any apples."

The weather is turning cooler and already some trees are showing a little orange, a great time for sports. Chuck and Ernie are playing basketball with the usual neighborhood kids with one exception. There is a new boy, and he's been bullying the others around. Chuck thinks he should teach him a lesson and Ernie is just the one to help him do it.

So Chuck makes a very nasty comment to the boy and gets the expected results. Within minutes they are down on the ground rolling around. The other boy, being a good deal bigger than Chuck has gotten the better of him and is soon on top of him, hitting him. Chuck is beginning to worry until he suddenly sees Ernie approaching, just in time. He waits until Ernie is within earshot and starts screaming.

"Ohhhh, he's killing me. My nose – it's broken!" Then to lend credibility to the whole thing, he bites his own lip and draws blood.

When Ernie gets close enough to see the blood on Chuck, he really believes his nose is broken. He doesn't even hesitate. He picks the boy up off of Chuck and lays him out. Chuck, watches the entire show as though it were entertainment, yelling even louder so that Ernie won't stop too soon. Finally, when Chuck has decided that the other boy has learned his lesson, he gets up.

"Okay, Ernie, that's enough. Let's go home."

Ernie picks up the other kid and tells him he is sorry, but he should leave Chuck alone. The kid walks off, nodding his head… not even sure what happened back there, but knowing he doesn't want to mess with the Davis kids again.

Chuck gets up, wipes himself off, and can't help grinning. Ernie has an idea that something not quite right just went down, and is pretty sure Chuck's nose is just fine. When they get home, they try to sneak into the bathroom to wash up, but one of the girls is in there, just taking her time and Mom catches them waiting there.

"What happened to you?" she wants to know.

"Awwww nothing." They both mutter.

"Now you tell me the truth, you two, have you been tangling again with those white kids? You know better than that. You could get into big trouble that way."

"This big kid was hitting me and Ernie wouldn't even come and help me right away. But finally he knocked him down."

"Ernie," says Mom, sternly. "You know that you boys should always stick up for each other." But Mom suspects that Chuck has more to do with this story than is obvious.

Tonight, though, Ernie is in high spirits, because while Chuck is planning revenge on some guys that have been bad-mouthing him, Ernie is planning his revenge on Chuck for todays deception.

In the morning the boys are in a hurry to get dressed. Mom is already calling them to breakfast. As usual, Chuck can't find his shoes. He prefers to go barefoot in the house, so his shoes are often lying around somewhere where he last took them off. Ernie calmly dresses as usual and starts down to breakfast.

"I'll be late for school," Chuck whines, "com'on and help me look for my shoes," as he gets down on his hands and knees, looking under the dresser and bed. Ernie sits back on the bed, in a very serious and helpful pose.

"Have you looked in the closet?"

"Why would I put them in the closet?" counters Chuck, in frustration.

"Look under the bed again, maybe you didn't look right before."

Chuck starts screaming and yelling now. "Where are my shoes?"

Mom calls up, "Com'on down you boys, it's late and breakfast is getting cold."

"Maybe you didn't bring them home yesterday. Did they fall off during your fight. Maybe the other guy took them home with him." Now Ernie is sitting there laughing and laughing. Finally the shoes appear just in time, and Chuck with murder in his eyes follows Ernie downstairs to breakfast.

After school the boys all stop at a friend's house where a group are gathering. Just as they are about to go home for dinner, one of the boys starts complaining that his coat is missing.

"I know I hung it up over there," he complains. "Who took it?" Immediately all eyes turn to Chuck.

"Hey! I didn't do it. Whatcha looking at me for. I wasn't even near the hook." Chuck protests, but even though he has already guessed who the culprit is, he never gives away Ernie. It is a pact of commitment more important than the pain of taking the blame for each other.

Ernie is sitting on the couch, having much too good a time over Chuck's predicament and one of the other boys notices him laughing.

"Hey, Ernie, you didn't hide it did you?"

The other boys scoff at that. Everyone knows that it is Chuck that is the trouble-maker. Ernie never does anything wrong…. And Ernie will never admit to it, but just sits there laughing.

Even though the kids like and respect Ernie, there are the usual childhood scuffles, especially since Ernie can hardly talk without a struggle. Maybe for that reason or just because of his character, Ernie is very sensitive also about others people's feelings besides getting his own hurt easily. He worries himself sick over how they feel about him or even each other. He can't stand to hear anyone say anything bad about someone else. He always jumps in with, "Oh, he's not that bad," or, "he didn't really mean that."

And because he likes everyone, he just ultimately expects everyone to like him. So it is a grave disappointment to him when those feelings aren't returned.

Angie, always there for her younger brothers, tries to diminish Ernie's disappointment in other people.

"They won't let me play," he tells her, amazed that anyone would be like that. "They say they don't like me."

Angie's heart aches for this younger brother/nephew.

"You need to be patient, Ernie. They'll come around. Tomorrow it will be different."

But Angie always worries it won't really be different. Yet, the next day when she looks out the window, he is already out playing with the offending child.

"How's it going, Ernie?" She can't believe it is really okay like she has told him.

"Oh, everything's fine. We're good friends now." He never holds a grudge and that makes it easy for the other kid to make peace with him.

Chapter 5

"But the sky knows the reasons and the patterns behind all clouds, and you will know too, when you lift yourself high enough to see beyond horizons".

Illusions, Richard Bach

Uniontown, PA 1949

Sandy Stephens and Ernie run across a large field near the river. John joins them and they start pushing and laughing.

"Com'on, Ernie, say it….."

Ernie just pushes him and keeps going.

"Say it, Ernie, say it…." Sandy joins in. "Bet you can't say funeral home…."

Ernie says nothing.

"Where does Sandy live? … where does he live? … com'on Ernie, … bet you don't even know."

Ernie racing ahead of them stops and turns, grinning, he finally tries.

"Mmunral fffffoam….

The others break up laughing and take off in a run. Ernie races after them and catches up with no effort at all. First he tackles one and then the other. The three boys roll around in the grass together laughing and all repeating in a chorus: "mmunral fffoam, mmunral ffoam. Then they lie down each one pulling up a long stalk of grass and chewing on it.

"Ccccom'on… do ya really ththink we'll mmmake the ttteam?

"Sure we will," says Sandy, "how good are we anyway! The Uniforms are so great… they look just like the major leagues."

"Yeah," Ernie agrees, "I cccan't wwwait to wwear one."

"Then we can march in the Midget Parade," concludes John.

Ernie sits up suddenly and stares at his friend. "Yyyour kkkidding. Ccccan we rrreally?"

"Yep," Interjects Sandy. "That's what the coach says and the kids did it last year."

Ernie gets a far off look. "Ssssome dddday, we'll ggget to wear the rrrreal ones. JJJust like jjjackie RRRRobinson.

"Yeh," contemplates Sandy, "Jackie got to play in the Big League, I'll bet we could too."

The boys lay there quietly in the grass for a moment, each one contemplating his own vision of the future.

Two weeks later the three boys are standing around with the other Little Leaguers, barely able to contain their excitement. There are the high school band members in wonderful uniforms with tassels on their shoulders, getting out their instruments and tuning up and there are majorettes in their little short skirts giggling and tossing their batons over on the grass, while kids on decorated bikes are riding up and down the road, looking for their friends.

Ernie, Sandy and John are all there, barely able to contain their excitement.

"Where's the coach," Sandy is looking around worriedly as others are beginning to line up.

A man comes racing up, out of breath with a bundle under his arms. "Coach is sick," he says, "but he sent me with your uniforms. Here, line up and you can put them on…"

"Com'on, guys.." says Sandy as he tussles for a place in line for the precious uniforms. John joins him, but Ernie stays behind, letting the other boys go first. Finally Ernie is the last one in line. When he arrives to the man, there aren't any more.

"Gee, I'm sorry kid," he says. "Don't know why we're short one. Someone must have counted wrong. Don't worry, there'll be enough at the game. You can march next year.

Ernie watches in shock as the others pull on their uniforms and line up for the parade. He stands there as they start off, the majorettes, then the marching band, followed by the kids on bikes.

"Hey, Ern…" calls Sandy as he passes strutting in his uniform, Ernie turns his head and moves off so they won't see the tears in his eyes. And some day they will be marching on without him again, but none of them can imagine it.

Chapter 6

Uniontown, 1952, summer

The large white house with the old fashioned summer porch is bustling with energy. Sunday is a very important day at the Davises. The door slams again and again as the children appear on the porch. The girls wear pastel dresses with hats and white gloves and the boys are in their best suits in spite of the heat rising off the pavement predicting a hotter than usual summer day.

The children race ahead down the street with Ernie in the lead. Twelve now, Ernie is taller then all but his oldest uncles. His size belies his true age, as he waits at the door of the church for his "Mamma", whom he still loves to sit next to. The church is full of excitement and activity as folks flow in, greeting each other cheerfully and loudly. This is no silent and subdued Northern White church, but the Baptist home of the Black population of Uniontown, the center of their social and spiritual lives.

The choir comes down the aisle singing out their anthem and swaying to the music. They find their places on the small wooden stage in the front behind the pastor, who, as the music dies down and they hum the final verses, calls them to worship.

"You've come to worship the Lord, and He is here with you.

"Amen."

"He hears your song and your laughter….

And he hears your every thought…"

"Yesss…

"Amen."

And Ernie's voice can be heard loud and clear responding, repeating and singing out in his off key enthusiasm.

Although all the older brothers and sisters are here this weekend, the clamor in the house is more subdued than usual after church. The tall and lank Ernie, still dressed in his Sunday best stands alone on the big porch, while the others are finding their seats at the large family table. He gazes off into the distance. Then Mom is behind him. She puts her hand on his hand that rests on the railing.

"You don't have to go if you don't want to, Ernie."

He looks at her and nods.

"Now, com'on in and have your dinner ..."

He turns to her and sees the look of sadness in her eyes and in spite of his awkward adolescence pulls her into a big bear hug.

She gets all flustered: "You com'on in here now, Ernie, and don't keep everyone waiting." She flutters her hand across her eyes and turns away.

They walk through the large living room to the dining room with the huge table and find the other 12 Davis sons and daughters already seated. The room hushes for a moment and then the others start chattering all at once, kidding and fussing at each other. Dad clears his throat and they bow their heads. Finally it is Ernie's turn and once again he chooses his favorite verse from his younger days, without hesitation and without a stutter: "Mica 6:6 "... to be fair and just and merciful, and to walk humbly with your God.""

Mom lifts her eyes and looks at Ernie. They are now slightly red and swollen.

A hand reaches out from beside Ernie and grabs a roll. Ernie's hand swiftly follows and three more hot rolls disappear into his big hand.

"Hey," calls out a brother further down the table. "Leave some for the rest of us." Then he grins and grabs several himself, while Angie hops up to refill the plate.

When she comes back, she stops by Marie at the other end of the table on the girl's side and says, "Well, I don't think Ernie should go. It's fine that he goes just for the summer, but he belongs here the rest of the year. He's always been with us. This is where he wants to be, isn't it, Ernie?"

Ernie starts to open his mouth, but nothing comes out. He looks down at his plate and gives it his full attention. He doesn't want Marie to feel bad. After all, she is his real mother. He has been spending the summers with her for years now, maybe it won't be so bad after all.

Marie is firm about her position. "Ernie is older now. He needs to be with me. It's right that he should be with me. You'll see. It'll be fine. After all, we'll be back for weekends and holidays."

Angie can't bear to see Ernie's discomfort and is used to protecting him. She jumps back in trying to make everything all right for everyone. "Well, of course..., I'm going to be a senior this year and then I'll be going away and getting a job and all. I guess we'll all be leaving, you know, moving on with our lives pretty soon. You'll be okay, Ernie, ...with sports and all. You'll get along with the other kids. You'll probably like it."

Ernie, who usually eats twice as much as the others, excuses himself from the table to get his bags. He lifts the large bag, as though it were a shopping bag and moves it out onto the porch.

Marie kisses her mother on the cheek and gives her a hug. "Don't worry, Mom. He'll be just fine. I want him with me. I've already waited too long. I'm married, I have a home and a job. He is my son, you know, and he's almost grown up."

Mom looks up at her first and beloved daughter, eyes filling again with unwanted tears. Very softly, almost under breath, Mom says as Marie let's the screen door close behind her. "He'll be right back, you know. He won't stay." Shortly, Mom follows them all out to the porch: There is nothing malicious about her statement, but she knows that Ernie, of all the children, hates being far from her or away from home.

Ernie is surrounded by the others as he arranges his things in the back seat of Marie's car. Then he climbs in the front wrapping his legs into the space in front of him. Mom walks slowly down the porch steps and over to the open car window. The others move back from her, still saying their goodbyes and teasing admonitions. Mom reaches in the car window and hugs and kisses Ernie.

"You be good now. Do what your mother tells you."

Ernie winks at Angie, who starts to cry. "Don't do that, Ang," he says, "or you'll have me crying too.

Ernie hugs his grandmother and waves. As the car pulls away, Ernie looks back at the family he has spent his entire life with and loves dearly and his eyes become wet with tears.

Chapter 7

Elmira, 1952, summer

Marie's duplex is in the East side of town right across from the high school. The school, Elmira Free Academy, serves the whole North side of the town. Elmira has a population of 50,000-80,000. On the Northside it consists of the East side, mostly Blacks and recent ethnic immigrant groups, and the West side medium to upper income and established White ethnics. Southside High School serves the homes south of the Chemung River, consisting of mostly Blue Collar white families. Notre Dame High School serves the Catholic families from all parts of the city. In addition, two northern communities, Elmira Heights and Horseheads each have their own schools and cater to lower/mid income levels and immigrant White communities. Elmira is a thriving small industrial city, home to American LaFrance fire engines, Remington typewriters, American Bridge and numerous other important businesses.

The Black community is well-established, but quite diverse. The old-timers had been there since the 1800s, some arriving on the Underground Railroad during the Civil War. Among them are professionals and highly respected families, but they live in a segregated area of the East side of town. A second influx of Blacks arrived from the Caribbean and added a new and less respected cultural group, sometimes in conflict with the "well-established" Black community.

The dynamics of this Northern city is quite different from what Ernie had grown up with in the Pennsylvania coal mining town.

The kitchens of her duplex have adjoining doors that are sometimes left open. Marie, Ernie's mother, and Lew Stark, her neighbor are talking about the challenges facing Ernie. They are sitting at her kitchen table enjoying a glass of freshly squeezed ice lemonade and some cookies just out of the oven. It is at least two weeks since Ernie arrived in Elmira and Marie has barely had a day off.

"I don't know what I'm going to do with Ernie. He jus' won't do anything. He sits around all day, just moppin' out there on the porch stump. I know he wants to go home, but he won't say anything cause he doesn't want to hurt my feelings. I'm afraid he won't stay after summer," laments Marie. She was so hopeful that this could work out, to have her only son with her, finally.

"You jus' leave it to me, Marie" responds Lew. "We'll get Ernie joinin' in in no time. I'll tell you what.... You know Buzzy's always actin' out, so he's been grounded for a while. I'll just bet he'd love to hang around with Ernie if I let him loose."

"Oh, would you?" Marie looks hopeful again.

Early the next morning Ernie is back out on the porch, baseball cap on head, chin in hand, just staring out into space, as if he didn't have a friend in the world. Suddenly Buzzy Stark bursts out the door onto the adjoining porch.

"Hey, Ernie, they let me out of prison. Com'on let's go play some basketball over at the Neighborhood House."

"Naw... I think I'll just stay here," Ernie replies.

Buzzy can't believe it, nor will he be put off. "Whaddya mean? You're just wasting your summer away. I don't get it. You've never just sat around here before when you've visited in the summer. If I don't get out of here quickly, Dad'll put me on house patrol again. Com'on, let's get out of here."

Buzz's usual enthusiasm is hard for Ernie to turn away from. He doesn't want to hurt his feelings. "Aw.... I guess so..."

Buzzy hits the ground running, "race you to the Neighborhood House..."

Ernie's not about to be beat at anything so his lethargy, that seemed pervasive before, is quickly left behind as he takes off, easily catches up and passes Buzzy, who, although older, is about 5 inches shorter than Ernie and whose legs only cover half the ground.

At first they don't even notice the white car following them, not until it comes up beside them and the White boys inside lower the windows. They lean out and start harassing them, keeping pace with Ernie, who has now slowed down a little so as not to leave Buzzy behind.

"Hey Nigger," they call to Ernie. "Where you running to?"

"You afraid of the boggy man, kid?"

"Ha, ha, ha....."

"You're so Black your mammies can't find you in the dark."

Then the car digs out, squealing, and leaving tire tracks as their laughter echoes after them. Ernie and Buzzy don't blink or look sideways, as though they never heard a word or saw the car. They enter the Neighborhood

House and amidst the greetings of their friends, already shooting baskets, the moment seems to be forgotten.

Several weeks later Ernie is on the phone to Angie, whom he talks with at least once a week. Marie, just behind the kitchen door, stops and overhears the conversation. As she listens she sighs her great relief. She is used to getting her way, but she just wasn't sure it would work out this time.

"Yeh, I guess I'm going to be staying for school."

"Well, Angie, I don't want to disappoint Marie."

"Oh, it's not so bad here. I've made a few friends."

Ernie hangs up the phone and sets up a game of checkers on the kitchen table, then he knocks on the door to the other kitchen. He calls to Buzz to come and play a game, then yells upstairs to Art, his stepfather, that he can play the winner. Marie enters the kitchen paying no attention to the boys, but she can't help smiling to herself.

Suddenly, while the wonderful aromas of food start dispersing through the kitchen, Buzzy throws up the board in mock anger and tells them they're all cheating and he's going home. He goes back through the kitchen door where his Dad is meeting with Rev. Latta Thomas and a group of other neighbors. They look up as Buzzy enters, while in the background they can hear Ernie's hearty laughter following Buzz.

"What's going on," his Dad asks.

"Oh nothing," Buzz responds. "Just Art saying that he's beat us again. As though he does it all the time." And he huffs out of the kitchen.

Lew returns to the church elders in his kitchen. "Well, we all agree on one thing, then. These kids have to go to college…. Every one of them."

"You're right," says the man to his left. Without college they're just going to keep getting the same old jobs. No one will hire them for anything but manual labor and half of those jobs are White only. They don't often hire coloreds. "

"Yehhh," another man pipes up, "and it doesn't make any difference if they finish high school or not. College is the ticket to a different life and white collar jobs."

"Well, that won't be easy," adjoins the second speaker. "The counselor spoke to my son when he was choosing courses last week, and I've heard he says the same kinds of things to the others. He tells them they should take the non regents courses, since they won't be going to college anyway. Can you believe that! He even said they'd be too difficult for him. Well, he's been getting mostly Bs and some As…. "

"Don't worry," says Lew. "We don't plan to settle for that. We have a plan to motivate the kids to push for the best they can do and we'll work on the counselors. Don't let them make those kinds of decisions for our kids"

"How are we going to change things?"

"We'll do it through the church," responds Lew. "Right Rev. Thomas?"

"You're so right, brother. The scripture tells us what to do if we pay attention. We've got something they are promoting in other Colored churches throughout the North and some southern communities. It's called Liberation Theology. It just means that we use the scriptures to teach our kids to go out and make something of their lives. Then we preach a sermon that goes along with that. We'll tell them right from the pulpit that it's their Christian duty to go to college."

"I'm for that!" Lew says enthusiastically, and the others join in in their approval.

Not even a week later, they put their plan into action. Ernie and the others arrive at the brick church early. There are always folks there to greet and lots of good energy going on. Inside the old red brick building there are wooden benches filling quickly with women dressed in bright colors wearing elaborate hats and men in their best Sunday clothes. Ernie slips into a seat on the aisle and watches as the chorus dressed in the usual black and white march down the aisle. They are singing as if they believe those wonderful words of promise and joy and swaying in unison to their music. The whole room vibrates with their movements and sounds of joy and Ernie can't help himself as he sways along with them.

Only a second of silence, then the pastor says a hearty "Amen!"

"Amen" responds the choir, now seated behind the pastor. "Amen, amen," shouts the congregation while Rev. Latta Thomas waits for them to settle down. He gives them a silent pause, a moment of anticipation, then he begins… getting right to the point.

"Now listen to the Lord's words, brothers and sisters," he says softly, while they strain to hear him. "The reading today is from Luke 19:12-27.

The church is still quiet except for the rustling of paper as many of the congregation open their Bibles to Luke ready to follow the reading:

"There was once a man of high rank, who was going to a country far away to be made king, after which he planned to come back home. Before he left, he called his ten servants and gave them each a gold coin and told them, "See what you can earn with this while I am gone. ......

"The man was made king and came back. At once he ordered his servants to appear before him, in order to find out how much they had earned. The first one came and said, "Sir, I have earned ten gold coins with the one you gave me." "Well done," he said; "you are a good servant! Since you were faithful in small matters, I will put you in charge of ten cities." The second servant came and said, "Sir, I have earned five gold coins with the one you gave me." To this one he said, "You will be in charge of five cities.".......

"And finally he got to the point of the message, "... to every person who has something, even more will be given; but the person who has nothing, even the little that he has will be taken away from him.""

As the congregation thinks this through, the choir breaks into song and many join in. Finally Rev. Thomas in his sermon speaks to the real issues:

"... If you will indeed experience that door toward the future and success...

"... If you will truly use those God-given gifts and multiply them...

"... then it must be through a college education. You cannot be satisfied with less..."

A thoughtful pause, then the older folks in the congregation break into approval:

"Yessir! Amen!! Ahuh! Amen!" while the choir brings the audience to their feet, everyone swaying and singing a favorite ... "Walk My Way"

Ernie stands with the rest, and the voice that so often fails him when he tries to talk, sings out loudly and clearly, if slightly off pitch. His eyes begin to shine as he finally sees a future for himself, a direction, an intent. Yes, he will use whatever he has.. in the service of God, and he will go to college. He must.

Ernie playing football with Small Fry

Chapter 8

Elmira, 1953, Fall

Young boys in uniform are arriving for the Small Fry football. They have been practicing for several weeks since the end of summer. This is their last practice before their fall games begin. Ernie and Ronnie Swain arrive in uniform on Ernie's bike. The coaches try to hide their laughter as they watch Ernie as big as a high schooler with little Ronnie, the same age balanced on the handle bars. The practice field is just over the bridge on the other side of the river and the team is made up of kids from both sides of the river.

Coach Mickey McDonald and Asst. Coach Gary May then turn to discussing what they'll do with Ernie in the games. He is only 13, but way beyond regulation size.

"He must be at least 5'10"" speculates Gary. "He long ago passed up our 125lb weight limit for carrying the ball. What're we going to do with him?"

"We can let him be a tackle, but it's a darn shame we can't let him carry the ball. What would we do with the other kids … he'd be running the ball all over and the game wouldn't be any fun for them."

"Ernie," Mickey calls him over. " I have some good news and some bad news for you. We're going to make you a first string tackle, but unfortunately we can't give you the ball to run with, cause you're so much bigger than these other little kids."

Ernie is clearly disappointed, but he nods and runs back onto the field and as soon as the whistle blows he races down the field after the kid carrying the ball. Within minutes he tackles him. They reform and he does it again.

"My God," says Mickey. "We can't let him do that. He's going to kill those little kids if he tackles them. What now?"

"Ernie!"

Ernie races back over, all smiles now. "Everything okay? This is fun."

"I thought you were going to kill that last kid, Ernie. Would you just hold him instead of mowing him down?"

Ernie doesn't seem at all put out by this reprimand, in fact he smiles back. "Sure Coach."

Ernie's back out on the field and the littlest kid on the team, Ronnie Swain, picks up the ball and starts to run. "Ohhhh NO," says Mickey half covering his eyes. He looks on in amazement, dropping his hands as Ernie reaches Ronnie and lifts him up into the air, holding him there and turns to the coaches waiting for them to blow the whistle. But Coach is laughing so hard he can't blow into the whistle, no matter how hard he tries, and Ernie just keeps holding Ronnie up in the air, grinning. Finally May grabs the whistle and blows it over and over. Ernie sets Ronnie gently down and goes back to the team that is getting into formation.

School is more difficult for Ernie than football, though. Each day he dreads going. He likes the kids alright, but isn't doing well with his teachers. One in particular makes him very nervous. She loves to ask the kids questions in class and Ernie for the life of him just can't answer. It isn't even so much that he doesn't know the answers, but he is totally tongue-tied when called on. No matter how hard he tries he can't seem to make even a word come out. His stutter has returned full force and he doesn't really know what to do about it except hang his head and avoid the teacher's eyes when she is looking for an answer. She takes this as insolence and finally sends him to the principal.

Ernie can't stand to have anyone angry at him and tries never to do anything wrong so as he enters the principal's office he is more upset and nervous than ever. The principal asks him why he won't answer any of the teacher's questions but Ernie remains silent. The principal loses his patience and raises his voice to Ernie. "Speak up, son. This is totally disrespectful. Answer when you are spoken to." Ernie can't help himself any longer and tears start streaming down his eyes. The principal is at a loss about what to do with this bigger than normal boy, a tough Colored kid, sitting there weeping and not responding at all. What is wrong with him? He calls his mother and asks her to come get him.

Marie leaves work and arrives at school. Her heart aches for Ernie and once again she is afraid he'll want to go back home to Pennsylvania. She tries to explain to the principal that Ernie is not being recalcitrant and difficult; he really can't make the words come out. She tells him that Ernie has had this problem since early childhood but now that he is in a new setting in a new school it has become much worse. Instead of stuttering, he simply can't respond, no matter how hard he tries. The principal gives her the name of a speech therapist in Syracuse and she promises to get Ernie help.

"Ernie, I'm taking you to Syracuse for speech therapy," Marie says a few days later. We'll have to stay there for a week or so."

"I don't want to go…" Ernie begs her to let him stay here, he'll just try harder. But Marie is adamant, and so Ernie goes and finally several months later he is able to respond in class without as much difficulty. The teacher, who meanwhile has been advised of the situation by the principal, makes a point of not calling on Ernie very often and not pressuring him.

In spite of Ernie's problems in the classroom, he is better than ever on the sandlot basketball court. He often plays pickup ball with men in their 20s and they spare him no special privileges for his age. In fact they tease him mercilessly.

"Gowan, Ernie.... You're too young for this crowd."

"Hey, man, your silver spoon is showing."

Then one of the men tries to trip Ernie, while another knocks him with his elbow. The third guy knees the back of his knee knocking him down, while the others grab the ball laughing.

Rollie, one of the popular Coleman brothers, Roland and Howard, who are really good at sports and leaders of their peers, takes pity on him and pulls him aside.

"You know they're only teasing, Ernie."

"Sure...."

"You just have to stay cool to beat them," he continues. "They really respect you, you know.... But as a Negro, it's a lesson you have to learn... we all have to learn it... You can't let THEM get to you... you've got to just grin and do better than THEM."

Now Ernie looks at Rollie seriously. He knows who THEM really is and it isn't the guys on the sandlot. Ernie is very aware this is a serious lesson he has to learn.

"I know." He responds, then goes back to the game. The others have continued playing. One dribbles nearby. Ernie grabs the ball, takes it to the hoop and puts it in easily. He looks back at Roland and grins.

Now Ernie knows how to deal with the aggression. He just jumps up again, grabs the ball back and puts it in the hoop, then laughs at their frustration. The more they pick on him, the better he gets. Every time he is successful, though, they pat him on the back, grin, and return to harassing him.

Ernie is no longer dreaming of Pennsylvania. He and Marie return often for family visits, but he has now embraced Elmira, his new friends there and living with his mother and stepfather. He can see they need him; and although it is very different being an only child, sometimes it is nice.

By the end of Ernie's second year in Elmira he has already become a very well known figure in sports and the Neighborhood House is the center of his life and the life of most of the boys and girls on the east side of town.

It is cold outside, but the gym is already warming up with the bodies that are pouring in from the street. This is a big game and the local teams have been practicing for it for some time. The Neighborhood team is playing the Hollow team. The Hollow team represents the kids on the lower east side near the river, while the Neighborhood team is made up of kids living around the high school. There is only one Black player on the Hollow team, Leo Hughey. Almost the entire Neighborhood team is made up of the African American kids. The kids from the two separate neighborhoods sit on different sides of the gym and are although some mixing, are primarily differentiated by skin color.

Play starts and Ernie immediately sinks a ball.... then another. As he easily dominates the game dumping one ball after another, the Hollow team becomes nervous. They huddle and decide that if they are to win, they've got to get Ernie benched. They agree that every chance they get they will force him to foul them. So they go for it. One after the other they back into him or trip over his feet or find other ways to yell foul. Each time it is called, the Hollow fans boo Ernie. Finally when his fouls reach five the referee blows his whistle and puts Ernie out of the game. Now it is time for the Neighborhood kids to boo and they boo the referee with vengeance.

"Put Ernie back..." they yell. They know he was sabotaged.

"We want Ernie," they start chanting. It gets louder and louder, while some of the fans rise up out of the bleachers and move onto the other side, pushing and shoving the other kids, who are now doing the same. The referees watch as things begin to resemble a rumble. They huddle and determine to put Ernie back into the game.

This apparently isn't a great solution, because now the Hollow fans start to go crazy again, pounding and stomping on the bleachers and calling out names.

The Neighborhood fans in retaliation zero in on Leo Hughey, yelling at him:

"Hey, Hughey.... What ya doing over there with them...?"

"You colorblind or something...?"

Ernie observes the crowd thoughtfully. The whistle blows, starting the next play. Ernie very openly and clearly knocks a player of the other team down. The referees puts him out again. Now no one can argue THAT foul. Ernie walks off the court, sits down on the bench and as the game continues without him, he grins to himself. Solved that problem.

Chapter 9

Elmira, High school, Fall 1954

Ernie can't believe he's in high school. He can't wait for the first football game. He has been practicing since August with Junior Varsity and has made the starting team. He is one of the only freshmen starting and is very proud of his accomplishment. He's finally in a uniform that counts sitting on the bench when the coach calls him in for the second time. Ernie is ready to put his all into it and show the coach that he made a good decision. Within minutes Ernie has the ball and is running down the field. The Binghamton boy grabs him and pulls him down hard. Ernie hears a snap and right away he knows what has happened. He can't believe that he hasn't even been able to complete one game.

Later in the afternoon when Varsity is playing, the local sports writer, Al Mallette, who has already been watching Ernie and waiting for his arrival on the high school scene, sees Ernie sitting at the top of the bleachers and waves. Ernie bounds down the bleachers, and with a great smile on his face thrusts his wrapped arm out like a trophy. Oh no, thinks the reporter....... More waiting.

Ernie's arm is still wrapped in sponge while he prepares for the basketball season. Against his better judgment, Coach Wipfler has not only let Ernie practice but has put Ernie directly onto varsity. Why lose a year waiting for him to put his time in as Junior Varsity he figures. Still, he is determined to keep him out until the doctor gives a written go ahead.

Ernie's not to be put off.

"Aw, com'on ccoach. Let me pppplay... ppplease. I kkknow I can help." Ernie is so anxious to get into the game he can hardly say the words. But he won't let that stop him.

"Ernie, you're crazy. You just got the cast off your arm yesterday. You're the only freshman on varsity. You can afford to wait. You've got four years left to play. Just watch this time round."

"Awwwww, ccccom'on. My arm's wrapped in sponge .. and Doc says it's fine now.... I've been practicing all along with my cast on.... And haven't done anything to hurt it. It'll be fine."

Wipfler can't resist Ernie's enthusiasm and finally gives in. "Go on in, Ernie, and get off my back. Go in for Bill at guard and I want you to play the point position. Stay out of the Center." Then he shouts after him as Ernie runs

Ernie playing varsity basketball as EFA freshman

out. "And take it easy on that arm of yours." Wipfler nods his head in false exasperation. He can't wait to see what Ernie can do in competition.

He's not disappointed. Within a few seconds Ernie makes his first basket and from then on, there is no stopping him. Coach just stands there with his hands on his head nodding it back and forth. He doesn't know what to do next. Ernie lays in one after another, a total of 22 points until Wipfler wakes up to his responsibilities and pulls him out. Meanwhile the crowd goes wild. With the cheerleaders leading them they begin chanting by the 12th point not stopping until Ernie is pulled out.

"Ernie, Ernie, he's our man, if he can't do it…. NOBODY CAN."

As Ernie leaves the court the crowd rises to its feet and gives him a standing ovation:

"Ernie Davis… Ernie Davis …. Ernie Davis…."

Ernie is elated, but confused. He just wanted to prove to Coach that he had made a good decision to let him in. But once he had started the momentum there was no stopping him. The season had begun and Ernie had become the "fair haired boy" before the end of the first game. All this in a town that never before had had a dark fair-haired boy. They love him already, but little do they know what is still to come.

Things are changing quickly in this period for African Americans. Ernie himself is impacting attitudes, the African American athletes are beginning to dominate some of the sports teams. A secret meeting is held by the cheerleading coach and the athletic coaches in which they discuss the need to have a Black girl on the cheerleading squad. And so it is done, at least for one year.

Chapter 10

Elmira, High school, Fall 1955

Ernie enters his sophomore year as shy as ever, but his classmates adore him and want to show him their admiration for him. So as the students prepare to choose their class officers for the sophomore class of more than 300 students, signs begin to appear advocating Ernie for President. All down the hallway… "ERNIE DAVIS, SOPHOMORE CLASS PRESIDENT." Different colored signs, but the name is always the same.

Two teachers on their way to the teacher's room for their break stop in front of a sign.

"So who is running against him," asks one.

"I don't know. These signs are everywhere. I haven't seen any others."

"I think it would be a nice thing if Ernie became class president, even though he IS Colored," says the first one magnanimously.

"Yes," agrees the second. "He certainly is a fine boy. He is always very polite in my class."

They nod in agreement, very proud of their open-mindedness. "Well, it WILL be the first time in the school's history that a Colored boy is elected to an office."

It is near the end of the football season of Ernie's sophomore year and he is on varsity playing first string. The weather is turning ugly in Upstate New York. Already by the end of Ernie's first year he was touted as likely to become the best basketball player EFA had ever seen and now they're seeing an Ernie who also excels in football. This year he has been playing end on the varsity team living up to expectations. So far this season he has been scoring well and impressing the crowds who remember him from basketball. Still, they can't let go of the idea that Ernie IS basketball.

EFA football team

Marty Harrigan is a very popular football coach. His medium sized solid figure can be seen pacing the sidelines, limping from an old WWII injury and smoking his mostly unlit cigar. Snow is beginning to fall and a light layer has already covered the grass. The varsity cheerleaders are dressed in their football outfits blue wool circle skirts that touch just at the knees and their heavy blue sweaters with a large white EFA printed across their chests. They wear blue shorts over their underpants just to be sure no one catches sight of anything inappropriate. On their feet are white bobby socks and blue sneakers and their bare legs often get chapped from the cold air of upstate NY. But they don't seem to feel a thing as they lead the crowd in one of its favorite cheers:

H.A..double R..I..G..A..N spells Harrigan

Proud of all the Irish blood that's in him

Divil the man that says a word agin him

H.A..double R..I....... G..A..N you see

It's a name born to fame   ......

Harrigan, our coach

And they jump into the air!

Coach Marty Harrigan

The crowd stands and cheers. Harrigan just bends his head slightly to nod at the crowd with a half smile, trying to feign disinterest. He moves up close to the assistant coach.

"You think you saw something when Ernie was an end don't you. Just watch what happens tonight. I've been training him for several weeks and I'm starting him as the half back."

"But he's only a sophomore," the assistant admonishes.

"That may be so.... " says Harrigan, but he's the size of a man, already over 6 feet tall with muscles in his legs you wouldn't believe. Just watch him run.

For several weeks now, Harrigan has had him over at his house using his own sons to scrimmage with Ernie and the results amazed even Harrigan.

Just as he finishes the sentence, he looks up to see Ernie with the ball, already whipping around the opponent's end and carrying it all the way down the field for a touchdown.

Harrigan jumps up and down forgetting his gimpy leg and yelling "go Ernie".

He turns to the asst. coach and slaps him on the back, "Damn, did you see that kid. He danced around the end like a ballerina and then ran like Hell. WOW! Just wait and see. We got ourselves one hell of a football player here. And a real nice kid besides."

The crowd is already bellowing a name that isn't that new to them...

"Ernie, Ernie, Ernie!"

"Ernie, Ernie, Ernie!" And the cheers go on into Ernie's junior year as he continues to career down the football field to touchdown after touchdown. There is no stopping him as he becomes better and better known in the area and even state.

By the time basketball season rolls around, it is becoming difficult to determine which sport Ernie is better at. Amidst cheers and shouts the EFA basketball team wins game after game undefeated and headed for the regional championship. There are many fine players on the team. The starters include quite a few African American players. Many of them could be stars on their own but Ernie outshines them all.

EFA varsity basketball starters spri ng1957

In particular, Ernie is an incredible rebounder, either grabbing the ball from the opponent basket or tipping it in his own. His outside shots amaze everyone, especially when they enter the basket without even touching the rim. And Ernie's jumping, added to his height, 6'2" by his senior year, makes him incomparable. No one can hold a candle to him. This is not always an easy position for Ernie to be in and he understands that humility in this position is more important than ever. It is hard for a star to take second place to a superstar.

Ernie doesn't forget his old friends at the Neighborhood House and still manages to play pickup ball with them. Now Howard Coleman has a bar called the Green Pastures and Ernie occasionally stops in there for a coke.

Ernie's famous jump

Ernie continues to be a regular at the Baptist Church and has given the youth group a new spirit. The other students and kids in the neighborhood follow him into the church and its youth programs as he becomes a leader there. as well. Even the White students start showing up for morning Lent services coming from the other side of town, before school on those days.

Ernie doesn't spend much time at home anymore. Art is drinking more than ever and he and Marie are having problems. Ernie loves them both and does worry about them. Not only is he terribly busy, but any free time now he is at his girlfriend's house, Betty Snowden, a senior. Her father coached Ernie in junior high and he has been invited into their home often ever since. Now he spends most of his free time there, getting help from Betty on his homework and having dinner with the family. Betty's parents sit in the living room while the two work away in the kitchen, arguing playfully and laughing a lot. They are so pleased that Betty has such a fine young man in her life and they love Ernie as a son. Ernie loves Betty and her family. He is also grateful for the help and the supportive home life he finds there. Especially he appreciates the help on school work, because he has never forgotten his commitment to go to college.

The atmosphere at EFA is mostly very positive, given the excitement of all the winning sports teams, some excellent teachers and a school and family approach to education that seems to be succeeding for many students. But the racial strife plus teen problems, normal at this age, are still underlying many events.

Ernie and his friends jump in a car after a winning game and decide to go to a party on the East side of town. One of the other "Members" in the car suggests they stop by Karen's house. She has invited them all over. Ernie immediately nixes the whole idea vehemently. She is White and he reminds them that her father has said he would kill any Niggers if they come to his house. The others don't think he means it.

"Man, you can't go out looking for trouble," says Ernie. And so they go within their own "Members" for their partying. In fact there are White homes where Ernie and his friends would be more than welcome, but it is difficult if not impossible to know for sure which ones, so mostly the Members have their own parties.

Ernie always avoids trouble when possible. His values won't allow him to create "situations" and his character won't allow him to be negative. Up against difficulties and prejudice, he tends to see the good in people, even when it isn't very obvious. That doesn't mean he doesn't notice injustices, cruelty and unkindnesses. When he sees someone else being treated badly, he steps in.

It is just this tendency that surprises the EFA students when they find out about the rumble that never happened. Frank Cox, a senior who starts on the basketball team is big, tough and often belligerent. Ernie's friends tell him that Frank has put together a small gang and they are planning a rumble with some others outside the football field behind the school. They have chains and other weapons and are already there. Ernie heads over and confronts Jim. Jim challenges Ernie and Ernie easily lays him out on the ground. That's the end of the problem. Students continue to talk about it for weeks, but when asked, Ernie won't comment on it.

The teaching tradition in EFA in the late 50s consists of many unmarried female teachers for the humanities, a few married teachers for language and such, and some male teachers that cover history, some sciences and, of course, all the coaching positions. There are no organized female sports teams except for cheerleading.

The teachers' lunch and break room is as much a place of gossip as the girls lavatory (bathroom). So two of the teachers are discussing the upcoming junior prom in hushed voices.

"I hear they're going to make Ernie Davis king of the junior prom."

"Well, I suppose that's okay if the girl who's the queen is colored too."

"Oh, I don't think so. It seems that they're expecting it to be one of the white girls.

"Well, that certainly won't do. What if they have to dance. They DO have to dance don't they?

"You're right. That would be terrible. Perhaps we should suggest that it would be better if he weren't elected. Maybe it could quietly be given to the runner up and make Ernie a runner up instead... or they could manage to put a Colored girl in as queen. I heard he goes with the Snowden girl, but I guess she's a senior so that wouldn't work.

"Of course everyone loves Ernie so much. He's a very sweet boy, although very quiet and not the best student. But well behaved. I'm sure he would want it this way too."

The night of the prom arrives and up on the stage sit Ernie with a

crown and the Rita Masone, a very sweet and pretty white girl, with the other crown being placed on her head. The two teachers stand in the back of the room horrified as the music starts up and the queen of the prom leans over and whispers something to Ernie.

VISITING ROYALTY: Jack Moore and Pattie Moore congratulate Junior Prom King Ernie Davis and Queen Rita Masone.

"I think they expect us to start the dance."

Ernie mumbles, uncomfortably, and sits awkwardly in his seat.

"I'mmm sssorry. I rrrreally ccccan't dddance.. " He stutters for the first time in a while.

Other students step out on the dance floor and start to dance as Ernie and the queen sit in their chairs watching. The teachers in the back, sigh their relief and go to find some more punch. The teachers are not the only ones who still find male-female contact between the two races abhorrent. Fathers of White girls are overheard at the games raving about Ernie and saying they would be happy with him as a son, but when the truth comes out, it is clear that they don't want him as a son-in-law.

Chapter 10

Elmira, High school, Late Fall 1957
Ernie's senior year

Elmira Free Academy

Ernie stumbles out of his bed in the duplex across from EFA. No rush, he thinks. I just have to cross the street to make it in time. Eyes closed he makes his way to the bathroom, and prepares himself carefully, combing his very short hair several times, although it is hard to tell the difference. Mom is in the kitchen calling him to come eat or he'll be late. She always has a huge breakfast ready for him, knowing that he is very hard to fill up. At the front door, Ernie checks himself in the mirror again and smooths his hair. Got to always look good, he tells himself.

He glances down at the letters on the table that have piled up, all with his name on them. He picks up two of them, one from Syracuse University and the other from Notre Dame and sets them inside his notebook. He wants to talk with Harrigan about them.

He looks at the clock then glances out the front window. Minutes later he takes off, slamming the front door behind him. He stops short at the edge of the porch waiting until he sees, Jeannie Conklin (one of the senior cheerleaders rounding the corner). He waits another minute giving her more of a chance as he hears the bell ringing from across the street. Already kids are at the windows of the second floor lifting them up and hanging out. The time is now. Ernie bounds down the steps just as Jean approaches his house and looks to see there are no cars coming down the street. They both cross at the same time and bound up the front steps. The boys leaning out one window of their homeroom are yelling for Ernie.

"Gaw'on Ernie. What's taking you so long.

"You can beat her, Ern....

Lay it on, Ernie.....

While the girls in rhythm shout...

Jeannie... Jeannie.... Jeannie.

They take the stairs two at a time almost running down Miss Loomis who is waiting at the top of them, hands on hips. She steps coolly in front of Jean, who comes sharply to a stand still with head down, not sure whether to laugh or quake in fear. Ernie nimbly escapes into the senior boys homeroom, where the boys are slapping him on the back and applauding. He falls laughing onto his desk/chair combination, barely able to fit his frame into it, puts his notebook down and sits up at attention as though nothing happened.

Meanwhile, Jean, as usual suffers the wrath of Miss Loomis who glares down at her as she slumps into her seat.

"Young lady, when will you be on time, and when will you learn to act like a lady? You are almost grown up. I expect more from you."

A bell sounds as Miss Loomis plods to her desk in the front of the room and starts reading off the role.

It is half past eleven in Mrs. Hutchinson's senior English class. The students are beginning to fidget with hunger and sitting too long.

"Senior papers are due in two weeks," she reminds them. "By now you should have all your research completed on cards. Your outlines are due by next Friday and I want you to pass in your cards with them, so I can see the kind of research you have really done. Don't forget to include a complete list of your bibliographies. Are there any questions?"

Every senior who plans to go on to college prays to find themselves in Mrs. Hutchinson's class. She teaches them everything they need to know to succeed.

A student in the back raises her hand.

"Do you want our name at the top on the right and should we also put our class number? What date should be put on the outline and what date should be put on the paper?"

Hutchinson patiently answers her questions, knowing that many students feel safer with details of what to do and just how to do it.

"Put your name in the right hand corner, your class number beside your name and the date directly under them. Use the date of paper due for both the outline and the paper."

Another hand is raised.

"Yes, Sandra."

"I couldn't find any books on Longfellow. Can I just use articles?"

"My, Sandra. That seems strange. No books on Longfellow. I never would have guessed. And I'm surprised you've found articles on him. They're not exactly common. Have you actually been to the library yet or just looked on your own bookshelves. None of you should have any trouble finding at least twenty books about the authors you are researching. Any other questions?"

She pauses... silence. "Hmmmm, let me see. Oh yes, there is one more thing." She ruffles in the desk drawer and comes out with a plate full of homemade cookies. The students sigh. Some make hunger noises.

"I know it's hard to make it through until the last lunch period... You can take the rest of the period to read the next chapter in your book."

As she passes the plate around the room, each student takes just one cookie, until one large dark hand appears out of nowhere and encompasses four of the cookies. She catches his eye for a moment and he grins sheepishly at her. She just moves on to the next student. She had already planned the extra cookies. Ernie has been in her class all year and she knows what to expect and just smiles to herself, glad that he feels comfortable with her.

In spite of the four cookies, Ernie arrives in the lunch line and can barely wait for the food. When he leaves it his tray is filled to overflowing with food. He arrives at a long table in the noisy cafeteria and sits down by his friend Will.

Will, another football player, looks at Ernie's plate and laughs.

"How do you manage to eat so much and not get fat."

"You just ggggot to live rrright." Replies Ernie who stuffs his mouth with one of the sloppy joes on his plate. Will looks up in surprise.... He hasn't heard Ernie stutter so much in quite a while. He realizes that he must be excited about something.

"Hey you hear from any colleges?" he asks.

Ernie pulls out the two letters he has in his notebook. "Lllook at these," he says. "I can't believe it. They are bbboth offering me ffootball scholarships, Notre Dame and Syracuse. I thought I'd sshow it to Coach Harrigan and get his opinion. I can't make up my mind."

"What about you, Will?

"Coach is saying that I might get into Syracuse. My grades haven't been so great and I had to stay on here to finish up my credits to graduate... but I'm hoping with him pulling for me... You know he went to Syracuse don't you?"

Ernie grins, "who doesn't. He never misses a game when he doesn't have one himself. I guess he's pretty tight with their head coach."

"Yeh, they say Schwartzwalder is tough but fair. Let me know what Coach Harrigan says. I've already been up there to visit. Hope you decide to go there"

"I don't know. I'm so confused. I've always thought I wanted to play for Notre Dame. And the guys that visited me from there were really great! But Harrigan made me promise to visit Syracuse before I make up my mind. He asked me to keep him informed about Notre Dame too."

"You know, S.U. has one of the best football teams in the country. Of course Jim Brown is leaving, but they've still got some great guys. You know, Syracuse has a good academic attitude too. Plus it's close to home. ..you going to the banquet tonight?"

"Yeh... of course."

"Did you know Jim Brown is going to be there."

"Yeh, that's cool."

Ernie scarfs down the last of his double meal. The lunch ladies turn a blind eye when Ernie goes through the line a second time. He particularly likes today's meal, sloppy joes.

"Will.... ?"

"Yeh..."

"If we both end up at Syracuse, will you room with me?"

"Sure..." Willy smiles to himself. He sees Ernie is finally bending his way. That would be the best, to be at Syracuse and have Ernie there too. He crosses his fingers behind his back and hopes really hard.

Ernie and Will are just picking up their papers and plates from the table when two cheerleaders approach them. They've been dressed in their uniforms all day in preparation for the sports banquet that evening. They love being in their outfits, knowing that every other girl in the school wishes she could be in their places. And the boys all seem to look at them differently too.

"Can you guys push these tables over to the walls," says Joannie, "We'll leave one in the middle for speeches."

Will and Ernie accommodate, then lean against the wall in the back. It's not cool to seem too involved. The girls hop up on the tables in the center and do a few cheers. The other kids are getting excited and yelling pretty loud. The echoes in the lunch room make it sound like thunder. Then Joannie points to Ernie. Com'on and say something, Ernie."

A couple of girls go over and grab his arms pulling him as he holds back.

"Speech, speech! Make Ernie speak!" The crowd picks up on it with shouts.

The girls pulling at Ernie look like a couple of little kids pulling a very big man. Without him seeming to resist, they can't even budge him. Finally they give up and the cheerleaders jump up on the tables again and do another cheer.

A little later in the day Coach Harrigan is leaning back in the chair in his office with his feet on his desk. He's talking on the phone.

"So, you think you'll be here by 7PM then, Ben. You're bringing Jim Brown and Ted Daily with you, right? Ernie was just in here. He showed me his Notre Dame acceptance. The guys from there were here last weekend courting him and apparently doing a good job of it too. He's leaning that way, but says he'll probably visit Syracuse anyway if I want him to. There is one thing, though. He's got a buddy here, Will Fitzgerald, a White kid. I've talked to you about him before. He's a really good kid, but had a rough time at home, stayed an extra year here at EFA. He's a linebacker. If you take him too, I think I can push Ernie your way."

"Yeh...."

"It seems Ernie wouldn't mind rooming with Will. He's kind of shy, you know... A little insecure. Wouldn't hurt him to have a friend right there. And you know how it is for these Colored kids. Hard to get them a roommate... so few of them."

"Great... you take care of that. Get Jim Brown and Coach Daily to say a few words to him and I'll make sure he gets there for that visit. I think we can do this. His basketball coach, Jim Flynn, is also from Syracuse, you know.

I think he's also had a talk with Ernie. Would you believe it.... the baseball scouts are after Ernie too, but I don't think that's a problem. He's committed to college and football. I think his pastor has played a part in that. He's talking all these Colored kids into shooting for college. Anyway... this is a fabulous kid. You won't be sorry for a moment to have Ernie there."

Ben thanks Harrigan for all his help in recruiting Ernie to Syracuse. Harrigan hangs up and breathes a sigh of relief.

Chapter 11

It had just begun to snow and thankfully Ben, Jim and Ted are almost to Elmira. The coaches are filling Jim in on Ernie. Jim Brown is one of the greatest athletes of the time, yet it took him until his Junior year at Syracuse to be played to the fullest. Jim had been belligerent from the beginning, but he had also had a lot of attitude from the others to overcome. Now as a senior, having risen to fame in a dramatically short time, Jim, was the most sought after running back in college. He had won all the big awards except the Heisman trophy. Up until this time, no Negro had ever been chosen and although Jim added this insult to his internal rage, outside he showed very little of these feelings. He often resisted the White world, but he knew the basics of what he had to do to survive in this honkie dominated world.

Although Ben knew Jim was an outstanding athlete in high school, he was not one to cater to moods or attitudes, so Jim had sat on the bench into his Junior year. Ben explained to his assistant coaches that it was because he had been late for practices and thought himself above the repetitive exercises. Finally, when the Asian flu was rampant and there were no more players to pull from, Ben called Jim from the bench. Jim didn't wait for another chance. He immediately ran the length of the field for a touchdown and didn't stop running for the rest of the game. After that, in spite of his early setbacks, Jim went on to break all kinds of records, make all the All Star teams and become one of the biggest names in college football. Now he had been offered one of the largest packages a rookie had ever had as a running back with the Cleveland Browns. Big, strong and sometimes mean, Jim was also very very smart and savvy.

Although Jim had some resentment towards Syracuse University, he also had some deep-seated commitments to the school that had finally given him a chance to excel. No one had seen anything like it. So he had agreed to go with Ben and Ted on this recruiting mission, even though he was not particularly excited about Ernie. Too many of these hot shot high school athletes he'd seen needed a lesson in humility and he figured Ernie would just be another one of those.

"So you think this kid is really good, huh?" asks Jim

"I don't think it, I know it." Ben responds. "I know one when I see one and I haven't seen one like this before, except for you, and maybe Avatus Stone. Bless his evil soul."

Jim looks askance and then lets it pass.

"He's broken all kinds of regional records and they say he's a really nice kid besides."

"Yeh, I've seen these "nice" kids before. They all think they're movie stars, just cause they're big shots in high school."

"That's not what I hear about this one. They say the kids and teachers like him so well they would all pick up and move the high school if Ernie told them too. Try to get him aside, Jim. Tell him to come to Syracuse...."

Then Ben turns to Ted. "So far we've got ALL his coaches on our side, Harrigan, Flynn, Wipfler. Even his lawyer, Tony DeFillippo. They're all S.U. Alums."

"Hot shit," says Jim under breath.

The car pulls up at the restaurant door and Jim unfolds from his side. He is immediately surrounded by kids who must have been waiting there for him. Jim takes whatever they offer him to sign on, pulls out a pen and signs them against the car. Finally Ben gets out and Ted drives the car off to park.

Ben and Jim enter the restaurant with a trail of people behind them. They are led to one end of the table, where seats are waiting for them. Ernie is already seated at the other end of the table. Jim recognizes him, of course, since he is the only other Negro sitting up front with them. Jim looks over at Ernie, studying him briefly. Ernie smiles back his sunshine smile. It's hard for Jim not to return it.

The awards have paused briefly while the Jim entourage has entered. Now Harrigan continues to hand out the letters to one player after another. Even the cheerleaders will get their letters in the shape of a megaphone with EFA written on it.

When Ernie arrives up front for his letter, Harrigan pauses a moment and then speaks up.

"There's never been a player like Ernie before and may never be one again, but what really makes Ernie great is not the way he plays ball, but the way he lives his life. Ernie never puts himself before his team."

Ernie bows his head, embarrassed to be singled out and mumbles his thanks, anxious to get back to the safety of his seat.

Coach Harrigan now presents Jim: "We're really honored to have with us today one of the greatest college football players of all time. Jim Brown has just accepted a contract to play with the Cleveland Browns so we'll be seeing a lot more of him in the future."

An excited ovation goes out as the students and their parents in awe of the celebrity status of Jim Brown are thrilled to see him in person.

Jim, this man bigger than life, whom they have only known as an icon now stands before them. "I'm pleased to be here in Elmira today... " he commences in his deep fine voice. It almost doesn't matter what Jim says. They are mesmerized and Ernie among them. By the time Jim sits down, the room echoes in applause. No question that his popularity continues to increase just from his presence. As the crowd rises to leave, there is another surge forward surrounding Jim as he's trying to make his way to the end of the table where Ernie is still sitting. Kids wanting autographs overwhelm Jim's movement, so he signals to Ernie with a wave. Ernie waves back. Jim shouts across the students, most of whom are at least a head shorter than him.

"Come to Syracuse..." he says.

Then he is swept out the door. Ben and Ted make it over to Ernie, though, while Jim is signing autographs. Ben pats him on the back.

"We could really use you on our team, kid," says the coach. "Com'on up to Syracuse and visit us. Bring your parents along. We'll put you all up for a couple of days. Jim and some of the others will take you around. I'll call you next week, by Thursday. "

"I'd really like that Mr. Schwartzwalder. Thank you for inviting me."

A week later Ernie picks up the phone and calls his aunt/sister Angie down in Pennsylvania.

"Hi, Ange. How you doing? .... You won't believe it. I just got a letter from Jim Brown, you know, Jim the great running back from Syracuse... yes... that's the one. He says he thinks I should come to Syracuse. Says they need someone like me, to keep the things going that he started there, you know, to open it up for other Black athletes .... I don't really want to fight battles or anything, though... just play ball. .. But most of all, Angie, I want to get a college education. Jim says that Syracuse will be sure I get that. And honestly, I really prefer being closer to home."

....

"Yeh, I'm getting offers from other colleges too. I got a call from Aubrey Lewis at Notre Dame... and they came to visit me here. I'm still not sure which way to go. So I'm going up to Syracuse next week to visit."

...

"Sure, I'll let you know what I decide. . .. Yeh, I know that the most important thing is to be where I feel most comfortable."

...

"Thanks, Angie, I'll call you as soon as I get back from Syracuse."

Chapter 12

Syracuse
Senior year in high school

Meanwhile in the Athletic Department at Syracuse University Ben is talking with his coaching staff to prepare for Ernie's visit. This is one he doesn't want to miss. Ben has a very good feeling about this kid and thinks that he may be the biggest thing to happen in his coaching career. Sure Jim was great, but Jim had some serious flaws. Ernie was malleable, willing, enthusiastic besides being a fabulous athlete with a wonderful healthy body.

"A little history," says Ben, "You remember Avatus Stone. Some of you knew him, others came later, but his infamy has remained. It made us wary."

The rumor was that Avatus was not only dating White women openly, but seeing both the mother and daughter. They even said that one tried to commit suicide. Interracial dating was no more accepted in the North than the South. Also Avatus was allegedly spending university money right and left. Eventually, given the prejudice against Negro players in the NFL, Avatus left Syracuse and the USA to play in the Canadian League. Avatus had been at Syracuse on scholarship, so the Administration and Board, in their great wisdom determined not to give any more scholarships to Negroes. It was into this atmosphere that Jim arrived. It is said that 44 of the influential men in Jim's Long Island community came together with enough money to send Jim to Syracuse University. No scholarships, but they wanted to see him play in their old alma mater. Jim took the, then available, number 44.

"So," continued Ben, "we couldn't give Jim a scholarship to play and when he arrived he wasn't very cooperative. I kept him on the bench most of the time, but finally he surprised me when I put him out there, and then, we couldn't keep him down, which was great for us, great for S.U. And great for Jim. Don't get me wrong. We all know he hasn't been easy, but he played well for us and grew up a lot. He is one of the greatest athletes we've ever seen. And Jim has other good qualities. He's smart as can be, among other things, and is willing to help us recruit Negro players.

Now we've got Art Baker and John Brown. They're both on scholarship and they're both really good and nice kids too. But I want to go for broke. There's one kid out there who can do what Jim can do, and he's a super kid too. "

One of the coaches nodded his head in disapproval reminding Ben that the administration wasn't going to be happy with too much recruiting of Negro kids.

Ben continued on, ignoring the negative thoughts. "Ted has already met him and he's pretty impressed too. His name is Ernie Davis and he looks like he's shaping up into something really special. In the sense that he's good at everything, he's like Jim. He first made his impression through basketball and took his team to the regional championship. Big league recruiters are after him for baseball, but he's committed to football and college. I want this kid and I want him bad. We're going to do everything we can to get him. No limits. Even if it means taking another player from Elmira with him."

Ted speaks up now. "I think you're right, Ben. I've got a friend down in Elmira. Says this kid is a kind of legend to them already. He can do no wrong. They're all wild about him."

"Jim's already agreed to spend a little time with Ernie when he comes up with his parents this weekend," says Ben. "He was a little wary at first, but just seeing the kid smile, he softened. Something about Ernie grabs people."

"I think we should get Art and John Brown to take Ernie around campus," adds Ted. "After all, they'll be here when he comes and will be playing with him. He'll feel better if he's with his own."

"Good idea," agrees Ben. "you guys understand now, don't you... when we get these Colored kids in here, we got to take care of them. We got to make sure they succeed, not just on the field, but in the classroom. When their moms call... you talk to them. They need a tutor ... you get it for them. I don't want any problems. We got to convince the Board that Colored kids are an important part of our athletic success in the future."

Later Ben calls John Brown and Art Baker into his office and coaches them on what to do this weekend. "Okay, you guys. Take this Ernie Davis all around and show him a good time. Tell him how good it is here. It is good, isn't it?"

They nod. And after all it was what was expected from them. These kids couldn't go to college if it weren't for the football scholarships. Mostly they are just glad to be here.

"If we've got Ernie," adds Ben, "we've got a chance at number one. We've got the makings of it already, but Ernie's the frosting on the cake. I'm depending on you."

And both John and Art knew what that meant. The most important thing to them was a chance at the national championship. It would be the thrill of their lives and important if they wanted to play pro ball.

John Brown takes Ernie, Marie and Art Radford around campus, then they go to a lovely lunch at the university cafeteria. For dinner the three from Elmira are entertained by Dean Faigle, the academic dean. The dean explains that Syracuse University has a very strong academic tradition and is not just focused on sports. Now for the important selling point. He tells them that when Ernie comes to Syracuse, although he is being recruited by the athletic department, his scholarship is an academic one. The school is committed to him and his education. He can keep the scholarship even if he never steps on the field as long as he passes his courses.

"No kidding," pipes up Ernie with enthusiasm. You mean even if I break a leg or something, I can keep my scholarship as long as my grades are okay?"

"I certainly do. In addition, we know you football players spend long hours practicing and sometimes you can get into trouble academically. We have a wonderful tutor program to help you keep up with things. We want you to succeed."

Later on in the evening, Ernie is finally alone with Art and John. The others are having a beer and Ernie is drinking a coke and having a hamburger in spite of his big dinner with the Dean. The Clover Club where they've ended up, is the local university watering post, and since drinking age is currently 18, most of the kids there are drinking beers. Music is fairly loud, but the boys have picked out a quiet corner in the back so they can talk. John and Art would be really glad to have another Member on the team and on campus. They often feel isolated. Their social life is significantly limited due to negative attitudes toward dating White girls, and White guys have a different attitude and approach to a lot of things. But usually the guys feel okay with teammates, at least on the field, and sometimes in a place like the Clover Club.

"Is it really like they're telling me?" asks Ernie. "I mean are they as interested in how you do academically as how you play."

"Next year they're red shirting me," says John. "That means I sit on the bench for a year and don't play, so I can stay five years and they can use me later. But I can still continue my education. They've done everything possible to help me and keep me here, in spite of lots of problems I've had. And man, I've been trouble too." John laughs at himself. "In fact, they've let some of the White players go for less than what I've done, but they're still keeping me."

"It's pretty good." Art isn't quite as enthusiastic as John. "There are some of the usual hassles, but mostly they leave us alone and let us play. I'd say it's probably the best treatment you're going to get in a Northern White college."

Jim Brown recruiting Ernie to Syracuse University

Finally the moment Ernie has been waiting for. He gets to talk alone with Jim Brown. He's got so many questions. He's glad he had time with Art and John, cause they are going to be there with him, but Jim is the one he is most interested in. Jim starts right out talking turkey. He holds nothing back, so it seems to Ernie. And Ernie admires him more for it, although he is slightly shocked by his frankness. Mostly the people Ernie knows don't really talk too openly about how things are. They just live with the prejudice and limitations. After all, it's been that way all their lives. Their parents have taught them to hold it in so they don't disrupt anything. It wasn't that long ago a Negro could be hung just for looking at a White person cross eyed. What if your eyes were naturally crossed... then you'd really be in trouble.

When Jim talked he pontificated, but it was all worth listening to:

"I'm going to tell it to you the way it really is, Ernie. I've watched you. They tell me you're a great ball player and that may be so, but I've also seen what kind of a guy you are. That's just what they need here."

"What do you mean," Ernie is surprised.

"When I came to Syracuse, they wouldn't give me a scholarship of any sort and wouldn't even let me play football. They kept me sitting on the bench until my junior year. They were mad at me cause I didn't always make scrimmage, but there's nobody out there who could catch me when I got that pigskin and ran. They got burnt by a guy named Avatus Stone. They just figured we're all the same. Got to find out if we're going to rape their White girls or steal their money. That's what they think we all do and don't ever forget it. It helps to know the mind of the enemy."

Ernie is a bit taken aback, but recognizes the truth of a lot of what Jim is saying to him.

"Well, I've learned you don't let them see what you're doing socially. You can go out with who you want... and there are plenty of White girls who want.... but you do it quietly. Take them to private parties, … that sort of thing.

"If you perform on the field and don't make a mess for them, they'll let you do almost anything you want. It isn't easy for us ... anywhere. Syracuse is ready now. I've taken a lot of crap to make up for Stone. I've fought the battles. Now you come in and give them what they want. It's up to us to make things different. To turn them around."

Back at home, Ernie goes where he can find the advice of his coach, another father figure for him. He wanders into the back yard of Harrigan's house. There are kids swarming everywhere. Harrigan's five sons are always excited when Ernie arrives. He is already the object of their hero worship. Harrigan shoos them away wanting to speak with Ernie alone.

"I don't know what to do," he's still saying. "Everyone keeps telling me to go to Syracuse University. I like the campus and the guys there. But there's still a part of me that wants to go to Notre Dame."

Harrigan gives it his last shot. He's pretty sure they've won him over.

"I don't want to tell you what to do, but I'll talk to you like a father. Of course, cause I went to Syracuse and know lots of folks there, I'm rooting for it, but there is one important thing they're giving you that Notre Dame isn't, and it's the most important thing in your life. They're going to give you an education no matter what. The other thing is also very important and that is Ben Schwartzwalder. Not only is he a really tough and fair guy. He's a winner. Ben is one of the best coaches in the country and perhaps one of the greatest coaches in college football history. If you play for him, you'll not only win, you'll learn, especially if you want to play pro ball.... you do don't you?"

"Well yes, if I was good enough. There's nothing I'd rather do. But I can't do that forever. I want to have another career too. I mean, I really want to get a degree and prepare myself for something."

"That's what I mean," answers Harrigan. "Syracuse is one of the few places where you can be sure to do both. If you want to go to Notre Dame, you should, but Syracuse is your ticket to a more secure future. The important thing is for you to be happy."

"I guess I also like that it's so close to home and Mom can come and see the home games plus I can get home on weekends when we're not playing. That really makes all the difference."

Marty puts his arm around Ernie's shoulder and they walk back toward the house.

"Now remember, Ernie, you're just a kid. You're supposed to have fun too. If you come home every weekend you miss half of what's going on. Not that we don't want to see you."

Ernie just smiled, knowing that Harrigan couldn't help it if he didn't understand that it wasn't going to be the same social life for him at Syracuse as for any White guy. No real parties, not much chance to date, so few Negro girls, and general exclusion. No, the fun would be at home, where it's always been.

Harrigan's wife already had the hot dogs made.... a pile high to accommodate all the kids and Ernie's huge appetite too. It doesn't take an arm twisting to get Ernie to help himself. He feels hungrier than usual, perhaps having finally made up his mind and lifted the burden of decision. It would be Syracuse. What a relief to have that figured out.

On the phone with Angie, Ernie can now be brief... no more indecision. "I've decided, Angie. I'm going to Syracuse. I sent them the letter today...."

.....
"Yeh, I think it's great too. Anyway... best of all, I'll be near home. Marie can come to the games and I can get home on weekends."

.....
"Thanks, Angie. How's it going for you...."

And Angie rambles on for a while with all the family news and things going on in her life. Ernie is happy to hear her familiar voice and feel the warmth of the love of his childhood home.

Chapter 13

Elmira, EFA, late Spring and Graduation 1958

Ernie plays out the basketball season with only one glitch. One of the Binghamton high schools starts a battle over the fact that EFA's starting team has four Negroes. The rumor has gone around among the African Americans, that Coach has put in one White guy and left Leo Hughey off the top line up in order not to have problems with other teams. In spite of that Binghamton students call the team names, yell at them and threaten a rumble. As usual Ernie convinces his team members that a fight isn't worth it. It is enough to beat the other team. All the EFA students there are furious at the treatment of their team, but follow Ernie's lead.

The whole Davis family is present for Ernie's graduation. They are all abuzz about his college choice commenting on how good the Syracuse team is and did he really talk with Jim Brown and what is Ben Schwartwalder like, and so on. Ernie basks in the limelight with those he loves, joking and fooling around as though they were all still kids.

EFA graduating seniors 1958

EFA yearbook
Ernie Davis and the Littlest Blue Devil

Chapter 14

Elmira, Summer 1958

Elmira has a wonderful variety of stores, clothes, shoes, furniture and others are owned by local merchants. The mall culture has not appeared anywhere but in a few very big cities. Bob Jerome owns a fine men's clothing store.

The store is owned, run, managed and mostly staffed by Bob himself. Bob's on the phone with Harrigan.

"Sure I know Ernie Davis.., who doesn't?"

"... Well, sure I'd like to have him work for me. Who wouldn't? Why would he want to work for me, though. He can earn a lot more working for a construction company or something like that. With his physique and power he'd be crazy to waste his time working for minimum wage in a clothing shop."

"You're kidding," says Bob... "You mean nobody will hire him because he's colored. I can't believe they don't have any colored kids working in construction."

"Sure I'll take him, but I can only pay minimum wage. He's a nice kid and a really great football player. I'm sure it will be good for business to have him in the store. What I can do, though, is give him pretty good discounts on clothes for college."

Within a few weeks Ernie is well entrenched in Jerome's. He is carrying a huge rack of clothes full of new suits across the main street from one of Bob's stores to the other. A small kid, Tom Wing is following along right behind him, trying hard to help, but not keeping up very well.

"Geez, Ernie, this is really heavy," says Tom as he tries to lift up one end of the rack. "I can't get hold of it very well."

"That's okay, Tom, you're doing just great. We're almost there."

Tom watches in awe as Ernie lifts the whole rack up over the store stump.

"Just hold the door for me, Tom, and we'll be done in a jiffy."

Tom is relieved to be able to find something he can do to help.

"Thanks, Tom. I couldn't do it without you."

Once in the shop, Tom and Ernie start hanging the different suits on shop racks and straightening things up. Two older teens enter the store. One of them points at Ernie.

"That's him!" He says, enthusiastically. "Geez, you mean if I buy a shirt here, I can say I bought it from Ernie Davis?" Wow," says the other and starts sorting through the short sleeve sports shirts.

Chapter 15

Syracuse, August 1958

The car is winding around the last hill and the city of Syracuse is in view in the far distance. Will is slouching in the right front seat, while Ernie drives. Will and Ernie haven't been talking much. Will is thinking about his high school sweetheart, Margaret "Mugsie" Burch, who had already been at Syracuse for a year. Maybe they could get back together. On the other hand, Ernie is thinking that he has done what he set out to do... he is going to college. A thrill goes through Ernie as he realizes that for the next four years this will be the center of his life. This is the road to his future too.

Ernie Davis and Will Fitzgerald preparing to leave for Syracuse University

He just hopes he'll do well. The car is loaded to the gills, overflowing with suitcases, bedspreads and other paraphernalia that Ernie's Mom thought they would need for their room.

"Whoa, Ernie... you missed the turn." Will pops upright in his seat.

Ernie grabs for the map and swerves the car almost ending up in a ditch.

"I don't know how I ever let you talk me into driving up here with you. I guess I thought your Mom would be the one driving."

"Oh yeh..." says Ernie. "Just stay cool man .. you'll be fine... You got to learn not to distract me. See.... I can drive with one hand only."

"I sure hope you run better than you drive." responds Will, his knuckles turning white as he holds on to the handles by his seat.

When they arrive on campus, Ernie stares right and left taking it all in, while Will holds tight. He takes the last corner a bit too fast and pulls up in front of the dorm. By now Will is covering his eyes. He peeks through his fingers.

"You can uncover, now," says Ernie. "I think we're here." Will checks out the directions, looks up at the dorm, back at the paper. He's putting off getting out.

"Yep, I guess we're here." says Will without moving.

Neither one says anything for another little bit. They just sit there.

"Well I guess maybe we should unpack the car."

"Yep, I guess so." But still neither moves.

Finally Ernie grins and hops out. Time to start life.

Except for Sadler dorm, the huge new freshman dorm on the hill, the campus is still fairly quiet. The freshmen football players are there early for pre-season training. The goon squad is also arriving, sophomores who will prepare for the freshmen coming in a few weeks.

After settling into the dorm, the thirty three freshmen, mostly on football scholarships head over to the Manley Field House on a bus for their first orientation. Many of the other players are leaving home for the first time too, and although they are all putting on a good show, most are fairly nervous. When Ernie arrives a few recognize him and undertones go around about him. Most have heard how great he is. They find him handsome, tall and muscular, but otherwise, not what they really expected. He is quiet and shy, completely unassuming and modest. Many of the young men were stars in their own towns and schools. That's how they got to Syracuse. But none of them could hold a candle to Ernie's reputation. His demeanor is strong and quiet, and he projects an image that in spite of his humility makes him seem a step above all the others.

The first few days are home sick days, but they don't last long because of the grueling schedule of double sessions and the August heat. This endless activity will fall over into the arrival of the other freshmen in three weeks and then the beginning of fall sessions.

Al Zak, the tiny gnarled equipment manager is on hand to greet the freshman team and it's not at all what they were expecting. He seems to have been delegated to bring the frosh down to size. The varsity team is already there and they've dreamed up a little show for the freshmen.

"You shithead," says Zak to a great big varsity linebacker towering over him, "What you been doing all summer? You're flab is showing." He punches the player in the stomach. The player grabs himself there and seems to grimace in pain. Other players back off and look like they're trying to hide behind each other. Still talking to the big guy he punched, Zak says, "You get out there and work that off or I'll tell coach to bench you."

Now Zak moves to the next player. "Get that damn smirk off your face or I'll wipe it off for you." He takes a swat at him as the player backs off and looks pretty nervous.

"Hey, Gary!" He calls over a big player. "You think you're some hot shit don't you? What happened to all the socks I gave you last year? You eat them for breakfast? No more socks for you this year. You can all go barefoot for all I care."

And then he turns to the freshmen who are already shaking. The older players huddle behind each other, smothering laughter as they watch the faces of the freshmen turn green. Ben is standing on the other side of an open door watching Zak give it to them. He sticks his unlit cigar in his mouth in order to stifle a smile.

"Okay frosh... you shits line up over here..."

Then Zak sees Ernie and Will off in the far corner, who haven't moved.

"What's the matter with you two, .. are you deaf?"

"Over here!!!!"

The others shove Ernie in front of them.

"So this is the big shit frosh who thinks he's going to be another Jim Brown, ...right?"

"No sir," says Ernie lowering his eyes.

"No sir, is it?" says Zak. "Where are your manners, kid? No sir Zak. It is."

"No sir, Zak," repeats Ernie.

Zak turns to the others. "... all you guys that were big shits in high school, don't think you'll be the same here. You're just dumb freshmen."

Zak throws his practice clothes into Ernie's stomach and walks on down the line. He sees that Ernie has dropped a sock. "See what I mean. You can't even catch a sock, how you going to hold on to a football?"

Ernie and Will retreat to put on their practice uniforms. Other freshmen follow as fast as they can get out of there with their uniforms. Once they're out of hearing the varsity players break up. Even Zak has trouble maintaining his harsh look as a smile creeps onto his face.

"Now get out of here all you shit heads. You better win all your games this year, every one of them." And Zak departs.

Joe Szombathy, almost a kid himself is Assistant coach to the freshmen and Les Dye is head coach. The freshmen pour onto the practice field and get started with the set up already underway. The coaches don't intend to waste any time. These kids are really green. High school football is a long shot from college ball. Les singles out Ernie. He is still not convinced that he is all they say he is. He just seems a bit too shy and quiet to make a "great" player. He decides to throw him in right away.

"Hey, Ernie." Les calls him out. Ernie bounces right over.

"Yes sir."

"You lead the calisthenics. Lead the warm up exercises."

Ernie runs off with a grin. He can't wait to get started. He gets up in front of the others without hesitation and puts them through such a rigorous work-out that everyone stands there with mouths hanging open. One exercise after another he leads the group with enthusiasm, strength and doing everything perfectly.

Ben comes up behind Les. "Well, what do you think."

Les turns to him. "You tell me." He points out into the field where Ernie is still leading the calisthenics. "I don't believe this guy. I've never seen anything like it in my life. He walks out here like a whipped dog after meeting up with Zak, and I say to Joe here, 'So this is the big star? The one that will follow Jim Brown? Doesn't look like much to me.' I figure.... well, we might as well break him all in one day, so we can start building him up again... so I send him out there to lead the calisthenics. The guy's an animal. He's working these kids to death and he's still got a smile on his face. He does everything perfectly... just perfectly. And ... darn it all ... he's a nice animal at that."

Ben grins and watches. "Not bad."

Chapter 16

Syracuse, September 1958

September is here and the 1878 new freshmen arrive along with the rains and cooler weather. The cooler weather is better for practice and the freshmen are so excited and so busy they barely notice the poor weather. By now the frosh football team members feel like old hands. They've gotten to know each other, they know their way around campus and Marshall Street hangouts, and they're not so sore from practice as they were a few weeks earlier.

The Goon Squad is well at work helping the freshmen find their dorms and settle in. Cars pull up with concerned parents and scared kids and are immediately welcomed by Goons sporting their big orange goon buttons.

There are a bunch of big guys hanging out too ... the football players, checking out the freshman girls and even hoping to make a little spending money by helping their Dad's cart the luggage up to their rooms. John Brown is the self-appointed mentor for Will and Ernie.

"So here's how you do it." says John. "You pick yourself the prettiest girl and go up all nice and polite to her father and offer to help carry her trunk up to her dorm room. You don't even look at the girl. Play hard to get ... you know what I mean?"

"Sounds good to me." Will is ready to go and has identified his prey. John is already off lugging a big trunk.

"This sounds like trouble to me" says Ernie under breath. He's thinking White girls, Black boys... trouble. "I'm outta here." But then he spies a rather homely overweight girl struggling with two big suitcases and looking side to side as the players neatly pass her up. Then just as she forlornly starts to move forward two strong brown arms reach for her bags and easily lift them out of her hands.

"Where to." Ernie grins down at her.

She points and he follows. Later in chapel where they are all entering for convocation, she sees Ernie in the distance with Art and John and waves.

"Uugh, Ernie," says Art. "Where'd you find that one?"

Ernie waves back pleasantly. "You know... you guys need your eyes examined. She's human just like anyone else." Art gives Ernie a surprised look, then shrugs his shoulders as they move on in with the others.

Next the boys check out the bookstore. Ernie gets all excited when he starts looking through the books for the business courses.

"Did you see these, Will? These books look really great. It's so different from the ole stuff we studied in high school. I can't wait to find out what courses I'll be in. Everything looks interesting."

"Hey, hey, .. Ernie. Slow down there. Not so much focus on the academic things. It might distract you from the more important tasks ahead, like girls and beer, you know..." says Will.

Tuesday noon is the freshman picnic. Will and Ernie sit apart looking a little lost, woofing down ham and cheese sandwiches. The goons jump up and start leading a bunch of cheers in preparation for the first freshman game of the season. Ernie almost forgets for a moment that all the faces around him are White. He's never felt quite so isolated before. It's not like anyone says anything, but he feels it. The culture is different. The looks are friendly enough but often pass over him, the way people do sometimes when they see a person with a handicap and don't know whether to stare or look away. It is just a moment, but enough to bring on the loneliness that he sometimes has been feeling here since he arrived. The feelings are short lived, though, as other players join them and the banter begins. The Goons jump up and start yelling for the frosh to "tip your beanie" as the freshmen raise their caps in unison, then they start again with the cheers and the songs and as Ernie realizes that this is for them, the football players and the games they'll be playing, he gets excited again.

By Thursday evening the fun and excitement has reached a new pitch. The Goons have gone to the dorms and gathered up all the freshmen willing to come to the massive pep rally and bonfire. A line of hundreds of beanie topped freshmen weaves its way across campus like a snake just as dusk sets in.

At Archibold Stadium Ernie and the others are suiting up in their game uniforms for the first time. Suddenly Zak appears and yells at them:

"Okay, you dumb shit frosh, get out on the field."

The players race out one by one as Ben calls out their names. They stand in a line in front of the crowd while the band marches into the middle of the field for an exhibition. Janet Smith leads them. They call the band, "a Hundred Men and a Girl."

Someone lights her batons with flames and she thrills the audience with fire baton twirling, while the band plays, "Down the Field" and the "Saltine Warrior". The placard section in the stand flips their cards and the word CHARGE appears in bright orange, then they flip again to show an Eagle's Head in honor of Boston University that will be the first varsity game this weekend. Finally the blue words appear on the orange: TIP IT FROSH and the crowd goes wild, waving a hundred orange beanies to the light of the huge bonfire that was just lit. With the reflections it seems like the whole stadium has caught fire.

Ernie stands still watching the spectacle, hardly able to believe that he is really part of this. Everything is perfect. Everything is wonderful.

Monday evening after their first game, Ernie calls Angie.
"Angie, How are you?"

......

"Oh, just thought I'd call. "No, no ...everything's fine... It's gggreat."

....

"Wwwell .. a little lonely maybe. You know. I'm the only Negro on the freshman team. If it weren't for John and Art, I don't know what I'd do. It's like a different world, and I'm not really part of it, but in a way, ... I'm at the middle of it. It's just ssso strange."

......

"Oh yes, I'm ggglllad I'm here. I just felt like talking to you."

......

"Oh, I'm managing okay. They give us $15 a month with our scholarship called laundry money, you know for movies, a coke, whatever. Next year we also get jobs that pay us $10 a week for 10 hours of work, like sweeping a hall or something."

......

"We can't really get spending money as part of our scholarships, too much like being a professional instead of a college amateur. Rules of the game, you know."

......

"So, how's it going for you...."

....

Chapter 17

Students crowd into the old Archibold gymnasium forming lines in front of the favorite courses and popular professors as they sign up for classes. There is a lot of wheeling and dealing as everyone tries to avoid getting stuck in such classes as Freshman English meeting at 8AM on Tuesday, Thursday and Saturday mornings. Although the football players get preferential treatment due to their heavy practice and game schedules, poor Ernie and Brian Howard end up with an 8 o'clock anyway.. Brian and Sam Colella two other frosh football players room two doors down from Ernie. So each morning Ernie and Brian have to get up while the others sleep in. They trudge down the hall, eyes half closed, meeting each other in the communal bathroom and not speaking until Brian starts his daily teasing of Ernie about being a hussy for using depilatory cream for the ingrown hairs on his chin. Finally Brian gives it up; all he can get out of Ernie is deep laughter. It isn't much fun to tease unless he can get a rise out of him. When ready to go, Ernie looks over at him.

"Hey, Brian, maybe you need a little more time; you look like you just got out of bed. It's a shame all that work at the mirror was for nothing."

One does have to admit, in fact, that it is hard to look as put together as Ernie always does. Ernie understands, especially being a minority, that it is important what first impression you make on people. And being originally from a coal mining town, he appreciates the saying "cleanliness is next to godliness".

Finally the Tangerines, freshman team, is ready for their first college game.. West Point, October 17. Ernie is ready to go in spite of his groin injury and some missed practice days as a result of it. Sam Colella is playing quarterback; Ernie is left half back; and Howard Brian is end. Will Fitzgerald, on the other hand is listed as ailing. Ben is really anxious to get Ernie onto Varsity, but there is a policy at Syracuse University that no freshman can play varsity, the main objective being to give the student time to adapt to college life and handle the academics. The game ends in a tie.

Next game the frosh win 34 to 0 with Pete Brokaw and Ernie shining. Ernie gains a total of 115 yards and Brokaw 97. By November the freshman team is no longer treated with the normal indifference it provokes as opposed to the varsity team. The Daily Orange runs a feature on Ernie with a picture that guarantees he is no longer just an unknown face on campus.

Ernie has entered into his golden period and he is not alone. The whole country is in its golden era, economic stability, streets paved in gold, happy family sitcoms on TV, some strides against racial discrimination; and for the young people -- college traditions mixed with more sexual openness.

81

At Syracuse, this is the beginning of an era of championship. After the football games, the boys crash the female dorms for panty raids, stealing trophy panties from the girls' drawers as they scream and hover and laugh.

Previously only the lounge area of the woman's dorm was open to "male guests" up until curfew (sometimes as early as 9PM on week nights for freshmen), now experiments in hosting boys in dorm rooms on Sunday afternoons are tried with a two hour open door visit and the requirement that both boy and girl must always have at least one foot on the floor. Girls are locked in their dorms after curfew and risk being kicked out of the school for breaking the curfew rules. Virginity is being challenged, but still defended by most. Yet plenty of girls can be found in the bushes by "Mount Olympus" dorm in hot desperate clinches until seconds before the last curfew bell. Virginity is still considered an attribute for the girl who wants to marry and the loss of it is usually a well-kept secret by the girl, but not necessarily by the boy who has conquered it. Guys are already savvy about condoms, now the girls take some control and learn about other methods of birth control. A local doctor's name, professor at the nursing school, is bandied about by the nursing students to their roommates as the place to go for safer birth control such as birth control pills, diaphragms or IUDs.

College students are between kids and adults, hula hoops are the craze as students meet in groups by the dozens with their bright colored plastic hoops slung around their hips, gyrating. At parties rock and roll still reigns supreme, along with beer that is legal at 18. Some students major in bridge and are looking for a game, morning to night, in the student union or in the dorm. The uniform of the day is knee socks, crew neck sweaters, tailored shirts with button down collars, khaki pants, crew socks, loafers, bermuda shorts, plaid pleated skirts, cashmere sweater sets, camel hair coats, and 6 foot long knitted scarves. You can see Liz Taylor and Paul Newman in A Cat on a Hot Tin Roof, Mary Martin in South Pacific, or Debbie Reynolds singing "Tammy" in This Happy Feeling, all lily white pictures. And, although divorce is no longer uncommon, it is mostly among movie stars and often an embarrassment to the children.

It was a Golden Era for some, but it was a fool's gold. It shone on the surface, but its value was questionable. Lots of people were left out of the "good stuff". Injustice, prejudice, segregation and indifference by military and corporations to the individual well-being and worth of people was common. It was a time of easy money for some and poverty for others; a time when the rich tried to appear poor and the poor wanted to look rich. While the well-to-do threw away their educations for a pile of beer cans and drunken partying that lasted whole weekends, the deprived struggled to get the college education that was no longer a dream but now a necessity for a decent job.

This was the end of one era and the beginning of another... that of the youth culture, the John F. Kennedy politics, strife throughout the world, fear of nuclear Holocaust, the healing helping of the Peace Corps, integration, marches for civil rights, and the beatniks (who protested everything in the establishment from deodorant to bras to fraternities). A time of posing important questions, some of which dealt with equality and rights.

The <u>Daily Orange</u> prints a series of controversial articles and letters about segregation in fraternities. Many claim they would be happy to pledge a "Negro" except their national organization would throw them out. Others sign petitions that say "We don't believe in prejudice" but continue to lock out minorities. Little actually changes as students express their "deep-felt commitment", but the students involved in these statements seem to feel better. Everyone believes that letting in just one person of color means they are integrated. No one yet understands the concept of tokenism. But at least this is the beginning of "consciousness raising" showing its face amidst the comfortable complacency of the 50s.

Then, true to a transitional period, some students protest and rebel while others continue going about the business of "having fun" in college. The University gears up for Colgate Weekend. This is a game that is totally unfair, between one of the big football schools, Syracuse and little Colgate, but it is a favorite old tradition of the school, so placards appear everywhere, especially on porch roofs of the fraternities and sororities: "ORANGE CRUSH", "THE ORANGE SQUEEZE", or "THE RAMPAGE OF THE SALTINE WARRIOR" creating great scenes in front of the words. On Friday night there are bonfires, raids and traditional shaving a giant S on the head of any poor thoughtless Colgate student found to be lurking in the vicinity. Colgate circulates a flier that warns their students of the peril. "Use your head and keep your hair."

After all the buildup one would expect the game to be a letdown, but now that Ernie's name is out among the students, there is a bigger than ever crowd coming to the freshman game, hoping to see one of Ernie's outstanding plays. No one is disappointed. Ernie is handed the ball and starts around the left end. Just as he passes the point of scrimmage he is accosted by three Colgate tackles, obviously warned to keep an eye on him. He easily stops in his track, cuts back at least five yards behind the scrimmage line, changes the ball from one side to the other, while giving a hip here and a shoulder there to throw off other blockers and then starts down the other side, making a 63 yard run. He is the sensation of the day, his team winning 22 to 12. By evening the parties are going like crazy all over campus. It is clear that Ernie is welcome everywhere, the hero of the day, but he is without a date. Although others are crossing the racial barrier for dating, Ernie isn't ready yet for that risk. There is too much at stake. Ernie has little time to socialize with focus on studies and football. He remains directed. He knows what he wants.

As soon as the other teams realize what a threat Ernie is to their defense, they focus it on him. Ernie never complains but spends a lot of time in the training room patching up little injuries and taking care of himself, hamstring pulls, tight muscles and the like. Ger Schwedes is a junior and is doing great on the varsity team as right halfback. He also has a reoccurring injury that requires the whirlpool, but with only three pools in the training room they have to wait in line. He decides to shorten the line, in conspiracy with Ernie, so he stands up and lowers his pants in front of everyone christening the pool. "Ugh" go the other players and from then on, they stay away from the pool that he and Ernie want to use.

Ernie and Will are always tired. There schedule is full of practices, team classes on plays, games and academics. Three to 6:30 every evening is practice and it goes on until 8 or 9 three nights a week. Some of the players deal with it by getting to class about 10 minutes early just to get their academic work done. Some of the profs understand and tell them: "Hey, you, get right down there in the front row." That way they can keep an eye on them. The coaches tell them the same thing, that when the prof sees them sitting there, showing up, asking questions and getting involved, they'll be more willing to help or overlook the small problems. The advice is good and Ernie tries to follow it, but he finds it very difficult, since he has been used to hiding in the back of classrooms so he won't be called on.

It's already late on a Wednesday night and Will leaves the room with a towel and toothbrush in his hand, while Ernie kneels down beside his bed and folds his hands as his mouth moves in prayer. Will nods his head in wonder as he leaves, but he has gotten used to this nightly ritual. When Will returns he hears the tail end of the prayer:

"Dear father, forgive my sins. Help me to be thankful for this opportunity. Help me make the most of every gift you send me. Our Father, who art in Heaven......"

Will stands quietly at the door until Ernie finishes. Ernie rises and climbs into bed as though nothing out of the ordinary has happened.

"Hey, man, put out that light and get some beauty sleep ... you sure need it," says Ernie as he turns over.

Ernie studying at Syracuse

Will and Ernie don't get home until ten the next night. They are both beat but still have classes to prepare for. They sit at their desks over their books and periodically one or the other nods off. There is a quiet knock on the door and almost before they can get their groggy eyes open to go there, in comes Jim Brown, very quietly. He's in an old sweatshirt and slacks and immediately plops down on Ernie's desk, ignoring Will completely.

"You know, Ernie..." Jim starts in right away pontificating and teaching his prodigy the political realities of college, football, and pros, "Don't think the battle is over yet, here. You've got a lot of battles to fight in this world and it's not going to be easy. You have to know how to handle these people. You give em what they want. At least on the surface and you put together your forces, ... your points. You pile them up .. like money in the bank, until you've got enough to cash in ... then you tell em what YOU want."

Will, very aware that his conversation isn't for him goes back to his books.

"You got it made. You're on scholarship ... all you have to do is pass to stay in .... Why you can break a leg and they still have to let you stay here. You got to get your education. That needs to be your goal. Yehhh you'll play in NFL for a while, but without an education, you can't get anything. Why even..."

A knock on the door interrupts Jim. Will opens it. Out in the hallway, shuffling quietly in their slippers, are over thirty pajama clad freshmen, whispering.

One pajama clad freshman appears to be the spokesman and explains. "We heard Jim Brown was here. We're hoping he'll sign something for us." And they had formed a quiet neat line far down the hallway, each one carrying something to sign: pieces of paper, magazines, books, footballs, caps, shirts, just about everything anyone could think of. As Jim patiently signs them all, he takes the time to ask each student a question, such as. " You a freshman? How do you like Syracuse? Where are you from? Having a good time?"

Ernie and Will watch in awe, seeing a side of Jim that isn't always appreciated. Jim stays on and continues his talk with Ernie.

The Daily Orange prints regular headlines about Ernie: "Freshman Racer Carries Team to Victory." "Freshman Team Undefeated. Ernie Makes Two Touchdowns." and finally, the obvious conclusion: "Ernie Davis: A Second Jim Brown."

After a winning freshman season for the first time in years, Ernie is tired but enthusiastic. He goes out for basketball and makes the team, boosting that sport too. As a result, he doesn't have much time to go to the typical college hangouts, such as the Varsity Club, the Orange or the Clover Club, but when he does arrive, other students are drawn to him like a magnet..

In spite of his time being filled, Ernie is homesick and manages to get home on any weekends when there isn't a game. Sometimes he and Will hitchhike or get a ride with Mugsie.

Life at his own home is becoming uncomfortable. There is too much drinking and then ensuing arguments, but Ernie barely notices. He is gone most of the time. Being family to so many in Elmira, he barely has time for all the dinners offered. He is still seeing Betty when she is home too, spending many of his Elmira evenings with her and her family. Even when he gets a haircut from Mickey Jones they invite him to dinner and he and Mickey cook up a cake that they eat in one sitting after gorging on Doris's spaghetti dinner. Then Ernie sometimes moves on to yet other friends, like the Coleman brothers and can't refuse a second dinner. He's like a bottomless pit and everybody loves to feed him. When he shows up for a visit at Jerome's shop, Ed takes his measurements for some new shirts and is amazed at the size of his neck.

"Why you're neck has grown 3 inches, Ernie. What have you been doing."

Ernie confesses that he's doing special exercises to develop his neck muscles. He doesn't intend to be put out of games with injuries, so he has to constantly build himself up. Ernie asks Bob Jerome to cut off the sleeves for him since he never wears them. He explains that he gets too hot in long sleeves. Bob measures and snips and explains the tailor will do the rest.

"By the way," he says, "There are some guys who have called about you. They want to buy you some clothes for college for next year."

"Why would they do that," asks Ernie.

"I guess cause they're alumni and they think you've done a great job this year. They just want to help you out a little. You know, kind of give you a reward."

"I'm not sure I understand," Ernie replies. "That doesn't really sound right to me.

"Sure it is," Bob reassures him. "It's done all the time. A kid does really well, they want to let him know they appreciate it. They can't give you money to help you out, that makes you a pro... so they buy things, like clothes. They want the kid from Elmira to look good."

Ernie looks over at the beautiful sweaters Bob is showing him, longingly.

"That's really nice," he says. "Thank them for me."

Then Bob calls him over to meet a kid standing by the counter where they had just cut off his sleeves. He explains he is a fan and is wondering if Ernie would mind signing one of his cuffs for him as a souvenir.

Ernie laughs a little embarrassed.

"You're kidding," he says.

"Well, sure, if you want it."

When he's done at Jerome's, he finds time to go up to the famous Elmira Reformatory, housing NYC hardened criminals. There he plays basketball with inmates and teaches them his techniques. He never talks about this. It is just one of his personal commitments.

At the first breath of Spring, before the buds even think of peeking out, the undergrads can smell the subtle change in the air. A little bit of the sun, reprieve from the terrible bitterly cold and snowy dismal winter days, probably all of 48 degrees, the students appear on the porches, the roof tops, the grass, still brown from the winter. They are dressed in tee shirts and shorts, and a few brave co-eds are laying in the still hazy sun in their bathing suits. As the sun warms things up a bit, the students in the Greek houses and the independent housing open their windows so the playful male-female warring can begin.

The second warm day in a row and Spring fever reaches an unbearable pitch. Students skip classes and organize themselves more enthusiastically with male-female touch football in the Walnut Street park. Finally the day culminates in Spring frenzy with a grand finale water fight. Anything goes: water balloons, hoses, buckets of water dumped from windows, wet tee shirts, straggly soaked hair and sunshine to celebrate it all.

Other students meander over to the rose gardens on Ostrom Avenue tended already by the elderly Italian gentleman. There they spread their blankets and lay down in each others arms or open their books.

Ernie playing basketball all winter was star of the team, but now basketball season is over. Still Ernie and his teammates have little time to sit on blankets in the park because Spring practice is well under way. Only three of the freshman team are likely to be allowed to play varsity. Others will be red-shirted, a system where the student must expect to stay at the university for 5 instead of 4 years, but in order to be eligible must not play one of those years. Ernie, not surprisingly is one of those practicing with varsity and clearly expected, not only to be playing, but also "starting" on the first string team. And what a team it is going to be!

Chapter 18

Syracuse, Fall 1959

After working at Jerome's again during the summer, Ernie reports back to Syracuse for three intensive weeks of double training sessions.

The coaches have an urgent meeting. Soon the freshmen will arrive and the team has to be accommodated with rooms. Because of their odd schedules and their out of town trips, they like the team members to room together, but they just don't know what to do about Ernie. Art and John Brown are already set up together. The only other new African American football player this year is John Mackey, but as a freshman his schedule is totally different and he needs to be in a freshman dorm to be well entrenched in college life.

"I just don't want Ernie rooming with Fitz again this year," says Ben in frustration. "We've red-shirted Fitzgerald, so he won't have the same schedule at all, plus he's going to be goofing off since he isn't playing and has an extra year on campus. We've already been through almost half the team. If Brian isn't willing, what are we going to do with him?"

The other coaches agree. There is a knock on the door and they prepare for another interview. In front of them is a long list of names and all but about ten on the list are crossed out. In comes Brian Howard, looking pathetically frightened. Brian thinks he's done something wrong, or maybe they're going to red shirt him. That's the last thing he wants. He sees his name near the bottom of a long list and is even more apprehensive as he sits down. They all look so sober, he can't imagine what he has done, but it must be something terrible. After much beating around the bush , Ben finally comes out with it.

"Well, what do you think? Would you mind rooming with Ernie Davis?"

Brian almost falls over. He's absolutely flattered. "Would I mind? Why this is one of the finest things I could be asked in my life. Would I do it? I'd love to. This is a great opportunity to get to know him better. He's such a fine person."

Brian is bubbling his enthusiasm and relief. He realizes of course what happened: the racial thing. Well, so be it. It opens up a door for him and he is thrilled. Later the coaches bring Ernie in and ask him if he is willing to room with Brian, but it is more of a formality. Everyone already knows that Ernie would never object.

The season begins and Schwartzwalder is determined to make this the ultimate team of college ball. Ernie can't wait to get started while most of the other team members moan and groan about the especially hard workouts.

Ben doesn't wait a moment to lay out his plans in the briefing room.

"You work, or you get out. The four key players of the starting team this year will be Ger Schwedes, Dave Sarette, Art Baker and Ernie Davis. Then he goes on to list the others. If you're good you stay. If you mess up you're out. There's someone just as good waiting in the wings to take your place." Some of those not mentioned nudge Ger and jibe him.

And the work includes hours in front of the blackboard with the chalk dust flying as Ben races through formation after formation. For some of the players this is the hardest course they will have this year. In fact, Ben thinks so hard and long about the plays he wants to do and is so unaware of what is going on around him, the players start teasing behind his back that his head is always in the middle of a huddle or a muddle. Ben, who is known for his absentmindedness, even forgot to get back on a plane once during a stopover when he got off to buy himself a magazine.

Ben decides to clear the air immediately of one particular issue now, early in the season.

"Okay. I'm going to tell it to you kids straight out. I know there's a lot of talk around here these days about prejudice, discrimination, segregation. Well, we're not talking about it here... cause you're worth as much as you put out on the field to me... no more ... no less."

"Well... I may be a little kinder in my talking with the Italian kids and the Colored kids, cause they're sensitive," says Ben, "but the rest of you Krauts and Pollacks should expect the worst."

At this point the African American kids and Italian kids clap and shout. The other kids boo.

"Okay.. okay. You Polish kids know you:re tougher, so you can take it when I call you a dirty Pollack and you Krauts... well, forget you... Schwaltzwalder isn't a mouthful for nothin'. I know what you're up to."

Then Ben aims a devastating look at Ger, who grins back.

"But mostly pay attention to what you're doing. It doesn't matter who you are. If I say you did it wrong. ... You did it wrong...."

In the dorm, Brian and Ernie are moving their things into the room. Brian is mesmerized by the massive amount of clothes Ernie is unpacking and neatly folding or hanging. He doesn't much care that Ernie takes up most of the closet, placing each hanger just far enough away from the previous one so as not to wrinkle anything. He lines up his shined shoes carefully in a row under the shirts and suits. In the drawers he puts dozens of carefully folded sweaters.

"What do you think?" says Brian to Ernie

"About what?"

"You know... how the coach is going to treat us." He doesn't want to be specific about the racial stuff. No one talks openly about that and he was a little shocked at Schwartzwalder's frankness.

"I think he's great!" says Ernie. "It's going to be a great year. I think we're going to win the championship..."

"Do you like him... the Coach?"

"Yeh! I think he really cares about what happens to us. I think he wants us to be more than just good fffootball players. I think he wants us to graduate too... walk away with a ddegree."

"I hadn't thought about that," says Brian pensively.

"Hey, Ernie. Tell me something."

Ernie has already finished his unpacking and now Brian has opened his one suitcase and dumped it all into one drawer... without folding anything.

"You're on scholarship, aren't you?"

"Sure I am," responds Ernie. "Aren't all football players poor? Why else would you go out there and get beat up every day," and he grins.

"Well, if you're so poor, how'd you get all those clothes?"

"Benefactors, Brian, benefactors. Here put this one on and let's go to dinner." Ernie throws Brian one of his beautiful new sweaters. Brian happily puts it on. Cool to be rooming with Ernie!!!!

It isn't long before Ben is bending over backwards for Ernie. He and his assistants can't resist him, his hard work, his tremendous abilities, his ready smile and sense of humor. Already as the year begins, almost like magic, they are mesmerized by the character and physical abilities of Ernie and will do anything to make his life easier and keep him happy. The fact that Ernie doesn't seem to notice any special treatment or expect it and is thankful for the smallest gesture of kindness or attention, draws them in even more. Generally speaking even his fellow players don't seem to resent what obviously has become special treatment and consideration of Ernie, because of his humility and kindness to them. Later, though, it becomes more difficult for those so used to being superstars themselves to so often give up the limelight to Ernie.

After initial meetings and practices it is time to get appointed uniforms and suited up for pictures that will be placed on game programs. Ernie arrives in the locker room and lines up with the others. When he gets to Zak, he is ready for the onslaught, having already learned that Zak's bark is worse than his bite. Zak hands him his uniform and tells him to suit up and get out of the way. Ernie's relieved that Zak seems to be a bit subdued at the moment. He finds a bench to put his things on and begins to dress. When he finally picks up the jersey he sees the number on it: 44. He is horrified.

He runs back to Zak who has already finished the uniform task.

"I can't wear this jersey." He hands it back.

"You what???" Zak immediately becomes ornery. "You can't wear this... a perfectly good uniform? What's the matter with you? You something special?"

"No," Ernie tries to explain. "This is number 44. That was Jim Brown's number. I can't wear that."

"Hey, kid. If it was good enough for Jim Brown, it's good enough for you. That's the one the coaches say you wear... then THAT'S THE ONE YOU WEAR.... any complaints?"

"No, I don't meant that... I just..."

Zak softens just a tiny bit for Ernie. "The programs for all ten games are already laid out with these numbers. If you don't get out there and get your picture taken in it, you'll have to answer to the coaches."

There are lots of arguments Ernie is thinking of to give Zak: he doesn't think he's good enough for Jim Brown's number; he thinks it's too soon for him to be linked to Jim Brown; and he thinks that maybe the number should be put away and honored. Ernie gets an idea... he goes around to the other players trying to exchange it with their jersey's, but no one will touch it. They treat it like a hot potato. Ger calls out to the players, "Hey get a move on it, guys. It's picture time. Make yourselves pretty. Ernie puts the shirt on a bit embarrassed, trying to hide it when he goes out. Zak watches him with a grin, the first in a long time.

Although Ernie is proud to be wearing Jim's number, - there being no player he would want to be more like-, it is a mixed blessing. He doesn't want to be thought presumptuous, that he would merit this shirt.

In practice the team is divided up into three groups and the groups wear different colored jerseys: white for the first team, orange for the second, maroon for the third and all others wear green. The "greenies" never get to play in the regular games, but they still play an important part in the success of the team. The greenies are made up primarily of players who are red shirted and guys who just want to be part of the bigger picture, but don't always have the skills. Jimmie Wright is the captain of the greenies and although a little guy, he has a brain big enough to make up for his physical size. Being a joker and having very little personally and professionally at stake, Jimmie gets away with murder, teasing and kidding everyone.

Usually Jimmie has Ernie in stitches, but now as they move over to have their pictures taken he calls after Ernie.

"Hey, wait up a minute."

Ernie slows down.

"So they gave you Jim Brown's number, huh?"

"Yeah."

"Don't you know what that means? It means you're a marked man. So you've got two counts against you. Nobody can live up to a Jim Brown, but everybody's going to expect you to. And just the number on your jersey is going to keep you from moving down that field. They'll be all over you... all the time."

Ernie's smile fades to a somber look. He recognizes the truth in Jim's remarks.

The grueling double practice sessions are coming to an end. The freshmen have already been on campus a week and now the other students are arriving. As usual Ben has been eating, drinking, sleeping and dreaming his plays. They are progressively becoming more and more complicated. The greenies are kept in the dark in order to test the strategies. Jimmie is not only their captain, but their leader and he is incredibly on top of it all. As a result Ernie can't seem to get through the greenie defense. He just can't figure out how they do it. One way or another, they always have the signals figured out and know which way the ball is going or whether Ernie is about to run. They successfully block play after play.

Ben is pleased with this challenge for his team. He's taken misfits from everywhere and made them into a perfect blend. Many of them are excelling brilliantly under his tutoring. But he is no easy task master and often there is frustration among the players.

Ben knows what he is doing, though. He had a chance to strategize with Jim Brown what to do with a fabulous runner. He also knows that he had failed to utilize Jim as effectively as he would have liked, but now he has another chance to put his theories into action. He will build a team around a great running back, and having another top notch one, Ger Schwedes enables him to build around two. Then he also has ferocious linemen that are going to scare the "Bejesus" out of other teams, just looking at them.

After the first game, Ben already knows that he has the national championship team in his hands. After developing their physiques with grueling exercises and practices, Ben fills their minds with plays, finesses, ploys and every kind of football strategy ever tried, plus some that no one ever thought of before.

Ben arrives at the blackboard early in the morning. The players are scrunched into the too small desk seats in the briefing room, snickering and even laughing out loud. Ben is scratching plays frantically on the board, covering everything in chalk dust, and then finally he turns to them with a murderous look.

"What is this about?"

Now they are all laughing openly as Ger points to his pants. Ben looks down to see that he still has his pajama pants on.

He stifles a laugh and mumbles, "Just wanted to see if you're paying attention," and goes right on explaining the next play.

Ben, as a survivor of two WWII invasions that left few other officers alive, now prepares his winning team as though they were going to war. Besides the normal calisthenics and briefings, they have to climb ropes, sprint half-miles and do other various difficult activities. Ben is hard-nosed, and working with him, they are all becoming hard-nosed too. In fact, they are quickly becoming known through the media as the Fearsome Four and the Sizeable Seven. The season is well underway with a victory over Kansas, thanks to Sarette's passing and Schwedes' running. Then the second game where the score was held to nothing, Ernie jumps in with a 77 yard run and then another 26 yards to a touchdown. Syracuse wipes out Maryland 29 – 0.

Brian and Ernie pack up for their first away game with slight trepidation. They travel to Norfolk, Virginia to play Navy. Three days away from school. The first day is traveling and relaxing, but neither feels a great deal like relaxing as they have dinner in the mess hall with the cadets, who sit perfectly stiff on the edges of their seats eating their "square meals". Ernie and Brian are pretty sure they wouldn't survive that, even though Ernie is highly disciplined in his sport. He feels even more sure of that when he hears the doors lock behind them in the grand fortress where they try to sleep. But the discomfort disappears from Ernie completely once on the field. He performs perfectly in a driving rain. Syracuse wins 32 to 6.

Before the sports year is very far along, Ernie is already making headlines. Al Mallette, the Elmira sports writer,93 dubs Ernie "The Elmira Express," not just because he runs so fast, but also because he can take out anything that gets in his way.

Ernie running the ball at Syracuse University

The rule for college ball of this period states that a player can be taken out and put back only once a quarter. This makes it impossible to have separate offensive and defensive teams. The coach is not able to change teams every time the ball changes hands. As much as possible, therefore, he must develop both offensive and defensive skills in all his players. For Ernie it means that he not only has to run with the ball and run to catch passes, but he has to also chase the other team and tackle players. As usual Ernie, fast, strong and determined, excels also at this and is able to take out three men in a play, all usually bigger than himself.

The wins pile up, the big cannon blasts as Syracuse scores again and again. Ernie runs, harder and harder. Syracuse decimates Holy Cross, Dave

Sarette and Dick Easterly both pass for touchdowns and Ger has a bright day for rushing and completing passes. Yet, Ernie's star is still rising. He is making touchdowns and running like a ballerina, dodging all the opposition tackles with seeming ease.

Ben calls the team together. He sits them in their too tiny seats and admonishes them to watch carefully. Then he starts scratching on the blackboard at a crazy speed with chalk dust starting to cover his arm and float on down to the floor around him. He lays out hieroglyphics that only a football mind can decipher and creates variations on their current plays.

"Now I want you to all pay close attention to this next one." A couple of dozing guys jump slightly in their seats. "This is special. This is Ernie's play and it's going to get us the championship."

Ben lines up the circles representing his boys in an unbalanced line, plotting his center, the weakest lineman, just off center to give more force to his stronger linemen. He brings his boys into a closed formation with tight ends and a tight wing back. Then when the opposition is least expecting it, instead of running Ernie on the outside to the right he runs him right down the middle through the opposition defense.

This play has a three way option that will allow the quarterback to make the decision at the last moment so that the other team can never guess which way the ball will run.

"Our team," continues Ben, "including the left back, Ger, will flow in one direction like this," and Ben quickly throws on a bunch of lines, arrows and circles to show the movements. "Then if it is clear that the other team is responding to that flow, the quarterback hands the ball to Ernie and he runs right down the middle for daylight."

The players are now sitting up and listening intently. It's brilliant ... if it will work. First of all... it had never been done before and secondly it takes advantage of Ernie's speed, his power and his fearlessness. They get it... when Ernie runs for daylight, it doesn't matter what's in his way.

So Ben emphasizes for this to work, his halfbacks have to be able to pass as well as run. That very same day Ernie and Ger begin their intense practice trying to make themselves as good at passing as most fullbacks and quarterbacks. Now the team is totally unpredictable equally capable of passing and running.

Day after day the team works on this play that will be the center of their repertoire. Ben never lets up and the players begin to grumble and complain. Out on the field it is only Ernie that seems to still be upbeat and ready to go. Ben sees the linemen missing their blocks and Ernie has to break a couple of tackles on his own just to gain 5 or 6 yards. Ben is really angry, constantly yelling at some of the linemen to start working, get their act together. Finally he throws his old hat down and stamps on it. Ernie seems oblivious to Ben's anger or even to the lack of interest and work of his other teammates. In his enthusiasm and excitement for having broken through the opposition he comes racing back to his teammates, patting them on the shoulders or backs as he goes.

"Great blocking guys!" he yells.

"Shut up, Ernie," says Ben. "You're lying! How am I supposed to coach these dumb kids when you're braggin on them like that?"

The other players get into it. "Yeh, Coach, listen to Ernie. He knows what he's sayin. He's tellin you right."

But because they know that Ernie isn't really telling it right and because they like Ernie and he's too good to them and patient with them on his special play, they turn around and prove to the coach that Ernie is telling the truth. They start working for him.

Ben Schwartzwalder showing Ernie a play.

Any more messing around, Ben no longer yells, he just throws down his hat and stares them down. Ernie... not really as oblivious as he seems, grins to watch the little coach stand up to these huge linebackers. Ben himself understands the benefit of the dynamics and knows that when he plays the bad guy and Ernie plays the good guy, the team gets motivated and comes through for Ernie. He's no dummy!

Zak, who is already privy to what's going on comes stampeding into the locker room like a herd of elephants, his grizzled old face in a mask of anger. He yells at the two players who have been goofing off most on the practice field.

"Okay, you shit-heads, what did you do with your socks after the last game? You know where they should go. They've disappeared!" And he continues ranting and raving at them that they are so stupid they can't even keep track of a pair of socks. For the second time that day, the two 240 pound bundles of muscle just hold their tongues and take it. Ernie, sitting quietly on the bench listening, sees Ben sneaking by the door with a bag in his hand (allegedly containing dirty old socks), he winks at Ernie.

So there is the humorous punishment and then there is the real punishment. Ben calls them into the training room and quietly informs them that he is going to make some significant changes of first string. He wants to move some up and others back to second.

The captain of the second team speaks up. "Coach, can you wait a moment so we can talk this over..."

Ben looks up in surprise and then nods his head. The second string goes into a huddle. They whisper for a few minutes then all sit down and the captain stands up.

"Listen, Coach. We don't need to play on the first string. We get to play just as much time as they do already. Why one of the newspapers listed us as the third best team in the country. We just got it going together now and we don't want to shake it up. Let's keep all the same guys working together how they are. Whatever we're doing, it's going right for us just the way it is."

"Why you're a bunch of crazies," says Ben and stops for a moment. "Well, ... okay. You got it. No changes.... for now, but if anyone sloughs off, I'm moving him right back to third string... Is that clear?"

"Okay, then... here's the score! No more messing around with this play. We're springing the "scissors play" on West Virginia this weekend and I want you to do it just right. You're going to knock the socks right off West Virginia. If they have any left on at the end of the game, I'll be surprised. Now, not a word of this gets out of this room."

"This is the way it's going to go: Easterly fakes a hand off to Ger, who starts around the end. As the defense moves toward that side ... Dick hands off to Ernie who plows right through the center. We'll use both his power and his running skill. After the surprise of it a couple of times, when they protect for the scissors, they'll leave their ends open. Then we'll go around. When they switch back to protect the ends, we'll push right through the scissors play again."

Art is very quiet. The play requires a lot of fakes to him, but Ernie gets the limelight. Art is good, but he sees the writing on the wall. This is going to be Ernie's show.

Several days later late in the evening, Ben is still in the briefing room, covering the blackboards with every conceivable configuration of the scissors play, obsessed with his thoughts. A knock comes on the door for the second time.

"What is it?" He responds gruffly.

"It's Ernie, Coach," replies the grounds superintendent.

Ben looks up sharply, worry etched in his eyes. "What about Ernie?"

"He won't leave. He's out there all by himself, kicking the ball, racing to get it, picking it up, running it down the field. I never seen anything like it. I need to put those lights off and go home."

"I'll tell you what, Sam. Tonight you let me take care of the lights. In the future, let Ernie practice 15-20 minutes after the others leave and then just turn the lights off. He'll leave when it's dark."

Ben finishes scribbling on the board and then walks out onto the field.

"Com'on, Ernie. These guys have to turn the lights off and go home."

"Sorry, Coach. I didn't realize it was so late."

Ben puts his arm around Ernie's shoulder and walks off the field with him.

"How's your Mom, Ernie? Everything okay?"

"Yeah, she's going to be here at the West Virginia game. I want to be at my best..."

"You're doing great, Ernie. Just great. Don't work too hard kid. You got to have fun too. How's school going?"

"Fine. I especially like my business management course this semester. Some of the readings are really good. They make you stop and think."

"Keep up the work, Ernie. Just remember that no matter how great you are at sports... you still need that degree."

"I know that, Coach. ...... Thanks."

Ben squeezes his shoulder and lets go. He stands there watching Ernie run into the locker room, then mutters to himself as he goes to turn off the lights. "Never seen a kid like this... Never in my life .... You can't run him off the field, .. even if you want to.... Nice kid.... Really nice kid...."

The weekend arrives. The team starts off pre-game with a big breakfast, including steak, potatoes and vegetables at Drumlin's Country Club. Then begins the skull session. After that they go to the locker room for ankle taping. Although they are all pretty confident, most of them are fairly nervous before a game. Some of them express it through rowdiness or excessive joking. Ernie likes quiet time and he pulls away from the others to prepare himself mentally. They exit for pre-game practice and drills, duck walks, leg lifts, jumping jacks and practice punts. They can see the other team doing the same, but they try to ignore them. They want to psych themselves up and that doesn't work as well when seeing their opponent hard at work too.

They are back in the locker room for last minute preparations.

"Okay, guys," Ben says, "I want you to remember, we're going to use the scissors play every chance we get."

Then it is Ger's turn. "Do the damndest you can!" He starts his 30 second pitch. "No matter what happens, as long as you've played your best....." Finally he reminds them, "West Virginia isn't a bad team at all, let's beat the shit out of them."

He calls Zak over to lead the prayer. They all bow their heads together. Then as they race out the door in silence, Zak pipes up with his familiar, "You dumb shits, you better win."

Out on the field, Ernie looks up into the stands. All he can see is a mass of Orange: orange scarves, orange sweaters, orange jackets, orange banners. He feels his chest swell with pride. This is his school, his game and he knows Marie is up there to watch even though he can't see her amidst the orange. He wants her to be proud of him and today is his day with the play designed to take advantage of his best abilities. He briefly remembers Rev. Latta Thomas telling them all how important it is to develop their God given abilities and use them as best they can. He is more than determined.

The scissors play is a great success. West Virginia doesn't know what hit them. But they know who is doing all the running and right through the middle of them. As the Syracuse score rises and the West Virginia players get frustrated trying to figure out what is really happening, they get abusive at the line of scrimmage, much of which is aimed at Ernie.

"Nigger!" they yell at him. "You nigger lovers," they direct at the other team members. "Kid Chocolate!" they name Ernie.

Every time they use a name like that Ernie and Art fly down the field faster than ever, determination written all over their faces. Ernie remembers well the lessons from the sandlot courts of his childhood with his older "brothers" and the Coleman brothers. Tough it out. Never let them know. And he just plays it out... faster, harder better. The scoreboard shows the results: 44 to 0. Ernie is the hero of the day!

Ernie had a terrific day. The team had made the scissors play work over and over. They were elated. Ben was quietly ecstatic. He knew it would work, but imagining and seeing it happen are two different things. Ernie gained 100 yards in this game just running the scissors play. All the fans who had loved to watch him run were thrilled over and over again. It looked like he was flying over the middle of the scrimmage, leaving the players huddled behind him.   Maybe he didn't wear a halo yet, but he sure as anything had wings.

To the rest of the world it looked like Ernie was having a great day ... and he was, because he came out victorious, but the motivation came from the opposition.   Little did the opposition know how much harder they were making it for themselves.

Ernie is riding his wave of victory when he meets his mother for dinner after the game. She is full of compliments for Ernie, but he can tell right away that something isn't all right. Finally she admits that she and Art have irreconcilable problems and that he is moving out, this weekend, while she is visiting Ernie. Ernie is devastated. He knows drinking has been a problem and he knows that they have been arguing too much, but he thinks they should stay together and work it out. Marie is adamant and simply changes the subject rather than argue with Ernie about it.

That week when Brian and Ernie are at their desks, trying to catch up on their backlog of work, Jim Brown shows up, walks in and sets himself on Ernie's desk. Ernie leaves his book open and listens as Jim talks.

"So how is it going in Cleveland," Ernie asks. "I hear your name in the news often."

"It'd be going great if those guys didn't get on my case so much. The way they treat players, especially Blacks is incredible. I mean, we're the guys who are scoring the points, bringing in the fans, and they just do the dictating."

Brian leaves the room with towel, toothbrush and toothpaste in hand.

Jim proceeds. "I already told you a little about Avatus Stone. Now let me tell you the whole story and how it impacted me. He came in on a scholarship, really talented guy, but after him, they decided not to give any more scholarships to Blacks. Like I told you, he didn't quite behave like their idea of a good little nigger boy."

"So ... when I came here .... they'd already made up their minds they didn't want any more of us. I didn't have a scholarship and they didn't want to let me on the team, but what could they do. I signed up; they had to let me practice, but they barely played me until my junior year. I was so pissed off by my sophomore year that I quit for a while and went home, but there was a guy there that convinced me to go back. I knew I needed the degree. I had to have it or I couldn't do anything I wanted. And I knew what I wanted to do. Pro ball, that's where the money is, but that's not all......."

Brian returns and starts getting ready for bed. Jim pays no attention to him. He goes on as though he weren't even there.

"There was a flu epidemic my junior year... everybody was down with it, so they finally let me on the field. I knew that was my only chance ... and there wasn't anything in the world that could get in the way of me and that goal. After that, they couldn't ignore me!!!! Remember you got to be the best. Better than the best, or they won't let you play at all.... you got to be bigger, ... run faster ... and be meaner. Don't forget that, Ernie."

"How'd you manage to get to Syracuse without an athletic scholarship," asks Ernie.

"There was one guy in my hometown... you know, ... the one who convinced me to return to Syracuse. He liked the way I played ... took an interest in me ... raised the money; 44 guys in all contributed. I was grateful... so I asked for number 44."

As Jim talks, Ernie packs up his books for morning, all the time listening and nodding. He looks at the clock. It's already midnight and Brian's in bed.

"Geeze," says Brian as he checks the clock too. "I've got an 8 o'clock tomorrow morning and I've got to go to sleep. But don't let me bother you. I'll just turn over and you guys can keep on talking."

Jim takes no notice. He acts like he doesn't even hear him. Ernie is the only one he is interested in. He barely loses a beat as he goes on... Ernie is still sitting at his desk, eyes drooping, then he gets up to prepare for bed.

"It's this thing with Paul Brown and Art Modell that makes everything harder. They're always at odds. It isn't a good thing that Modell bought the club and then keeps Paul on to Coach. "

Ernie, finally ready for bed, crawls in, leaving the sheets and blankets tightly tucked in. He barely disturbs the covers. He turns out the light over his head, but stays leaning on one elbow, not wanting to be rude to Jim.

"You had a great game today. I was there. That new play of Ben's is a stroke of genius. Makes you look real good. But don't get confused by all this attention. No matter how big a hero they make you, don't ever forget that they won't ever let you forget... for them ... you're still a Nigger. You got to be careful. You push em to the edge and then step back just a little. But they're never going to accept you ... and you don't have to ever accept them. Just play their game when you have to. Some guys pretend they're buddies with them, but that's not for me. I don't know anyone I respect who is friends with them. I'm not pretending. I'll follow their rules when I have to to get what I want, but I won't kiss ass ...."

The next morning Brian calls over to Ernie, who also has an 8 o'clock.

"Hey, Ernie."

"Yeahhh."

"When did Jim leave last night?"

"Geez, I don't know for sure. I think I fell asleep too. I guess he let himself out."

Brian bounces out of bed, grabs his things and starts out the door.

"Hey, Brian," Ernie calls after him.

"Yeah?"

"Take it easy, boy. You crazy? You got to be withdrawn in the morning. Don't jump around like that. You know..., you better watch yourself... you could break a leg or something."

Brian laughs as he goes out the door.

Ernie slides neatly out of bed leaving it as though it had never been slept in, struggles into his robe and then goes for the door, never opening his eyes.

Syracuse University is the rage. It is the most watched football team this year. All the newspapers are following its games: Pittsburgh 35-0, Penn State (also undefeated) 20-18. Now Syracuse is in the lead nationally. They are the team to beat. But that won't be easy.

Ger brings the latest paper into the locker room.

"Hey did you guys see this. How do you like that. This one says we ought to be playing ourselves to find out who's number one."

The second team members slap each other on the back and let out whoops.

Just then, Ben walks in.

"Don't you kids listen to what they write in the papers. Why you kids can't even beat the greenies in scrimmage.

"Yeh," shouts out Jimmie Wright and other members of the greenies start patting each other on the back too.

"Hey, Ben," that's not a fair comparison," the first two teams gripe. "You wear us all out and then bring them in fresh."

"Com'on guys, stop making excuses. If Jim can figure out all your weaknesses, what makes you think the opposition team can't."

"Just remember this. When you're at the top of the mountain there's only one place to go, down. And everybody, but everybody, wants to be the one to bring you down and take your place. You can bet they're going to be watching you through a microscope. If you've got a weakness, they'll find it. You're going to have to work harder to stay where you are than you had to work to get there in the first place."

The laughter of the players and patting on the back slows down as the players begin to contemplate what Ben is saying and understand the truth in it. Ernie's face too changes from amused to somber.

After all that, Ben throws a surprise at them. "Practice is over for the day. I want you kids to get a little extra rest and relaxation. Don't you get too lax, though."

The players exchange amazed looks. He has been working them to the edge all year. They can't imagine why... now that the pressure is on .. he should be letting up a little.

Back in the coaches' office Ben is describing the scene to the other coaches.

"You should have seen their faces. I know we've been driving them really hard and they need the break. I just don't want to let up too much. But last time we wore them out before we ever got to the Cotton Bowl. I don't want to make that mistake twice. We've got to keep the energy going at just the right pitch. Balance ain't an easy task, is it?"

"Ernie's looking good. We want to keep him right where he is, but we're going to have to be careful with him. The other teams are catching on to what we're doing with him and he's going to be their prime target. He's already taking too many hits. We don't want him injured. He's essential to the team."

Chapter 19

Excitement is at a high pitch as the weekend arrives. Although the traditional Colgate vs. Syracuse game is a highlight of the season, as usual, Colgate is really no competition for Syracuse University's football team. After all, Syracuse is clearly headed for the national championship and Colgate is just a medium sized men's school. The attraction is with the weekend social activities involved. The newspapers have already picked up on the inequalities of the two teams and inappropriateness of the competition more than ever this year, but once again the students seem oblivious to it.

Signs adorn fraternity houses: Beat Colgate, Scalp Colgate, etc. with pictures on the roofs such as a tube of toothpaste with an orange guy squeezing it. In front of one of the houses there is a large group of guys while others run to join them. It looks like a brawl. When they separate, out steps a guy with a brand new haircut. The mohawk (a tuft of hair left down the middle of his head). He looks dazed but unhurt. Chances are he already knew what was to come when he stepped on campus for a spy expedition.

Snakes of students weave through the streets and end up in a field with a huge bonfire going and cheers being led by the cheerleaders.

The day after the game, Ben sits in his office with Coach Sims. He puts down the newspaper and holds his head in his hands. Then he lifts his head and looks at him.

"So they're calling me Atilla, the Hun. They say we're ferocious and that we shouldn't be allowed on a football field. That we knew we could decimate Colgate, but it was too extreme. So what are we supposed to do? Try to lose?"

"Nah... just laugh at it. We got a national victory to think of. Maybe take it a little easy on guys like Colgate that aren't in our league. Otherwise, we can't let up, ...not for a minute."

So far, except for the first game, Syracuse had managed to keep the other teams to 0 or single digits. The fans are a bit perturbed. They want to see at least a little excitement or competition. Sometimes there are hazards to being too good. But it isn't going to last forever. Soon the other coaches will catch on and counter attack.

When asked about Colgate, Ernie told the press that the team already knew they were running toward the national championship, but that they weren't trying to run up their scores for a national record. "We try to keep the scores down, ... win, yes, but not crucify the other team."

Meanwhile, Ernie is missing home. The social life at Syracuse is so limited. There are the few Negroes on the team, maybe a handful of other Negroes in the school, and even looking at a White girl who looks back might jeopardize his plans, or at least that's the way Jim tells it and Ernie is sure there is some serious truth to that. Jim's solution, however, is to do what you want, but hide it good. Ernie's solution is stay clearly out of trouble... racial trouble.... and keep focused on the goal.

Art Radford, Ernie's step-dad, has already seen to it that Ernie has a car. He knows it's important for him to get home. Only ... what a car! It's an Edsell in very poor condition. If there is one thing that can get Ernie's goat, it is his car. Will Fitzgerald often catches a ride home with him, but he doesn't have as much to leave for or return home for. After all, he is White and can find his own entertainment on campus.

So Ernie gets into the car on the hillside, lets it roll to the bottom, and if the motor is running by then, off he goes home to Elmira. On his way to his own house he stops at Mickey Jones' house.

"Where you going," asks Mickey

"Goin home," replies Ernie.

"Whaddya mean, goin home. You home right here, right now."

So Ernie doesn't miss a stroke. "What's Doris cookin tonight?"

"She's going to have collard greens and made some bread,"

That is all the invite Ernie needs. He sits down at the table between the two of them and eats all two dozen of Doris's rolls. He tells them about Syracuse, his games, his classes and Jim Brown's visit. And as he devours everything on the table, Doris asks him about his personal life.

"Well, you meet many girls?" She knows how shy Ernie can be.

"Man," he grins, " I have to beat them off with a stick," but he never talks about the girls in the same way lots of men do. He always treats them with respect within or without earshot. Mickey knows that Ernie is just joking, but he thinks it is truer than Ernie will admit. He has walked down the street with Ernie before and seen the girls throw themselves at him. Ernie doesn't take advantage. What Mickey or some other guys would have done with that set up! It was kind of weird with Ernie. He wasn't a wimp or holier than thou, that wouldn't have gone down well with anyone. It was just that Mickey sometimes almost felt like he was in church. You always watched what you said and how you said it in front of Ernie. You didn't want him to think badly of you. He had high standards and somehow as a guy.. friend, you tried to live up to those standards when he was around.

Although Ernie had made his family in Elmira out of all kinds of family and friends, all ages and all races, he couldn't forget his childhood family. He continued to have calls and visits with Angie, Chuck, Willie, Walter and the others, and especially with Mom and Dad, who now lived in NYC. Dad had had to leave the coal mines. His health had suffered from the years of breathing coal dust. He had contracted black lung disease. Mom wasn't in perfect health either, so Ernie went to see them in Brooklyn when he could.

Back at Syracuse Sammy Fraternity is having some very serious discussions. Ernie's name has been proposed again as a possible member. Sammy, a national Jewish fraternity is ready to be on the forefront of racial integration, or at least some of its members are.

The fraternity members love having a winning football team, but have mixed feelings about asking the star of the team to join them.

Racial attitudes in the 60s are confusing at best. There are a small number of White students who are vehement about openness, integration, and equality, but few of them have a real understanding of what this means and of the hidden attitudes among their friends and colleagues. There are an equal number of students who have just as strong or stronger attitudes against Blacks in any form. Then there are those who superficially want to get on the bandwagon of integration, but underneath are still very uncomfortable about getting close to a "Negro." Many sororities and fraternities sign non-discriminatory statements to send to their national headquarters, but few of them stand behind their signatures. The excuse for not inviting someone of a different racial background is that the Greek group will be forced out of their national organization. Sammy members, on the other hand, seem ready to take this risk.

The President of Sammy is ready to take a straw vote. It is understood that six "no" votes can keep a person out. As he counts the hands in the air against letting Ernie into the group, six go up.

"Okay," says the president, "do you want to reconsider? .....Let's open the floor for discussion and then we'll take a final vote."

There is murmuring in the back of the room. The anti forces are pretty confident they can keep Ernie out. Many of the other members are relieved that they won't have to oppose Ernie openly because of the already six votes against him.

The members state their thoughts:

"He's not our kind. We'll get a bad reputation for letting him in. I don't care how good a football player he is."

"I don't have anything against Colored people, but I think it's hypocritical to just pledge a name. You know he won't be active. He won't be comfortable with us."

"I hope none of you guys where you come from ever have been attacked or beaten up by Niggers. I hope you're ready to lock your personal things up every night and sleep with your wallet under your pillow. Once you let one of them in here, you'll never be safe again."

"I think Ernie is a better man than most White men I know. I would be proud to be his brother."

"I think it's time we stopped talking about not being prejudice and started acting on it. I'm for inviting Ernie in."

The president waits a moment or two but because there are no more comments, he calls the vote.

"The question is called on Ernest Davis of Elmira, New York as a candidate for Sigma Alpha Mu pledgeship. All those opposed....?"

Several hands go up immediately and a couple follow. The president counts them. Before anyone can put it all together, He announces the result.

"Only five votes against Ernie, he is now officially invited into membership of Sigma Alpha Mu."

Those voting against Ernie look around confused, wondering what happened to the sixth vote. They were convinced he was a shoo out. After most of the brothers leave the room, the president and several others gather in the front of the room and give each other hearty pats on the back. One of them was the sixth no vote in the straw vote. They pushed Ernie through by letting the fence sitters think they didn't need to show their true attitudes. It was a ploy and it worked. Ernie is the first Negro in Sammy.

"I can't believe we pulled it off," says the guy who set it up.

"We know we're doing the right thing, but it sure is going to raise hell with national."

A week later Ernie is crossing campus with John Mackey.

"I understand how you feel, John. I was the only Member on the frosh team last year. It's lonely out there in a field of White.... Listen, next year when you're with varsity we can room together. Then there'll be four of us."

A Sammy passes near and waves at Ernie. "Hey, Ernie, great to have you join SAM. Looking forward to having you aboard."

Mackey looks worried for a moment. "Hey... aren't you going to end up living there then. How do you feel about joining a fraternity, anyway?"

Ernie explains that he thinks it is something they ought to do when it's possible.. break through the barriers. "I don't plan to live there. After all, I'll still be living with the team. Hey, you didn't think I was going to leave you all alone to grab the best girls did you. Not in your life. I've got to keep a watchful eye over you." Ernie jostles Mackey playfully.

The wind is bitterly cold and howling through the Pennsylvania hills as the teams run out onto the field. Ernie shivers and wonders how they will survive the icy chill in the air, but soon he is too engrossed in the game to notice. Ernie does well against Penn State in defense and blocking, but Penn has developed a fairly effective defense against the scissors' play since their scouts had observed the West Virginia game. Ernie can't seem to gain much ground. He has already passed Jim Brown's yardage record for his sophomore year, which wasn't hard since they hadn't played Jim much that year. But that isn't his focus anyway. He is thinking about the team and winning and he knows that being the decoy this time around is what is going to make it work.

Sometimes Ernie's enthusiasm gets in his way, though. When Penn State kicks off in the second half, and the ball is headed out of bounds, Ernie intercepts the ball around the 5 yard line and then steps out with it at the 6 yard line. His teammates chide him, not entirely sorry to see him make a mistake and a somber Ernie goes on with the game. He does make a touchdown in the fourth quarter, but then Penn runs the ball for 100 yards. At one point Ben had decided to break his self-imposed seven minute rule of playing the first and second team only seven minutes each. Now he is not so sure that was a good idea. The game is won but only by a slim margin, 20-18. After that the rule gets engraved in cement, seven minutes in, seven minutes out.

In spite of primarily acting as decoy in this game, however, Ernie manages to take 44 hard won yards.

Ernie's friends, on the other hand, aren't satisfied with the use of Ernie as a decoy. They had come to watch Ernie run and thought that Ben was slighting him. They were also confused by Dave Sarette's plays when he was acting quarterback. He could rarely see far enough to pick up the coaches signals, so he had to get them from Ger in the huddle or just play it his own way. Often he ended up calling his own plays (which actually was the way it was supposed to be in 1959). His calls were somewhat simplified from what Ben might have tried to do. Some of Ernie's African American friends thought there was hidden prejudice in the limited play of Ernie. According to Ben, he was trying to save Ernie from injuries. Ernie was too important to the total outcome to run him out in a game like this. Prejudice in the North was like that: so difficult sometimes to discern. How much was discrimination, how much was simply the best choice of the moment. With so much semi-masked and blatant racial injustice, it was easy to assume the worst and often true.

At the Penn game there were lots of photographers taking pictures during the plays, especially of Ben as he called them. Unfortunately Ben didn't take notice of them, used to the media being everywhere, he didn't realize it might be scouts from other teams.

When Ben gets to Boston, he calls plays from the Bench as usual. Ger watches for them and then passes them on to Sarette in the huddle. Sarette plays them out. But every play Syracuse tries to run, the opposition has the right defense for. By halftime the score is held to 12-0 in favor of Syracuse, nowhere near as good as it should be given the difference in abilities of the teams. Ben is so angry by halftime that he can't even come to the locker room and his hat has been stamped to pieces. But by the end of the first half some of the S.U. Team had been watching the Boston bench and saw that every time Ben gave a signal, the Boston coach followed with one to his team.

So Ger goes to the coach with their conclusion.

"Coach, they're on to our signals."

Coach sets Norm Lemieux down on the bench near him and continues to call play signals, meanwhile Norm signals different ones unobtrusively, the right ones. It works. Syracuse scores another 34 points in the second half, winning 46-0.

As 1959 is drawing to a close and 1960 is in sight, a new language is dawning. Familiar words take on new meanings, reflecting new attitudes: relating, consciousness raising, commitment, concern, in depth, sensitivity. It is the end of a certain kind of innocence, but one that cheated many people out of a good life, such as unmarried pregnant young women thrown out of their homes, homosexuality hidden away and ridiculed, Negroes limited in homes, jobs and educational opportunities. Instead it was the beginning of new sensitivity and concern, a kind of humanity that demanded respect and love of others. It was also the beginning of an era of hopeless war, in which everyone was the victim, and a time when everything was questionable and everything was questioned.

But Ernie's life was still part of the old era and not quite part of the new. At the beginning of his college career, academic life hadn't changed so much from what it had been 20-30 years earlier, but by the time he would finish, it would be rapidly changing and in many ways Ernie, whether he chose it or not, was in the forefront of those changes. There needed to be a Jim Brown to come out fighting and tough it out, and an Ernie Davis to soften the blows of change. Ernie still felt uneasy in the White world that surrounded him at Syracuse. On campus, companionship was limited, teammates could be pleasant acquaintances, but mostly friends were Blacks, such as John Brown, Art Baker, and John Mackey. With them, he could be himself and not stop to think about his image. They threw parties and invited local Blacks, Blacks from nearby universities such as Cornell, Colgate, Oswego and Cortland. Those White teammates they sometimes included felt honored. The parties were always fun. But Ernie didn't purposely isolate himself from Whites. At times he actually seemed to be color blind, treating each individual as he would a friend without regard to his color or race. He was an individual and enjoyed one on one relationships judging people on their human worth and not limiting his friendships to Blacks only.

Chapter 20

As the year progresses Syracuse has a special opportunity for recognition, they go to California to play a nationally televised game with UCLA. At last they are acknowledged as the greatest team in the nation, not just of the year, but of the decade.

After beating UCLA the coaches gather in Ben's office.

Ben's laughing hard now. It's so exaggerated he can't take it seriously any more. In fact, it's putting Syracuse right where they want to be... at the top.

"We're beasts, crunching our bloody jaws, with huge creatures plowing down our innocent opponents." Ben paraphrases the current media comments on Syracuse.

"UCLA has a few monsters of their own. They just don't like losing. They make us sound like something out of a science fiction movie. Well, call us what they want.... we're on our way to the national championship. The only route to that is through the Cotton Bowl. We've got the invitation. Do we want to take it?"

That seems like a crazy question for Ben to be asking, but Szombathy takes it seriously.

"I don't know. You remember what they did to Jim Brown a few years ago. No buses. Couldn't find a hotel that would take us. When we did get one, they wouldn't let him in the swimming pool and restaurants. This year we have three of these boys and I don't see signs that attitudes have changed much."

"You're right," responds Ben. Can we put these guys through that kind of stuff. It doesn't seem right. But if we don't go, we throw the championship down the tubes. And you know we finally have a team that can make it."

"Let's turn the decision over to the kids." he adds. "It's their game. And it's their year. Let's see what they want to do."

When Jim Brown had gone with the Syracuse team to the Cotton Bowl in 1956 he had not only been treated badly off the field, but the press had all but ignored him. The Texas press had not even mentioned his name, although much of the Syracuse victory had been dependent on his superb showing there. It was bad enough to be called names and not allowed in any public places, but to be treated with such disdain, as though you didn't even exist is the worst of insults. In private, Ernie, John Brown and Art had already expressed their views with each other. It wouldn't be fun, like Florida would. They didn't really want to go. They knew they would be subjected to every kind of discrimination. Their movements would be limited. Most restaurants would be closed to them. No public transportation except the back of buses would be available and that too would be questionable. They would be hassled, harassed and threatened. They would have to be there a whole three weeks in some podunk hotel and watch while the other players moved freely and enjoyed themselves. It wasn't a pretty picture. And it wasn't fair. But they also knew that they needed to play Texas and beat them in order to confirm their national supremacy.

"So," says Ben to the big boys all crowded into the seats in the training room. "It's up to you. Just remember that we're a team and we've got to think of everybody."

"I say we go to Florida where we won't have a hassle, instead of staying in a third rate hotel in Texas," says a tackle.

"I don't want to be treated like dirt in Texas," adds Art. It is his senior year and he wants to have fun at one of the Bowls.

"Geeze," comments a tight end. "This is our one chance at the national championship. We've worked too hard to get there. I don't give a damn what hotel we stay in. I think we should go to Texas."

"I vote for Texas," Ernie stands to give his approval. "It's the only way we can be national champions. How can we settle for anything less."

"Let's take a vote," Ben puts a halt to the comments after listening to a few more differing opinions. "Let's see a show of hands... how many want to go to Texas?"

All but a few hands go up and the decision is made.

A huge satisfied grin spreads over Ben's face. He's glad Ernie supported it. That probably made all the difference.

Chapter 21

Ernie's benefactors make sure Ernie is dressed well for this special event. Newspapers in the area all show pictures of Ernie, Art and John boarding the plane in Syracuse. They are dressed in elegant winter coats and fedora hats, looking more than spiffy and feeling the excitement. What the press doesn't show is their arrival in Houston Airport. Most of the team gathers their luggage at the pick up and piles into cabs, while Ernie, Art and John are left standing at the curb. Within minutes, Doc Manley, an alum who has accompanied the team pulls up in a rental car and picks them up.

"Okay, guys, pile in."

They throw their bags in the trunk and get in with Doc. As he pulls out he lets the cat out of the bag.

"This car's for you guys," says Doc.

"Geeze, thanks."

"Cool..."

"That's great...."

Maybe it won't be so bad after all.

"It'll give you some flexibility." Doc tries not to make a big thing of the situation. It's always hard for the White guys to know what to say. So usually they don't say anything, but often there are awkward moments and silences.

A couple nights later, Ben is pacing in the lobby, looking at his watch when Ernie, Art and John slink in, trying to avoid him.

Ben is furious now. "Do you guys know what time it is?" He tries to keep his voice down, but his anger is obvious.

"Yeh..."

"Uhmmm"

"Sorry, coach...."

"That's it! No more car! We tried to make it easier for you, but you blew it. Do you think just cause you have some problems here that gives you a right to break the rules.???"

Ernie knows how to talk to Ben so he moves forward and in a low voice discusses it with him, while the other two move on to their room.

"You're right, Coach. We understand that you should probably take the car away from us. If it was the other guys it wouldn't be such a problem, but you know we can't do anything here without a car. We know we shouldn't have been late. It won't happen again."

"Well...." Ben is such a pushover for Ernie. "You just make sure it doesn't happen again. I'm depending on you to keep these other guys in line, Ernie. You can be sure that next time I'll really take it away. I mean it!"

Ernie is relieved. Once Ben has disappeared he goes to the room and tells the guys the outcome. John gives Ernie five. "Good going."

Art on the other hand has mixed feelings. He's glad they still have the car, and he respects Ernie's character, but he resents that Ernie, just a sophomore, gets his way with Coach every time.

And get his way, he does, for the next day Ernie comes begging to Ben again.

"Com'on, Coach. All I need is a little practice." Ernie is begging to be allowed to do the kick off and it's not even his expertise.

"Bob will probably be healed in time for kick-off," Ben tries to put Ernie off, but Ernie gets an idea in his head and he doesn't give up.

"Yeh, but you need a back up, ... just in case. It won't hurt for me to do a little practicing, will it?"

Ben gives in again. "Aw, go on out there Ernie and shut up about it."

An hour later Sims stops Ben.

"Hey, Ben?

"Yeh?"

"Did you tell that kid he could go out there and practice kicking."

"What kid? ... Oh, you mean Ernie. Sure... why not? Keeps him happy."

"That's not all it'll keep him."

"What do you mean?"

"It'll keep him right out of the game." Sims points over to Ernie sitting on the bench rubbing his thigh and holding ice on it. He's got a painful grimace on his face. "Hamstring injury."

"Oh shit!" Ben throws his hat down.

Three days later in the training room, Julie, the trainer, is massaging Ernie's thigh. Ben comes in with an unlit cigar hanging out of his mouth and stands over him.

Finally he asks Ernie how it feels. Ernie's reply is affirmative. "It's just great. No problem." Until Julie hits a particular spot on his thigh and Ernie lets out a yelp. Then he smiles with a cringe as Julie keeps hitting the spot, just to make a point to both of them.

"Great coach... Uhh .. I'm sure... I'll be just fine for the game. I'm all set."

Julie on the other hand doesn't pull any punches. "It's no good, Ben. We can't fix this before the game. I've done everything I can, ... ice, whirlpool, lineaments, wrapping... These hamstring injuries are really tough. These things don't heal over night, you know. There's no way you can put him in the game. Not unless we could find a brace of some kind to keep it tight."

Ernie is horrified. This isn't even funny... Not play in the Cotton Bowl. No way. He'll figure out something.

"No, really, Coach. Julie's exaggerating. I'm just fine. It doesn't hurt at all."

Julie knows right where to push and figures another reality check for Ernie is a good plan. Ernie jumps, trying to maintain his smile.

Ben doesn't want to play an injured Ernie and spoil him for the rest of his football career, but on the other hand, too many plays depend on Ernie. He can't imagine going into this game without him. Texas is a really tough team.

"Don't worry, Ernie. We'll get you in if we can. We'll find a way, but you'll have to take it easy."

"Julie, ... I want you to go out and hunt for some kind of elastic or brace. Get a girdle if you have to."

Ernie grimaces again, but this time it isn't for the pain.

Ernie limps on and off the plane to Dallas, barely able to walk. Ben is by his side, every step of the way, just like a nursemaid. As soon as they get in, Julie takes off and goes store to store, finally he goes to the biggest department store he can find and gingerly holds up several girdles for size. An amused saleswoman comes over to help.

"Is this the biggest you've got," says Julie.

"What does your wife weigh?" she tries to stifle her surprise. "I'm afraid they don't come any bigger than that. Surely this will fit her."

116

"It's for a football player," Julie mumbles.

"Unhuh..." she doesn't seem convinced.

As she cashes it up. Julie makes the mistake of getting in deeper and deeper trying to explain...

"He's very big.."

"He's got a hamstring injury..."

"You know... an injury to the thigh..."

"We need to keep it tight.."

For the game ... this afternoon, that is...."

"You know... the Cotton Bowl."

"Thank you very much, sir." The saleswoman hands him a bag and quickly turns to the next customer, a woman who is truly big enough to fit into the biggest girdle.

"Can I help you, ma'am?"

Julie doesn't find it as difficult to buy Ernie some long underwear. As Julie walks out of the store holding tightly to his precious purchases, he mumbles under his breath. "Next time Ben gives in to Ernie's begging, HE gets to go hunting for girdles...."

Julie arrives breathless and pulls out his purchases. Ernie, who is getting his pre-game massage... groans when he sees them.

"I've never worn one of them before, but I suppose if it'll get me into the game, it's worth it."

Ben watches him struggle into it from the doorway. "Okay, Ernie. Hurry up. You're starting."

Ernie lets out a whoop and almost jumps off the table, but Julie holds him back.

The fanfare begins, music, bands and the stadium quickly filling up. The Texas players run out onto the field amidst a roar of approval. The Syracuse players run out a few minutes later to hollers and applause from only a limited part of the stands. Many buses came down with fans, but it was a long expensive trip for many to take, in spite of their enthusiasm. Any Blacks that came with the Syracuse team are limited to one end zone area. Ernie is still limping having a little trouble keeping up with the other players. You can see that every step he takes is costing him, but his mouth is in a stoic line. Obviously Ernie doesn't do the kick off and he holds back a bit on the first plays, saving himself. By the third down, when it looks like Syracuse may lose the ball, Ger looks over at Ben and sees the sign for a pitch out pass. He passes to Ernie and Ernie goes for it. He takes off at full speed around the end. He's no longer limping. It would be difficult to even guess that he has an injury.

Ben's mouth falls open, then he yells as loud as he can: "NO, ERNIE, JUST GET US THE 10 YARDS!"

Ernie is running like crazy.

"SAVE IT, ERNIE. YOU'RE GOING TO RUIN YOUR LEG."

Now Ben takes off, still screaming at Ernie and starts running right down the field after him.

"SLOW DOWN, ERNIE," Ben screams. "ERNIE, YOU'LL KILL YOURSELF!"

"SSSLLOOWW DOOOWNNN!"

Arms reach out and grab Ben, pulling him off the field just in time to avoid a penalty. The coach must stay between the two 35 yard lines.

Ernie never hears a thing. He doesn't even know that Ben followed him. All he can hear is the wind blowing in his ears and the thumping of the pain in his thigh. All he can feel is the intensity of his determination to make it to the goal line, no matter what!

The cannons go off as Ernie throws the ball up into the air and limps off the field. The crowd goes wild. Now that the adrenalin of the run is wearing off, Ben sees the pain setting in, but also the exhilaration on Ernie's face.

The canon goes off again. Rumor amongst the Texans has it that the canon, which belongs to Alpha Tau Omega and has been used for years at games, was a Civil War canon that had been acquired solely for this game just to aggravate the Southerners. So a group of Texans go after it, shouting at the students carrying it. Syracuse students guarding their canon hide it under coats and blankets, carrying it constantly to new locations. To them it's a great game.

Dick Easterly tackles a Texan and ends up rolling over to the Texas side where the players jeer him. "You Nigger Lover!!!"

No one helps him up, a traditional courtesy extended to opposition players by most teams. Dick just smirks at them, picks up his split helmet and

118

walks away. He's amazed at the blatantness of their attacks, never having experienced so much of this before.

Now the Texans are shouting again at the Syracuse fans:

"Get out of here, you Nigger lovers."

"What do ya want? ... another civil war?"

"Why didn't you leave your canon at home?'

Then a White player spits at Art Baker.

At halftime the famous Syracuse band, One Hundred Men and One Girl marches out onto the field, Jan carrying her flaming batons. When she drops one, the Texans shout and applaud in glee to see her humiliation.

The Syracuse team is steaming by halftime. When they return to the field, there is no holding them back. They have been taking spitting and abuse now already for half the game. No more is going to be tolerated. John Brown is up front in the line of defense, face to face with a sneering White Texan. "You Black Bastard" hisses the player and more spitting arrives at John's face. Enough is enough, John takes a jab at him and suddenly there is a free for all. The Syracuse and Texan players pop up from the benches and race onto the field. Only Ernie and Ger stay back. Ernie is still nursing his injured leg and Ger heads over the field to the Texan captain, whom he knew from previous meetings.

"You grab your guys and start hauling them off and I'll grab mine," says Ger and they head into the mayhem.

As Ger heads off the field with most of the players ahead of him, he stops the guy in front of him.

"Hey, would you believe that?"

"What is it?"

"Don't they know they're part of the union? Look at their color guard. They're dressed in U.S. Air Force uniforms, but they're carrying three Texas flags and two Confederate ones. Looks like they forgot the U.S. Flag?"

"Yeh, that's not all they forgot. They forgot where their asses are," yells another player back to them.

When the game is over, Syracuse wins 21 to 14, the Syracuse stands go wild as the Texans boo. A few Texan players walk over to the Syracuse players and put out their hands. Several walk up to John, Art and Ernie and apologize for the Texan behavior.

That evening, Syracuse's first team sits at the head table in the ballroom of the Dallas Hotel at a full house for the awards dinner. The game official takes the podium.

"Now it is my greatest pleasure and honor to present to Ernie Davis of the Syracuse team, the outstanding player award. Ernie scored 16 of the 21 winning points. But even more outstanding was his 87 yard touchdown run, the longest in bowl history. I am told that he did that in spite of a hamstring injury. A really amazing performance today, Ernie."

Ernie stands up, almost unbelieving that this is really happening to him.

"I am both surprised and honored to receive this award, but I can only accept it for the entire team. I was just lucky to be in the right place at the right time. There is little I can do out there without the support of everyone else. I think we played a fine game out there today and I'm proud to be a part of this undefeated team – number 1 in the country."

The overflowing ballroom resounds with applause as Ernie sits back down beside Art and John, glowing with the excitement of the evening.

A quarter hour later, as desserts are being brought out, a man steps up behind the three and Ernie gives him a flashing smile. He bends down on one knee and whispers something to Art and John. John in turn whispers something to Ernie. Ernie's face changes dramatically from open happiness to a closed mask. The three whisper with each other for a moment, then throw down their napkins on their unfinished desserts, rise from the table and leave.

Dean Faigle, also at the head table, glances over at them just as they depart. He follows them out of the room, then returns about five minutes later.

He goes right to Ben and Chancellor Tolley and tells them that someone has told the three to leave at the end of the invitational Awards Dinner and prior to the opening of the doors for the dance, a public function.

The coach and chancellor were shocked speechless for a moment. They couldn't believe it. They had been careful to set up an agreement with the Cotton Bowl officials that there would be no discriminatory practices in the events they controlled.

"Who told them that?" asked Ben.

"They don't know who it was," said Dean Faigle.

The three discussed the matter, shocked by the turn of events and caught by surprise at their embarrassing and offending predicament. Finally they decided on a course of action.

Ger leans over and wants to know what is going on, where the other guys went. When they tell him, he starts to get up himself. "We're all out of here," he says, furious.

"No, no," Ben puts his hand on Ger's shoulder and stops him. "We've had enough civil wars today, just stay where you are and don't even tell the other guys. We don't want to cause a scene. We'll leave with the guys, make sure they have a good evening. Just tell the others they went off to their own parties."

"I'll go with them," says Ger.

"No, you stay here, or they'll notice something is up."

At the end of the evening the Texas players got an idea of a prank, which added one more seed to the controversy. As part of their prize, the Syracuse team was given an open tab that they could use at the hotel bar. Many of the players had left early and gone to parties of their own. The few that remained used very little of it. After they had all left, the Texas players came in and ran up the tab to an outrageous sum and then signed the names of the Syracuse players, especially Ernie Davis.

Chapter 22

Back at Syracuse Tolley walks into Ben's office and throws the newspaper down on his desk, along with a pile of letters.

"It doesn't matter what you do. There's no pleasing them."

Ben is clearly frustrated. "We took every precaution we could, except refusing the invitation to play Texas. We couldn't have been number One without that victory. They assured us the boys would be allowed to attend all related activities. How could we know that they'd throw the dance open to the public and exclude them."

"I know, I know, Ben. It isn't your fault, but now they're calling us every name in the book. And they're not even slapping the wrists of the Texans, who were the ones who caused all the trouble."

Tolley pulls a letter from the top of the pile.

"This letter is from a Mr. Campbell of Austin, Texas. He makes stupid rash statements about our players' remarks to the press. Why it was their players who spit on ours, called them names I would never dare repeat, and charged outrageous bills against our names."

"Sometimes the injustice of it, just makes me so tired."

"Well at least you were able to explain it in your letter to the Pittsburgh Courier. We probably would have gotten even more criticism if we had insisted everyone leave. At least we left, appropriately."

"Perhaps so, Ben, but I can't help wondering. Did we really do the right thing?"

"We did the best we could at the moment. That's all I ask of the boys. And that's all we can ask of ourselves."

"Well, anyway. We must be doing something right. Look at this letter from one of the referees of the game. He has nothing but good things to say about our team's conduct."

Ernie is asked to appear on the Today show. He's a bit concerned about it, but they promise not to ask him about the racial issues in the game. And then, of course, they do anyway. Ernie, a kid who could hardly talk, growing up, is now up to the challenge.

"I was not in the game at the time of the incident. I only saw a Texas player apologize to John Brown at the banquet."

But Ernie gives a different slant on it to his friends. "Texas wasn't the cleanest playing team we faced." For Ernie, who tends to make excuses for everyone's misbehavior, that was saying a lot.

On the other hand, a little later, Al Mallette of the Elmira Star Gazette quotes Ernie as saying, "All that other stuff they're saying. ... I think they're just trying to make a big thing out of nothing..." Ernie doesn't like controversy and will avoid it at any cost. His way of handling it is to play harder and win bigger and that's just what he did in Texas.

The Syracuse team and Ernie Davis' name are on every avid football fan's tongue now. Even Ed Sullivan invites him on his show. And as he appears more and more, his fans grow in leaps and bounds. Even the wave lengths of the television manage to portray his warmth and sensitivity. Once the public begins to see him in person they all become fans.

At Syracuse everyone recognizes him and calls to him as he crisscrosses campus, attending his classes. Ernie tries to respond to everyone. Everyone wants to claim him for a friend, and Ernie treats most people as though they were long lost friends. In Texas he sent postcards to Elmira and Pennsylvania and bought gifts for everyone, nieces, nephews, friends and even acquaintances. Ernie feels the energy of all he has and wants to share as much as possible of the goodness of it with others.

Ernie goes to visit Angie as soon as possible, anxious to see his nephew again. He has a special gift for her son... the Cotton Bowl watch. Then Ernie admits to Angie what really went on in Texas. Even his own team was responsible for some negative behavior toward the Members. The hotel wouldn't let the Negroes use the elevator, so they had to stay in a room on the first floor. There were four beds in the room and the White player assigned to their room with them refused to stay there. Mike Neary, on the other hand, was happy to take the fourth bed and share the room with them claiming, "I don't care where I stay."

"Well, I don't care," Ernie refers to the player who wouldn't stay in the same room with them.. "I'm not going to worry about that, cause that's their problem, not mine." And with that, Ernie wiped the incident out of his mind.

But there are other concerns Ernie has more difficulty dealing with. He can't stand to disappoint other people and will go to many lengths to avoid it.

Betty Snowden, a year ahead of Ernie in school had already graduated from nursing school and taken a job at a hospital on Long Island. They are still attached to each other in many ways and often Ernie goes to New York to see his grandparents and visit Betty. Sometimes she comes up for college weekends or they see each other in Elmira. But Ernie isn't sure that he is ready to pin himself down to her. Still they had been together so long and friends since they were in junior high school. Ernie had never purposely hurt anyone in his life, yet he didn't know how to free himself up to enjoy college and get to know other girls without hurting Betty.

"I think Betty and I both need a change," he tells Angie. Angie agrees, but doesn't know what to tell Ernie to do about it. So Ernie puts it off.

Winter seems particularly harsh after being in Texas three weeks. The campus is covered with snow. Students are calling after him and waving to Ernie as he zigzags across campus, following the tracks that other students have worn into the snow. Ernie hears the faint bell in one of the buildings he passes and takes off with his books under his arm like a pigskin. He slams into the hallway amidst mud and slush, then puts on the brakes by the door of a half full room and tries to slip in unnoticed.

No such luck.

Ernie in class at Syracuse University

"I see Mr. Davis has decided to grace us with his presence," comments the professor. "Better late than never."

Then the philosophy professor continues to ramble on. Ernie pulls out his notebook and pen to take notes. His freshly typed paper falls out onto the floor.   When he picks up his report, he rereads his last sentence with satisfaction.

"I came to one conclusion; to do injustice is more disgraceful than to suffer it."

Ernie smiles as he looks out the window at the still falling snow. He likes this class. It makes him think.

Later Ernie is in Professor Hoole's class.

"A leader is best when people barely know he exists." Ernie scribbles his notes frantically. He loves this class. Later he writes at the bottom of his class notes: "I feel that this was a very interesting lecture and that students taking this course should pay attention to the characteristics of a good leader.."

It's too late in the season for the football players to be on the S.U. Basketball team due to the Cotton Bowl. So a group of players decide to barnstorm, informal games. Ernie has trouble even with this, though. His leg hasn't healed as well as he would like and now he is also getting some back pain. He suspects maybe he had an additional injury during the Bowl game when a knee swung up into it.

Ernie and the other football players are used to injuries and they especially happen to the stars, who are targeted. But this was lasting longer than usual. Ernie thought of Jim Brown and marveled at him. It was hard for him to believe that the "man of steel" played four years and only once suffered as much as a bruise, or at least that was the legend.

Ernie, on the other hand, spent more time than most in the training room, in the whirlpool and on the massage table. Now with this new persistent injury he was going to have to take it easy and heal, but that's hard to do when you are also trying to keep in shape.

After one pick up game, a bunch of the football players have congregated in one of the dorm rooms. As Ernie starts to enter, a White player slams the door in his face.

"They don't allow no Niggers in here."

Ernie easily pushes the door wide open and quietly says:

"Come outside with me."

"You bet," at first the other player swaggers arrogantly.

The others follow them out, surprised to see Ernie react. When the truculent player sees the anger in Ernie's eyes and a posture in him that is unfamiliar, he begins to back up. Ernie hits him once and he goes down. Ernie picks him up by his shirt and shoves him up against a wall.

"Do you want to say that again?" He asks him, once again in a subdued voice.

"I don't know what you mean, Ern. I was only kidding."

"Don't you ever talk that way around me again..."

The player nods.

"Do you hear me?" Ernie raises his voice.

"Fine, Ernie. I hear you. I'm sorry."

The other guys are standing at the door stretching to see around and over each other. Some are left with their mouths open. They had never seen Ernie get mad.

Ernie walks away, past the door where the others are standing. He is nodding his head and talking to himself. He doesn't even seem to notice them anymore.

"Hey, it's stupid to get mad. Whaddya get mad for, anyway. You can't do anything about it. Just stupid.... That's all!"

When Spring practice starts, Ernie still isn't allowed to join in the contact sessions, at least in the beginning. The doctors never did locate the problem so it keeps reoccurring off an on through his college career.

Chapter 23

After working at Jerome's again and enjoying total celebrity status Ernie returns for summer camp. Sadler is a new dormitory, conveniently located just behind the stadium. John Mackey and Ernie's room is more like two rooms, allowing them a good deal of privacy with a partial divider separating their beds, desks, closets and little mirrors. Mackey and Ernie choose to sleep so that they can see each other and talk with each other with their heads at the end of the beds. It's great for Ernie. It reminds him of the years he and Chuck shared a bedroom. In fact, Mackey reminds him of Chuck.

They are very compatible, both neat and particular, hanging their shirts in the closet just an inch apart, lining up shoes precisely underneath. It is their social behavior that is quite different.

As is often the case, far fields look greener, especially for guys when it comes to girls. This is true to Ernie and Mackey. Ernie is ready to start looking around, and Mackey wants to go further. He's not interested in the African American girls on campus. So one evening, Ernie decides to accommodate his three friends, Art, John Brown, and John Mackey, by getting Betty to bring up three friends with her for the weekend. Ernie usually enjoys being alone with Betty, so off they go. He doesn't much like parties or crowds. The other Guys are pretty much enjoying themselves until they realize that the girls aren't going to put out for them, so they decide next best thing is food and take the girls out to a local African American restaurant, Ben's Kitchen.

As they enter the restaurant Mackey pulls Art aside and whispers that he doesn't have enough money to feed the girls. Normally in the 50s the guys buy for the girls.

"Don't worry about it," Art assures Mackey and Brown. So they both assume that means Art has enough money to cover the girls' meals. They follow the girls in and enjoy a fabulous meal. Art gets up, pays for his meal and then walks out. Brown, not knowing what else to do, follows, covering only his own meal. There sits Mackey with the three girls and only enough money in his pocket for his own meal. He isn't happy about the circumstance, but he doesn't see any other options, so he up and pays his meal and follows the other two out.

The girls are angry and insulted, so the minute they get back they go to find Betty and tell her. When Ernie hears the tale from Betty he gets so angry he can't talk. He goes to his room and finds Mackey there. "I cccan understand ttthat Art and the ooothers mmmight do that. BBBBut I would nnnever have expected yyyou to gggo along with them. You knnnow I would gggive you the Mmmoney bbback."

"But, Ernie, I didn't have any money with me," Mackey tries to explain.

Ernie hears nothing. He is too angry. "Mmmy gggirlfriend's friends cccome dddown and you tttreat tthem like gggarbage."

Mackey can't believe how bad it makes him feel to disappoint Ernie. It seems like there is nothing more important than having his respect and now he's lost it. At least for the moment.

Ernie stamps away like a little boy, hating himself for losing control. What a waste of energy. Mackey hears him all the way down the hall, talking to himself again.

"What'd you do that for?"

"You don't need to do that."

"It doesn't matter that much."

The attitude of most of the football players toward girls, especially those on campus was not good. They lacked the kind of respect that was just second nature to Ernie. When they hung out with him, they sometimes improved, but they would easily slip back into old behaviors, often encouraged by old style coaches in various settings who didn't want the boys messing around with female relationships. They thought it distracted them.

Mackey enjoys rooming with Ernie, the big man on campus and he doesn't mind when a bit of the star rubs off on him. After all, Mackey himself is better than good. Why he would be running as half back already in his sophomore year if he didn't have to wait for Ernie to leave the spot. In fact, Ben had offered to red shirt him for a year and then to come up behind Ernie and wear the 44 number as half back. But Mackey didn't want to follow any one. He wanted to be his own man, so he chose to be tight end and be running to his hearts content, starting his sophomore year.

However, there are some things for which he doesn't mind following Ernie. One day out in Ernie's car by himself, he gives a White girl on campus a ride to her dorm. She recognizes Ernie's car, but doesn't really know what Ernie looks like up close. She thinks Mac is Ernie. Mackey thinks it is a great joke. When they get to the dorm she doesn't want to get out. She asks him to drive her around for a while. Mackey never one to turn down an opportunity obliges her. Finally he parks in lover's lane and makes passionate love to her. Or in other words they have sex.

As he returns her to her dorm and let's her out he says, "Oh by the way, I'm not Ernie Davis. I'm John Mackey. Thanks for a lovely time."

She is horrified, turns pale and blanches, while John laughs at his big joke. It's one, though that he knew better than to tell to Ernie.

In the fall of 1960, Ernie and his Negro friends find movies a great relaxation. Ernie is shushing them throughout the news clips. Khrushchev pounds his shoe on the podium at the United Nations, while the Presidential candidate Jack Kennedy is speaking on social justice, followed by clips of racial incidents.

"Hey guys, don't you have any respect. This guy may end up being your next President." Ernie is admonishing them during the cartoon.

"Don't make any difference what he has to say, Ern," answers John Brown, "It doesn't change what goes on in Biloxi or what went on in Dallas last year for that matter."

"Dallas was just a situation," Ernie responds. "Those guys were just upset about losing."

"Don't go making excuses for them, Ernie. You can't always make excuses for them," comments Mac. "Hey, man, you comin to the Members party tonight, do a little twistin'. The Niggers are playing."

"The Niggers, you kiddin me? Why do they call themselves that...?"

"Cause we can call ourselves what we want to... nobody else is allowed to do that though." answers Mac.

"Sure I'll be there," says Ernie. I'm kinda getting the hang of the twist and I need a little more practice."

"Yeh, you sure do need more practice, Bubbles, so you can twist right on down that field." Brown responds, raising himself a little from his seat and wiggling his butt. Ernie starts laughing so hard, the audience around him turns and shushs him now.

Ernie scrunches down in his seat, wiggling as he goes.

"See, Ern," whispers Mac now that the main show has begun... "that ole DDI is coming out again. If you don't control that DEEP DOWN INSIDE, you're gon ta git in a lotta trouble one of these days. They're goin ta discover the real Ernie and then it'll be all over for ya."

Ernie breaks up now and scrunches down even further relieved that the music of Ben Hur rises up over his laughter.

After the movie the fellows head on over to the party. Theres lots of girls, mostly Black from nearby neighborhoods, but some White college girls too. Several recognize Ernie and come up to him trying to drag him out on the dance floor, but he won't budge. Later he is twisting with an African American girl, while Mac waves to him from beside one of the White girls.

In the dorm room Mac is already in bed, while Ernie is shaving.

"How can you do that at this hour, man. You crazy or somethin."

"Listen, Mac. You got to look good. You can't let it go. If I do this at night, then I don't have to worry about it in the morning."

"Hey, man, what you gotta look good for. You don't even know how to treat the girls right."

"Yeh, man, you goin to teach me somethin. I saw all those chicks runnin away from you the minute you got near them."

"Listen, Ernie, if I had all those White girls so hot after me, I'd know what to do with them."

"I'm not goin to mess with that, Mac; it only means trouble." '

By now Ernie has climbed into bed and turned off the light. Mac can see a light flashing against the wall on the other side of the partition.

"Ernie?"

"Yeh?'

"What's that, a flashlight?"

"Yeh..."

"Wassa matter? You afraid of the dark?"

"Naw, ... I jus don wanna disturb you. Keep you from getting your beauty sleep, you know. It's so I can read in bed."

But the light flashes against the wall again and also against the wall on Mac's side of the room.

"Hey, DDI..."

"Yeh...."

"You're too big to be afraid of the dark."

"Hey, Chuck...," says Ernie, and then laughs.

Sylvia Cole is a lovely sheltered Black girl who has attended only private schools in Washington, D.C. She did her first two years at MacMurray College in Jacksonville, Illinois before transferring in to Syracuse her Junior year. John Mackey knew of her, but he wouldn't ask her out. He didn't think she fit into his group of crude and streetwise friends. She wasn't hip enough for them. One day he borrows Ernie's car to go over to her dorm and get some records from her group. She asks him for a ride to the Student Council meeting.

"Why don't any of you guys date the girls on campus?" she blatantly asks him.

"Well, do you want a date?" Mackey kids along with her.

"Yes."

"You've got it."

"When are we going out?"

"Friday," he says.

"What time?" she's determined to pin him down.

"8:00 PM"

A few days later, when Friday arrives, Ernie corners Mackey.

"Hey, I understand you are taking Sylvia out tonight."

"Well, where d'ya hear that?" Mackey hedges.

"Well, don't worry, I just understand you are taking her out."

"There ain't no way in the world I'm going to take her out."

"Well, did you make a date with her?"

"Well, I didn't mean it. I was just kidding, man."

"Well, why would you do that, man, she's a very nice girl. Why don't you go out with her?"

Now Mackey is really feeling cornered, but he's got some quick answers. He can handle this. "Two very simple reasons. I don't have any transportation and I don't have any money, that's why I'm not takin her out."

"Well, if that's all." Ernie is ready for this one. "Here's five bucks and your car," says Ernie as he points to the keys.

"Are you serious, Ern? Well, for five dollars and the car, you know I'll take her out."

And so Mackey's fate is sealed... Sylvia and he quickly become an item.

Ernie is standing at the mirror in the bathroom applying medicated powder to his face. Mackey enters the room and reminds Ernie they're only going to a movie.

"I just want to look good. You gotta care about the impression you're going to make. You see, Mac, you don't appreciate the finer things in life. It's important to always look your best. You don't know who you'll meet and people make decisions about you, just by looking at you."

When Ernie leaves the bathroom, Mackey stands there looking at himself. He splashes some water on his face, looks again, then pulls out his comb and reluctantly starts working on his hair, mumbling.

"I don't know why I let him do this to me. I don't want to compete with him anyway. I look just fine the way I am..."

With that, he throws down the comb, looks in the mirror again, and then tries once more. Finally he makes a face at himself and goes back to the dorm room.

In their dorm room, they are both looking through all their jacket pockets for money. Mackey finds a quarter first.

"I've got one. Now all we need is a second quarter for you. You know, Ernie, for a guy that looks like a million dollars, you sure are poor."

As usual Ernie laughs and agrees. Then he finds his quarter and they hit the road.

They're sprinting down Salina Street to the theater when they are approached by an elderly decrepit looking woman. Ernie slows down, but Mackey calls to him they'll be late.

"Please, just a little money for a cup of coffee." The woman holds out her hand.

"Hey, Ernie, com'on. I hate to be late."

But Ernie stops and walks back to the woman and reaches into his pocket.

"No, Ernie, don't give her your only quarter. Com'on... we're going to the movie."

But Ernie pulls out the quarter and hands it over to the woman.

Now Mackey is really angry. "Whaddya do that for. Can't you smell her! She'll just use it for more booze. Now we can't go to the movie."

"I don't care what she uses it for. If she didn't need it, she wouldn't ask for it."

"Ahh, shit." mumbling, Mackey pulls out his quarter and shoves it into her hand. He stuffs his own hands in his empty pockets and turns around to go back to the dorm.

The coaches are sitting around the training room and Sims is reading a newspaper article. He reads the headline out loud to the others. "Ernie Davis, Elmira Express, 100 Yards Per Game."

"Ernie's a marked man, Ben," he adds. "We've got to do something."

"They've got at least six men on him every game," adds Coach Day, "and they're trying to injure him when they tackle him."

"It's expectable," says Ben, "You don't think they're going to just sit there and take it, do you?"

"So... maybe we need to just use him as a decoy for a while, let things die down a little. He's just too visible. Give him a break before they break him."

Ben's adamant, "We've talked about this before. We'd ruin him as an All American if we did that. He's on his way to some outstanding records. Let's try some new plays that draw attention away from him, but still keep him running." And Ben steps up to the blackboard.

Ben explaining a play to Ernie

Even though by the time Syracuse plays Penn State, they have 15 straight victories, Ernie's fans aren't exactly satisfied with how things are going. People are asking why they don't play Ernie more. They are beginning to worry that he won't get the chance to run enough to make All-American again this year.

Some of the explanation is printed in the newspapers: "Davis Caught in the Unit System". The article explains Schwartzwalder's theory about playing each team, the first and the second about seven minutes. It appears that Ernie by luck, just happens to be on the field mostly during defensive plays so he doesn't get to carry the ball during those times. Ernie would love to be playing more offensively and running with the ball, but being a good team player he's not complaining, except for saying to Mickey Jones that he wishes he could play more.

Although the track record is still good, this team doesn't seem to have quite the charisma of the '59 team. Their wins are not as striking as the previous year. The consensus seems to be that this team is missing some of its vital components and the chemistry is not quite the same. Ernie is worried about his performance in the Penn State game. Even when he does his best, if there is only one thing he did wrong, he focuses on that.

The criticism from the press is that the Syracuse team is becoming "fat, complacent and big-headed", which Ernie takes personally and seriously.

Chapter 24

One aspect of Ernie's life, however, is about to become pleasanter, if not more complicated. The Sadler Four, the African American football players, had seen Helen Gott on campus since the beginning of the year. They all agreed she was the most beautiful girl on campus and several had already tried to date her. She is a freshman from East Orange, New Jersey and seems to these guys a little out of their range. Although she is African American, her father had been a military Colonel and they had always lived in a mostly White community. Her cultural experiences are totally different than theirs. In many ways she seems naive, but still sophisticated..

Although Ernie has been out with various girls at Syracuse, he has always considered Betty his girl and never gotten serious over anyone. Helen is different from the beginning. When Ernie finally gets the nerve to ask her out, they see each other regularly and he refuses to double date with others or speak lightly of her. He obviously is taking this girl seriously. With the onset of this relationship, comes a very difficult dilemma for Ernie. For another guy, it might not have been such a big problem, but Ernie knows that Betty has some future expectations about their relationship and he hates to let her down. Besides that her family has been a home for him since his first days in Elmira. He would be letting everyone down including his Elmira friends.

"They'll think that now that I'm a big star, I think I'm too good for Betty," he tells Mac, "but that isn't it at all. They all think we should get married, but we've grown in different directions now."

"Well, I think now we both need a change," Ernie tells Angie again, but he puts off saying anything to Betty about it.

Marie calls Ernie at school. She hasn't seen him in several weeks.

"Ernie, you have to come home. I need to talk with you."

By the time he gets off the phone Ernie has guessed what she wants to tell him and he is determined to be too busy to go home for a few weeks. He simply doesn't want to hear it. But Marie calls again and insists, so he complies.

"I'm getting a divorce from Art," she tells him. He argues with her about it. At first Ernie was not enamored of his stepfather, but through the years his affection had grown for him. Ernie had had to bring Art home from a bar now and then, when he couldn't make it on his own, but now Ernie loves him and he doesn't want to see him hurt, or to see him alone. Cheery Art had made him plenty of breakfasts and sung in the shower, and been at his games for him.

On the other hand, Marie is adamant that she needs to do what is right for her life. So Ernie vows to himself that he will give a little extra time to his stepfather, now when he needs someone who cares.

Art has already moved out of the house into a rented room not too far away. Next time Ernie comes home, Art has moved again and he hadn't told anyone that he was going or where he was going, but that doesn't stop Ernie. He shows up on Art's doorstep.

"How'd you find me, Ernie? No one knows where I am."

"I'll always find you," Ernie gives him a big bear hug, then adds:

"You had anything to eat yet? Let's go get something."

So off they go to eat and talk and talk and talk. Art asks all about Syracuse, how things are going, how he is playing, and how his social life is. Ernie promises to come back soon.

In the bleachers, the Pittsburgh fans are going wild waving their flags and shouting. The Syracuse players leave the bench enthusiastically but little by little return subdued. They continue to shout each other encouragement, though.

"Way to go"

"Hit those guys."

"Com'on."

Finally their shouts diminish until they mostly sit there subdued. Ernie fumbles twice, and others make some errors. Ben pats him on the back after his second fumble.

"Ernie, you couldn't help it. Those dumb guys aren't blocking for you."

Ernie just hangs his head. He doesn't know about the others, but he knows he shouldn't drop the ball.

Halftime and the Pittsburgh band marches out onto the field amidst thunderous support. After halftime, the Syracuse team just trudges out, while Ben stands on the sidelines with a stony stare, players kneel by the bench, but don't shout any more encouragement. Then the nasty jeers begin coming from the bleachers above Ben.

"Hey, Kraut, what's happened to your warriors?"

"The ole man's leading a bunch of invalids."

Ben never moves a muscle or acknowledges he hears. It's hard to be at the very top and start going down. Some of the reserves can't take the harassment any more and head up into the stands, grab one of the guys who was shouting and beat him up. The game is over with defeat. The team leaves the field with helmets in hands and heads down. People are throwing things at them as they go through the passageway.

"You're a bunch of junk."

"What a fuckin team."

"You guys are so full of shit, you deserve to lose."

Someone throws his program at their passing heads.

"I'm just sorry it's not a rotten tomato," he shouts after him.

Minutes later in the shower there is silence except for the water running. Some of them, including Ernie, splash their faces with shower water to cover the tears.

"Okay, guys, get in here a moment," calls Ben into the shower.

Guys with towels around their waists and various stages of undress gather around Ben in absolute silence, expecting the worst.

"So what?" His voice booms. "It was bound to happen sooner or later. Don't let this one throw you. It don't mean nothin. We've got three games left to play and you can go a long ways down or a long ways up between now and the end of the season. I know you kids. You're going to beat Army next week with your hands tied behind your backs...."

The group perks up almost immediately. A few begin to cheer Ben, but looking around decide against it and move back into the showers and amongst the benches. Although still quiet, the spirit is a bit raised and in the locker room, some team members begin to kid around a little again. But Ernie isn't in the mood for any kidding. With head down he dresses and prepares to leave, but they're not about to let him go without a bit of jibbing, trying to get a smile or a rise out of him.

"Oh, you played today?" says one of the players, pushing Ernie a little.

"Oh, you weren't sick?" says another. "I didn't think I saw you out there."

Ernie sees Fitz later in the day. "Com'on, let's go home."

"Naw," says Fitz, "I got a big date tonight."

"Well, I'm going to get out of here and go home," so he goes alone to Elmira.

Ernie sees Fitz when he gets back Sunday evening just before he leaves he says, "Oh, by the way, you know, on the way down, coming through Nedrow, I ended up in a field. I lost control of the car and went over 30 feet from the road."

Fitz lets out a sigh of relief. "I thank my lucky stars I didn't go with you."

It's hard for him to believe that Ernie, who is so coordinated on the field can't seem to get it together to drive a car and stay on the road. Another time when Fitz had been riding in the back seat, just before Sullivanville, Ernie got tired and lost control of the car. They started sliding sideways down the middle of the road and finally ended up in the ditch.

Sometimes Fitz would try to take over.

"Do you want me to drive?"

"Naw, naw, I can drive."

It was hard to decide which was worse, the car, or Ernie's driving.

Poor Ernie, when he gets into a car, has too many other things on his mind to pay attention to where he is going. Ernie never tries to hide the accidents, but he doesn't seem to make much of them either.

Matter-of-factly, he tells his Mom, "I was talking and saw a car veering to the right or maybe it was to the left and I panicked. Before I knew it, I was in the field."

Marie never quite understands how he gets himself into so many of these situations, but mostly she is beginning to be sorry they had bought him that broken down Edsel and is scared she will lose him.

Sunday a week later, the phone in the hall rings and someone calls Ernie. He doesn't recognize Marie's voice at first, then he realizes who it is.

"It's Mom," she says. "She had gone to church this morning like usual. She hadn't been feeling well, apparently. After church, in the kitchen with Mary, she told her she was going to change her clothes and then Mary heard a noise, as though something had fallen. She found Mom on the floor. She had died of a massive heart attack."

"Oh no, not Mom," is all Ernie can say.

Marie leaves Monday morning to be with the family. Ernie joins them on Wednesday. When he arrives, he is more emotional then they've ever seen him. He sheds tears for the loss of Mom, but also for the loss of his time with her, when he left home and he was still a kid. He hadn't had enough time with her yet. He loved her so. Ernie cries. Then he and Angie talk in the hallway.

"I wanted to do so many things for her. I wanted to show her all the love that she had given me, to return some of it. Let her see my love and appreciation. When I finished school, I was going to help her out. That's what I was working for, to make her proud of me and be able to give back to her everything I could."

The funeral is Friday, but the family stays on through the weekend. Saturday afternoon Syracuse is to play Army at the Yankee Stadium right there in New York City. Ernie has never missed a game, but the last place Ernie wants to be in this moment is on a football field. Ernie knows, though, that they need him more than ever for this game after losing their last game to Pittsburgh.

The family convinces him to go, but he hesitates again as he stands there saying goodbye to Angie. He is terribly upset.

"Dddo you think I'm ddddoing..." he starts, but she interrupts him.

"Of course you're doing the right thing, Ernie. Mom would want you to go. You know she always said, 'if you're a part of something either be a part or nothing at all. Go on.... Ernie."

That afternoon his "brothers and sisters" are all in the stadium to watch Ernie play Army, but the game is a dismal disappointment. Ernie had missed the practices all week, plus the coaches know he is being targeted so they use Ernie as a decoy, pretending to pass off to him over and over, but not giving him the ball. His frustrated family is furious:

"Give him the ball. Give him the ball, you jerks."

"I can't understand it. Why don't they ever hand it to him?"

"What's the matter with them that they're not using Ernie?"

"Look at that, 9 to 6 in favor of Army. All they need to do is hand it to Ernie. He'll do the rest."

"It's always like that! He's getting too good for them. They don't want to see one of Us be better than Them."

And they're not the only ones questioning the wisdom of the Syracuse coaches.

In the Army locker room a reporter asks the coach, "How do you feel coming out on top of Syracuse."

"It was a tough game and we had trouble moving against Syracuse, but our boys played well," he responds. "I don't understand, though, why they didn't run Ernie. If Syracuse doesn't want him, then I know what to do with him. I'll run him right into All-American."

Finally the team rallies itself for the following games.

In Miami for the final game of the season, the team stays at a hotel with a whites only pool. No Negroes allowed. The night before the game, one of the players yells to the others that they'll all meet at the pool. So John Brown says they'll see them later and reminds them the pool is segregated.

"Well, then, we'll integrate it..." says the White player.

So they all get on their suits and arrive at the pool. The White guests, already in the pool look shocked as all the players enter, including the four African Americans. Ernie and Mackey who can't swim, enter from the shallow end. Everyone else exits the pool and a few leave in anger, until a White kid jumps back in, then others follow.

Art Baker is frustrated by the whole situation and he finally claims he won't play where there is discrimination. The next day they are still trying to persuade him as the others are dressing for the game.

"Com'on, Art," says Ernie. "We need you. This is an important game for us."

"You know where they seat the Members?" exclaims Art. "In the end zone only. We get to play to entertain Them, but we can't even watch from a decent seat. I won't be a part of it."

"Think of the team, Art. You can't let them down now. They're not the ones discriminating."

"Yeh, Art," adds John Brown. "We knew what it would be like before we ever came. We knew what Texas was like."

"You don't pay attention to it," advises Ernie. "It doesn't deserve your acknowledgment."

"You guys coming," calls Dave Sarette

"Yeh, we're coming," responds Mackey, "and we're going to run them right into the ground." He slaps Art on the back and they all head out the door and off to the game.

That day Ernie determinedly runs so much in the game against Miami University that he carries the ball about 26 times. Syracuse is victor, 21 to 14. The whistle blows and thousands of orange pompoms fly up into the air. After the game Ernie is exhausted and sweating, but as a crowd of kids surrounds him for autographs Ernie stays until he signs them all.

Ernie sits on his bed in his dorm room with letters spread all around him. Mackey is at his desk.

"Hey Mac," says Ernie.

"Yeh."

"I don't understand it. They keep putting me on these All-American teams and we had such a lousy season."

"You know, losing two games for most people isn't a lousy season."

"Yeh, but I didn't play all that great this year. I had a few bad games out there."

"What do you expect, Ernie. With every tackle in the country gunning for you, your 44 is almost iridescent, and in spite of that you managed to remain the leader in the country for rushing."

"Well, I guess so, but there are so many other good players out there."

"Don't knock it Ernie, just enjoy it." Mackey goes back to his studies. There's a lot to catch up on and he's already way behind.

The final tally of Ernie's statistics surprises him. He has surpassed himself in every category and is considered one of the best backs in the country and one of the most versatile backs in history.

Ernie is getting behind in studies too, but he is invited to banquet after banquet for awards or just appearances in response to his growing fame. His free time has dwindled down to nothing.

The wind is blowing like crazy, there are freezing temps and the snow coming down heavily as Ernie and Fitz head off to Elmira after the Hitchcock award banquet. The back seat of the car is taken up with the huge 5 foot Boston Touchdown Club Trophy. The two are discussing the banquet and Roger Meras' 61 home runs that got him the Hitchcock Award. There is 3 to 4 feet of snow in the fields with drifts over 6 feet deep, just your usual Syracuse winter in upstate NY.

Now the snow is blowing so hard, it is covering the road as quickly as the road crews can take it off. When they get to Cortland they hit a stretch of road that is open on both sides with fields. The drifts are shoving their way back onto the road seconds after being cleared.

Two cars in front of the Edsel is a snowblowing machine trying to clear the road, and the going is slow. The truck stops suddenly and so does the car in front of Ernie. Ernie, as usual, more engrossed in his conversation with Fitz then in the driving, fails to stop and runs right into the back of the car. Ernie and Fitz pop out quickly, concerned about the other occupants. The two women are on their way to work at Smith Corona, but they want to stop and call the state trooper, so Fitz finds a phone and they wait at the cars. It looks like the Edsel has finally seen its last days.

When the state troopers arrive, they find the four in 10 below zero weather with the snow flying all around them.

"License, please," he says to Ernie.

"Ohhhh, Ernie Davis, well better get out of this cold. Let's get into my car." So Ernie and Fitz sit in the back of the troopers car while he fills out the report.

"Ernie, how far behind do you estimate you were when you hit the brakes?"

Ernie had barely seen the car stop and only hit the brakes at the last moment.

"Well,,, I...I ... I .. a...a ...a.. I... a...," he can't seem to get anything meaningful out.

"You were at least 180 feet behind, weren't you, Ernie?"

"Yeh."

So he writes it up that Ernie had skidded, and certainly it was true that in the end he had skidded, since the conditions were so bad.

Then the trooper gets everything out of Ernie's car, including the huge trophy and puts them into his car, along with Ernie and Fitz.

"Now, how are you guys going to get home?"

"I guess a bus."

"Well the bus might have left, so we'll go down the highway and double back to stop it," but when they double back they end up back at the station. People surround them as they get out of the trooper's car, everyone seems to recognize Ernie.

"What's the matter?

"What happened?

"Is something wrong, Ernie?"

Soon there are at least 50 people surrounding him, all talking to him, while Fitz goes and buys the tickets. They board the bus and leave the lemon of a car to be carted home later. It sits for many months in a garage in Elmira, allegedly being repaired, but is hopeless and finally abandoned for buses and hitchhiking.

With football season over, Ernie, Mackey and other football players again form an informal team, but the Syracuse basketball coach begs them to join his team for the season. And they do.

Next time Ernie sees Fitz, he again asks if he wants to go home.

"Sure," says Will, "shall we walk this time?"

"How about hitchhiking."

It's another snowy evening, but not nearly as cold as the night of their accident. They stand out on the highway headed the right way for Elmira with their thumbs in the air. The cars speed on by.

"Hey, man, We been standing here for over an hour and I'm freezing to death. Its time for me to hide behind a tree."

"Whaddya mean, Ernie?" Will feigns ignorance.

Ernie doesn't answer, but stands back behind a tree off the road a bit, and sure enough a car stops almost immediately. Fitz races over, opens the door and leans in to tell the driver where they're going, while Ernie pops out from behind the tree and starts to climb into the back seat.

"Hey, what the..." and the driver starts to accelerate the engine to take off without them with Ernie only half in the car and Fitz at the window. Fitz speaks up quickly:

"You don't mind if my friend, Ernie Davis comes along too, do you? You know ... the All American from Syracuse."

"Why .. sure... yeh, I've heard of Ernie. So you're the guy they're always writing about. Have I got some questions for you... Do you think I could have your autograph for my son? He's quite a fan of yours. Wait'll he hears that I gave you a ride."

The guys hop in, as the man chatters on, with Ernie giving him short but polite answers.

The Edsel sits in the garage a long time and finally is trashed. Ernie manages to get a 58 blue Oldsmobile that finally runs and so is back to driving home instead of hitchhiking.

The rest of the year Ernie visits his family in New York City as often as possible. His appearance is always a special occasion for the family. They all adore him and realize that they always have. There was a special quality about Ernie even as a child and with age that only matured and became more apparent to them. Ernie inspires his whole family and they measure their successes on what Ernie has done and how he does it. Everyone wants to be around him and when he leaves they hate to see him go. It is as though he were yellow flowers lighting up the table and they can't bare to part with the brightness they bring to their lives. Even when Ernie is just passing through, they all seem to have a second sense and show up without being called. To his family, Ernie is real and warm, but almost too good to be true. He is someone they can really believe in, who lives the life of his beliefs and doesn't just talk them. In fact, Ernie never does talk about the way he lives his life, nor does he declare his religion to those around him. He just lives his life in a way that everyone who knows him understands the meaning of it. And to Ernie, his family and friends are his sustenance. They breathe fresh air into every setting. He is a very happy young man.

So when Ernie arrives Chuck and he go into Manhattan on the town. When they walk into a night club, everyone knows he is special, maybe an aura about him, even if they don't exactly know who he is. They turn their heads and watch him. By now Ernie is used to this and barely notices. Everyone waits on his words, although he doesn't say much. They just wait there, even when he says little, as though they know they should listen, so they won't miss something very important. Maybe what they aren't realizing is that he is already saying it, loud and clear, by the way he dresses and respects himself, holds his head high, treats others with respect and concern and deep interest, and by the 100% he gives to his sports and other endeavors.

Then Ernie laughs, at first just a quiet one, as though he has a secret, a private thing, but then when he bursts into an unguarded loud one, it is so contagious that Chuck and the others nearby have to laugh too. The mirth inside them is ignited by Ernie's spontaneous joy in life.

As new people come up to speak with Ernie, he goes back into his shell and Chuck does the talking for a while, but soon he opens up a bit. Everyone knows how he attracts the girls and Ernie let's them all kid him and think he has a lot of them, but he doesn't run after the girls and he takes relationships seriously. Ernie is too afraid of hurting someone and he already knows that sooner or later he will hurt Betty, in fact he is already hurting her even if she doesn't know it yet. And he feels that hurt, deep inside of himself.

Ernie is so sensitive about hurting others that Chuck, who is anxious to confirm that he and Ernie are still close like they used to be, plays some head games with Ernie. He pretends to be angry or upset about something to see if

Ernie will care. Ernie sometimes comes back to him 10 to 15 times to be sure he is still okay. Finally Ernie says: "Oh, you're crazy, there's nothing wrong with you." But he still worries a little and waits around to see if Chuck IS okay.

Although Ernie seldom expresses opinions in public, possibly due to his childhood stutter, he is a deep thinker with well thought out opinions on many things. Chuck finds that out now and then when they go out together in the evening. When they come home, after Chuck has been expressing himself verbosely Ernie turns to him.

"Why did you say that. You couldn't possibly believe that stuff." So Chuck sits down with him, listens to Ernie's ideas and is impressed by the seriousness and preciseness of his thoughts.

Chapter 25

The fifties sewed the seeds of unrest. In the sixties, the seeds begin to sprout into buds: the buds of racial protest, political brinkmanship, and social individualism. While Blacks and Whites sit together at the Woolworth lunch counters in the South, flower children declare, "Make Love, don't make War." But governments aren't listening to the long-haired generation as the words fly between Khrushchev and the newly elected Kennedy. More troops are sent into Vietnam to "defend democracy against communism." Nothing has changed much, but everything is changing. Students stop washing their hair, wearing deodorant, or make-up and young men grow beards and long hair. New words or new meanings to old words begin to reflect the new atmosphere: the Establishment vs. Anti Establishment, holocaust, sit-ins, busing, backlash, awareness, commitment, relationship.

In a way, Ernie is part of the Establishment, but in a way, he isn't. Ernie's hair is still cut close to his head and neatly parted. He is the clean cut All-American boy next door, only he isn't next door if you are White, and most people don't think of a Black boy as an All-American kid. He plays football, basketball and baseball, almost as American as apple pie. He listens to his elders and respects them, even when they sometimes don't merit that respect. He goes to church every Sunday and gets down on his knees at bedtime to thank God for his gifts and joys in life. Ernie IS the fifties. He is the son everyone would want; he is the player every coach dreams of; he is the student every teacher would like in class. But one thing that breaks that 50s image, Ernie is Black. He just happens to be Black, African American. Here is the kid who doesn't want to upset anyone, and he upsets the whole applecart and no one minds because he does it so gracefully, the same way he runs down the field, like a dancer. Yet they still can't see him married to their White daughters or swimming in their southern pools or eating in their Virginia restaurants or employed in their construction crews.

Ernie's very existence is upsetting to a system that already finds it exceedingly difficult to justify itself. It places in jeopardy any attempt to categorize and label people based on skin color, or hair color or any other foolish color.

Ernie is unable to escape the reality of the times and the country he lives in. He strives to be Ernie Davis in excellence and succeeds, but his Blackness follows him every step of the way and he knows it. Still he chooses to not allow it to stand between him and his goals. "That's their problem," says Ernie, when the issue arises. His philosophy dictates that he should not waste his energy and time on something that is not within him to change (the attitude of others) **and** *yet his very character and existence do change those attitudes, over and over again.*

The beginning of Ernie's senior year he arrives at the quansit houses for preseason practice. Ben is already focused on Ernie. This is his last chance to get the most out of this unusual athlete and to give him the opportunities he deserves. He recognizes that this team has outstanding talent but needs to be developed the way the 1959 team was -- with a special spirit.

Right from the beginning, though, things don't point to another national championship. Almost immediately the players begin to suffer injuries in practice. Ernie, in particular, is still having trouble with his thigh muscle and his back where he had been injured in his sophomore year. He spends a lot of time in the training room, which, however, is not unusual for a big star who sees a good deal of action. The team has lost some of its exuberance after its winning streak in '59, but Ernie is still at the pinnacle of his fame. It hadn't been easy to follow Jim Brown, but now Ernie has arrived with a name of his own and is recognized for who he is both on and off the field.

Before the season even begins, the media is already plastering Ernie's name over the entire country. He is featured in magazine and newspaper articles and is named already to preseason major All American teams. His name is even being whispered as a possible Heisman trophy contender.

Although Ernie doesn't object to the attention it does stress him out a bit. The expectations have been put so high that he is worried about his ability to live up to them. And if there is one thing Ernie doesn't want to do it is disappoint ANYone. Now he has an entire country to satisfy. Being a great football player requires more than just personal skill and determination, it requires the backup of an excellent team. He knows that his teammates are capable of that, but the outcome also depends on the consistent good health and well being of all.

Ernie's health seems excellent in most respects, but he is annoyed by some little problems. His gums bleed frequently and he hasn't yet found time to see the dentist. He is also having somewhat frequent nosebleeds when he is hit hard, but this is not entirely unusual. For the rest, though, he is keeping himself in superb shape.

Right at the beginning of the season Ben calls Mackey in for a serious talk. Mackey is a junior and has two more years to play at Syracuse. These are his very important years for his future football career. Ben makes him an offer.

"Look, Mackey, I want you to replace Ernie when he graduates."

Ben thinks this should be exciting news for Mackey, but the reaction is different than he expected.

"I'm not going to sit around on a bench and wait until Ernie graduates." protests Mackey.

"Well, you have two options: You can either be a second string halfback and wait and we'll give you all the publicity and buildup when you wear number 44, or you can be first string tight end."

"You've got it." Mackey doesn't take a moment to decide. "I'm your first string tight end." Mackey is clear in his own mind that he wants to play with Ernie not after him, and he wants to be a player in his own right, not the shadow of another. Mackey is a great athlete on his own and would never be playing second string in another school. He and Ernie are still rooming together and although they tease and laugh, they are also competitive.

In the first game of the season with Oregon, Ernie is pitted against the All-American quarterback, Terry Baker. He suffers two sprained ankles and a painful shoulder injury, but runs the team into a 19 to 8 win and gets a Silver Cup as the best player in the game.

Ben enters the training room and finds Ernie being worked on by Julie. His shoulder and two ankles are already wrapped.

"My God, Ernie. You look like a truck ran over you."

"That's what it felt like. How many guys hit me? I thought the whole team was on top of me every time I carried the ball."

"That's about right. You got to take better care of yourself out there."

Coach Sims enters the room, checks out Ernie and the two coaches retire to a corner and speak softly.

"I can't believe we're starting the season this way," says Ben. "I just don't know what to do to protect Ernie. We've got to work a lot harder on our front line. They can't let so many guys get through to him."

"Right, Ben. We'll work them to death this week. We also need to run Brokaw more. Distract them a little."

Ernie who's aware of the gist of their conversation speaks up. "Don't worry, coach. I'll be fine by next week. I'll just take it easy for a few days."

Next weekend in the locker room, Ben is giving the final words to the team.

"You kids know that West Virginia is a formidable foe, but they don't have a chance against the likes of you beasts."

"Atta way."

"You said it, Coach."

"Hurrah!"

Ben then pulls Ernie aside and has him put his ankle with the worst injury up. It's already wrapped, but he bends it a little to either side.

"Does it hurt?"

"No not really," responds Ernie as he cringes.

"You know, Ernie. You better take it easy this time. A sprain needs more than a week to heal and you can't even favor it since both ankles are injured."

Ernie grins, "that way, I won't have to limp."

Over in the West Virginia locker room, the WV team is getting their last advice from their coach.

" Now I'm not going to tell you guys to do anything wrong. I want you to play a nice clean game out there. But remember, if you don't get Ernie out of the play, you don't win. I hear he's got a couple of bad ankles, so go kind of easy on him." And he winks.

A few smirks and laughs for the players know exactly what he means. Once Ernie sees the light of day and is running with the ball, it is almost impossible to stop him. It's not for nothing that sports writer, Al Mallette has nicknamed him, "The Elmira Express."

The players line up on the field, while Ernie, still standing next to Ben, is like a horse harnessed and ready to run. Ben hesitates only a moment and then waves him out onto the field as a starter, nodding his head in exasperation. Ernie almost gallops out there, but it is a bit lopsided due to pain in both ankles.

The two teams look at each other with the ferocity that their animosity of two years ago has left with them. John Brown is in the front line and ready for any indication of a repeat. He doesn't intend to take any crap from them.

Ernie carries the ball in the first play and is quickly tackled by a 240 pound linebacker. Once Ernie is down, the tackle sits on top of him and pulls his leg up from behind. He twists as hard as he can, then lets go. Ernie gets up and walks away without a backward glance.

The next play that Ernie carries the ball, the same guy is on top of him doing the same thing to his ankle. Still Ernie doesn't say a word, and walks away without indicating to the referees that anything at all happened.

Finally the third time this linebacker has Ernie down and is going through the same torment, Ernie turns his head looks him in the eyes and says laughing... "What the...."

That's it. The other player can't keep it up. He lets go of Ernie's foot and begins to laugh too. "I'm sorry," he tells Ernie as he climbs off of him. "I just can't do this to you...."

Ernie gets up and runs back to the bench, grinning. The other players watch him confused. He grabs a towel and wipes his face. When he drops it back down, there are blood stains on it. Ernie searches in his bag, takes out a piece of cotton and turning away from the others, stuffs it up his nose. Then he returns to the bench as though nothing has happened..

The final score of the game is 29 to 14, another Syracuse win.

Back in the dorm Mackey and Ernie are in the bathroom.

"You should have seen how surprised he was when I started laughing. He just couldn't keep it up..." Ernie's telling what happened out there to Mackey.

Ernie starts brushing his teeth.

"I wish I had seen his face... I can't believe you... If it had been me, I would have blown him away the first time he tried that."

Ernie spits in the sink and answers. "No man, that's not the way it's done. You got to stay cool. Never show it hurts....."

"Hey, look at the blood in the sink. I saw you had a nose bleed. Isn't it any better?"

"Oh, that was nothing. I just got hit a little hard. Right now, it's my gums. They been bleeding lately when I brush."

"You ought to see someone about it. You could lose all your teeth."

"I'm okay," Ernie brushes any concern aside, but knows he needs to see a dentist one of these days. Growing up the Davis kids almost never had to see a doctor or dentist. Mom kept them in good shape with the good ole remedies.

Newspapers are talking about Ernie all the time. Such headlines as "Davis: Best Running Back in History," or "Elmira Express makes longest pass for SU," continue to make Ernie a targeted man.

Humor is still Ernie's middle name in spite of all the stresses, so when Jack Moore, a skinny white friend who started with Ernie in high school basketball, wrote that he wanted to come and see the Pittsburgh home game at Syracuse, Ernie sets it up. When Jack arrives, he goes right to the players window as directed, retrieves the card Ernie has left there for him and goes immediately to the gate, entering without a problem. When he looks at the card afterward, there is the name, John Brown and a picture of the big, Black lineman on it, the most unlikely match to be found. Jack laughs a lot, but is surprised no one tried to stop him.

Pittsburgh as always was not going to be easy. By halftime Pittsburgh is ahead 9 to 0. Ben standing on the sidelines throws his hat down over and over, and finally gets so upset he begins to stomp on it.

In the locker room he goes for a change of strategy for the rest of the game.

"Okay, guys. I know you're worried cause of the beating you've been taking out there, but 9-0 doesn't mean anything at halftime. You've got half the game left and they're not as good as you are, so what're you waiting for?"

He continues. "We know Ernie's a marked man, but we're going to use him anyway. Up til now, he's mostly been leading the other guys off track. Now I want you to hand him the ball. They're not going to be expecting it."

A great big grin on Ernie says he's ready. In fact, he can't wait.

When Ernie enters the game, Easterly passes the ball to the great #44 over and over and he runs two touchdowns in a row and a total of 119 yards gained. The final score is 28 to 9.

After this game, things begin to look dismal for the team. Syracuse is sustaining injury after injury, so much so that Ben begins to avoid contact during practice in order to keep the injuries of the remaining players down. Still Ernie never misses a game and Ben isn't sorry. He needs him more than ever now. Easterly breaks his hand and is out for three games. At one point there are as many as eight starters out when they play Penn State. Ernie almost single handedly manages with the help of the third and fourth teams to hold it to a controlled loss. In the Penn game there are moments when it seems like there are as many as ten Penn men attached to Ernie when he moves.

The problems of this season make a lot of people wonder if Ernie's chances for All-American might be thwarted by the difficulty of giving the ball to Ernie with so many opponents on him. But Ernie holds his own. When he does get the ball, even with four or five pursuers on his tail, he forges ahead, barreling through them or dancing around them, to gain yard upon yard for his team. Some even suspect Ernie of taking ballet lessons he is so adept.

Many people feel that Ernie is better than ever. His statistics certainly show it. Everyone knows that Ernie is often out there in the field carrying the ball single-handedly, but there are lapses for Ernie that might not be apparent to the casual observer. Those who know Ernie's perfection, who play close to him, notice the incongruity of the occasional errors he makes. Ernie himself is only too aware of his shortcomings and takes it very seriously. When someone teases him about a mistake, he feels bad and beats himself up afterwards.

Notre Dame is one of those games. Ernie makes one major error that impacts the outcome of the game. It is not a typical Ernie Davis play. He knows better and he is devastated. So he makes up for it in the rest of the game and Syracuse is ahead until Sweeny is called on a foul. There are actually some questions after the film of the game is viewed about a miscall, but Notre Dame refuses to concede the game and Syracuse loses its chance at the Orange Bowl.

Typical of Ernie, he works even harder for the Boston College game, rushes 90 yards, defends against a 2 point conversion and flies 63 yards with an intercepted pass.

So now as the awards begin to arrive, there is no doubt that Ernie deserves what he is getting. And he is getting them all.

Chapter 26

Mid November brings a barrage of mail to the Athletic Office and all of it talks about Ernie Davis:

John Bently sends a telegram on November 14:

"Ernie Davis is one of the most powerful runners we have met this season. When a player runs up 122 yards on 22 carries as Davis did against us, you can't help but have respect for his ability."

Tom Nugent, head football coach of Maryland sends a telegram on Nov. 17:

"Ernie Davis is the best back we have played against. Our squad picked him #1 on our All Opponent Team. He is outstanding on defense as well as a great runner."

Val Pinchbeck, the Public Relations Officer calls Ernie into his office.

"You should see all the letters we've gotten about you. They're all complimentary. You've even got the opposition coaches raving about you."

"I'm not sure I've done anything special," responds Ernie modestly. "There are lots of good players out there."

"Yeh, but not all of them are gentlemen too. And there aren't very many who have won all the honors you have... in October you were named back of the week for Sports Illustrated. I just got this letter from Sport Magazine, naming you annual top performer. You are on at least three All American lists and more are coming in. We've got letters from all over the country, organizations wanting to present you with awards of one sort or another and wanting you to come speak. And best of all, you are a top contender for the Heisman Trophy."

"Wow! I don't know what to say."

"Do you think it would be okay if I wrote some thank yous here and sent them off. I don't want people to think I don't appreciate their recognition," adds Ernie.

"Sure. Why don't you sit down over at that table and write out what you want to say," Val suggests. "We'll have it typed up for you and you can sign it.".

The season is almost over and Ernie is named All-American by at least eight magazines. Along with the awards come the obligations, the honors, the celebrations and a schedule that keeps Ernie running morning through night and back into morning again, plus a need to keep up his academics so he can graduate. He responds to all letters and all invitations personally although briefly, but with a polite respectfulness and appreciation of the honors or kindnesses bestowed upon him.

In spite of these demands, Ernie is practicing every day for the Liberty Bowl game, writing papers and being requested to travel all over the country making appearances, speeches and accepting awards.

Mackey watches as Ernie tries to cope with all this attention. He crawls into bed at 10 and turns off his light. Ernie is working with a tape recorder:

"I want to tell you how honored I am to bbbbe hehere, tttoday."

He grumbles at himself, rewinds and begins again.

"I want tttto ttell you how...."

Ernie stops the recorder, rewinds and begins again.

"I'm really happy to be here tonight. It is such an honor ."

He smiles... he got through it all; he plays it back and then goes on.

"I'm really happy to be here tonight. It is such an honor. I don't know if you realize that I was born in ppppennsylvania..."

Ernie stops the recorder and starts rewinding.

Mackey pulls the pillow over his ears.

"Com'on, Ernie. You'll be just fine. You always are when you get in front of an audience."

"You don't understand, Mac, you got to always present yourself at your best. You got to be prepared, man. If it doesn't come easy, then you work at it."

"Well then work at it tomorrow when I'm in class. I can't take one more...'it's nice to be here tonight...'"

He groans and hides under the pillow again.

"That's okay, Mac. I've got to stop now, anyway. I've got an exam tomorrow."

"You're kidding! You're going to start studying now? How can you keep these hours and still keep up at practice?"

"You gotta do what you gotta do."

With that Ernie opens his book and starts studying. He closes down at 2AM when he falls asleep over his book in his bed.

The next day Mackey and John Brown find Ernie back on his bed struggling to keep his eyes open with a textbook in front of him. They're carrying a newspaper.

"You've made the news again, Ernie. They're all talking about whether or not you're going to win the Heisman Trophy," says Brown.

"Ah, that's just talk. I don't have a chance. I didn't even have a good year. Too many injuries. Too many mistakes."

"Hey, man," says Mackey, who is still reading the newspaper. "Here they say you may be the first "Negro" to win it."

"If Jim Brown didn't win it, I'm certainly not going to."

Mackey continues, "You're not the only Black in the running. They're also talking about Sandy Stevens, the quarterback from Minnesota and Bob Ferguson of Ohio State."

"You're kidding.... hand me that paper! Sandy Stevens? That's great! I haven't seen him since two summers ago."

"You know him?" asks Brown.

"Know him? We grew up together, played baseball in Little League in PA, dreamed of the major leagues together."

"Well," Mackey notes, "it looks like you're both going to play with the big boys now, but not in the diamond. I understand NFL is watching both of you."

"Hey, let me see that paper again. Does it say any more about Sandy?"

Ernie leans off the bed to grab the paper, but Mackey slips away, rolls it up and passes it to John Brown. Ernie gets into it and jumps at John who passes it back to Mackey. John holds Ernie down as Mackey opens it and begins to read.

"Ernie Davis: top contender for the Heisman Trophy. Can a Negro win the election? ...."

"Whaddya think, Ern, can a Negro win the Heisman Trophy? Can a Negro carry a football? Can a Negro run down the field? Can a Negro....????"

Ernie interrupts. "Man, I don't worry about those things..."

Ernie grabs away the paper, looking for information about the other players.

"... there are lots of great players out there. Let's see who else is being considered.."

Ernie receives the news with mixed feelings. He's not convinced that he had such a good year. Ernie knows the other contenders, and truly expects the trophy to go to Bob Ferguson .

Sportscasters all over the country speculate, as they always do, on who will be the victor, but this time the racial question takes front stage. Once again Ernie, who wants to be simply Ernie, and not a protester or campaigner, is pulled into a major racial debate. He wants to be recognized for what he did, not what-he-did-against-the-odds.

So the newspapers didn't hesitate to ask the fundamental question, like John W. Fox, "Can a Negro win the election?" A silly question taken out of context, but apparently a question that was relevant to that era. To Ernie none of it made sense, but being of that period of time, he regarded it, as he always had... as ..."that's their problem.".

"Shhhh, here he comes."

All is quiet in the athletic office as Ernie enters.

"Hurrah!!!" they shout.

"What the...." Ernie doesn't understand right away.

Ben puts his arm around Ernie and hugs him. "The Heisman Trophy..."

"Nah..." says Ernie

"YAHHH," says Ben

It finally sinks in and Ernie lets out a whoop. The others all join in, grabbing him, hugging him, slapping him on the back, shaking his hand.

Ernie is the recipient for the 1961 Heisman Trophy. He was made the victor in a 1-2-3 balloting by 840 electors around the country. Yet, that victory had long been determined along the way by the greatest football coaches in the country who had keyed their defenses against him; and by players like Gary Kaltenback, lineman for Pittsburgh, who when asked, "who is the toughest team the Panthers had to face?" responded, "Ernie Davis."

So Ernie wins the ultimate recognition, the coveted Heisman Trophy with 824 points, Bob Fergusen comes in a close second with 771, then there is the Texas sprinter Jimmy Saxton in third place and Sandy Stephens, Minnesota quarterback, in fourth place.

Ernie stands quietly for a moment and then speaks to them all. "Winning the Heisman Trophy is something you just dream about. You never think it could happen to you."

Every child has a fantasy, but so few ever see the culmination of them, especially at such a young age.

"It's the biggest thrill of my life," Ernie tells the throngs of reporters who are parked on his doorstep and barrage him with phone calls.

"How do you feel about being the first Negro to win the Heisman trophy?" asks a reporter waiting in his dorm lobby. There it is again, the perennial question.

"I feel very honored to be chosen, but surprised. There were so many good candidates."

"Ernie, do you think Jim Brown didn't get it because he was a Negro?"

There it is again. Inescapable.

"I think Jim Brown was a great player. I'm surprised he didn't win the Heisman Trophy. I'm surprised I did."

"What are your plans now, Ernie? You can just about pick your NFL team."

"I'm not thinking about that yet. First I have to graduate, that's the most important thing. Meanwhile, I've got a lot of traveling to do and some All Star games. I'm going to be pretty busy for a while. But of course I want to play for the NFL... who wouldn't?"

December 6, Wednesday morning, Ernie has barely been able to sleep the night before. He shaves in the morning instead of the evening which is his usual custom, and spends hours in front of the mirror trying to get his hair just right, which always stays in place anyway since it is so short. He puts on his sports jacket that Jerome's has gifted him especially for the Heisman Trophy dinner. Finally he settles for the image that stares back at him.

His entourage includes Chancellor Tolley, Lew Andres, Val Pinchbeck and Ben Schwartzwalder. Ernie and the others are ready in plenty of time, but the plane isn't. There is a blizzard in Syracuse and planes aren't taking off. They are all lined up at the airport with the sweating Ernie Davis and Syracuse contingent inside one of them. They finally do take off, but the trip from Syracuse to New York City, normally a short and easy one, is grueling. The dinner being held at the Athletic Club in honor of the Heisman Trophy winner is on hold while Ernie is awaited. Bob Hope entertains with a monologue.

"I want you to know that I carried the ball faster than any of the kids on the block when I was young."

"I raced into the kitchen, picked it up and out of the broken glass on the floor then got out the back door before my mother could even make it from the living room to the kitchen after hearing the crash."

Laughter.

Someone comes up behind Bob Hope and whispers in his ear.

"They tell me Ernie's plane has arrived at Idlewild. They say there aren't any taxis available cause of the storm, so Ernie decided to sprint over here. He ought to be arriving at any moment."

More laughter.

After a few more jokes and a lot of laughter, Ernie slips in the door at the back of the room, his overcoat still wet with snow. Someone grabs the coat and hat off him and pushes him toward the podium in the front of the room. Bob stops talking and the room becomes silent. The spotlight swirls and stops on Ernie picking his way between the tables. He lowers his head in embarrassment as the room breaks out in an ovation, a few people standing and then the entire room rising in his honor.

When he arrives at the head table in the front, he tries to go for his empty seat, but Hope puts the mike in front of him.

"Thanks," says Ernie. "Sorry to interrupt, but glad to be here, finally."

Laughter

"Yeh," says Hope, "I'll bet you're glad, Ernie. Rumor has it that Ernie is fearless when faced with seven 240 pound tackles, but is helpless in front of two stewardesses who try to fasten him into his seat belt on the plane."

Introductions follow with Ernie being lauded for his accomplishments and his character. Comments from other coaches and dignitaries are also read. Finally the Trophy is presented to Ernie and then the master of ceremonies backs away from the microphone again, motioning Ernie forward.

"I want to thank my mother and grandparents, all my coaches, especially Ben Schwartzwalder and Marty Harrigan, my teammates, without whom I would never run a ball, my friends, and Syracuse University for giving

158

me the change to do my best, both academically and on the football field. Most of all, I thank God for giving me the ability to excel."

"Thank you all very much for this honor."

Ernie receiving the Heisman Trophy

The next day Ernie arrives at the Press Club luncheon in honor of him and is seated at the head table. Within a few minutes a man steps up behind him and whispers in his ear. He immediately turns to Val, who is sitting nearby and whispers something to him. Val nods his head, picks up the 50 pound Heisman Trophy sitting on the table and they get up. Ernie approaches the President of the Press Club.

"The President of the United States is at a hotel nearby and has asked to see me."

Then the two race out with Val carrying the huge trophy. They arrive quickly at the nearby Carlyle Hotel only to encounter an immovable police line.

"This is Ernie Davis," says Val, holding up the trophy. "The President has asked to meet him."

"I don't care if he's the Pope," responds the despondent policeman, "my orders are no one goes in here."

Disappointed Ernie and Val grab the next cab back.

At the Press Club, Ernie sits down to enjoy his chicken. He's savoring the first morsel when he spies his high school coach, Harrigan, slipping in the door at the back, and then leaning against the wall and lighting a cigar. Ernie rises from the table, goes back to Harrigan, shakes his hand hard and insists he come forward and sit at the head table right next to him. Harrigan's face turns red.

"Coach, I'm so glad to see you. You have to come up front with me."

"Naw, Ernie. I'd rather just stay back here."

"Com'on, Coach, You're not going to make me go through this all alone are you?"

Harrigan follows him up front rather reluctantly, but pleased.

Just as Ernie takes his last bite, a man appears again at his shoulder and whispers to him.

"The President sends his apologies. He heard you tried to get through the lines and couldn't. He says he'll be at the Waldorf Astoria for about a half hour and he'd love to meet you. He'll be sure you get through this time."

"Here we go again," says Ernie to Val.

This time Val grabs Dick Harris who is acquainted with the President and the three race out to hail another cab, massive trophy again in hand.

There is no problem at the Waldorf Astoria. Obviously the President was sincere in his wish to meet Ernie. He goes right through with entourage and meets the President as he is coming out of the Anteroom where he was meeting with Pierre Salinger and the Association of Manufacturers. President Jack Kennedy greets Dick Harris whom he knows, and then turns to be introduced to Ernie. As they shake hands flashbulbs go off, Val sticks the trophy in front of them, the picture eventually to become an icon of the era.

"Congratulations, Ernie," says the President. "I've watched you play several times. Thought you might like to join one of our family games of touch football this summer. We could use a guy like you on our side."

Ernie laughs, "Thank you Mr. President. I hear those are pretty exciting games."

"Do you think you might end up in Washington like me? How would you feel about being the first Negro to play for the Washington Redskins?"

Ernie lowers his head in embarrassment. "I really haven't given the racial issue any thought .... But of course I wouldn't mind playing for the Redskins."

Satisfied and not completely aware of the awkwardness of the question, the President shakes Ernie's hand again. "I've heard you're a fine young man. Good luck to you. I look forward to seeing you play some more."

President Kennedy congratulating Ernie on the Heisman Trophy

As soon as Ernie gets a chance, he finds a pay phone in the lobby and dials up Angie.

"Hi, Angie, how you doing?"

"And how are the kids?"

"Angie, you'll never believe it.... guess who I shook hands with. President Kennedy. No lie..."

"Oh, it was great. I really can't believe all this is happening."

"Yeh, I think Jim Brown should have gotten it before me. But you know.... He had some problems at Syracuse I didn't have. He didn't play a good deal of his earlier years there. Maybe someday we'll get to play in the backfield together. He's been talking to me about playing for the Cleveland Browns."

"Yeh. I'd really like that. Can you imagine Jim and me in the backfield together? That'd be outstanding... "

Ernie sees Ben at the other end of the lobby, looking around for someone... he can guess that someone is probably him..

"Sorry, Ang... Ive got to go now."

Off he runs across the lobby and almost knocks Ben over, thrusting his hand out at him.

"Coach, Coach.... Shake hands with the hand that shook the hand of President Kennedy."

Ben smiles as Ernie pumps his hand.

Back in Syracuse life goes on. Mackey finds Ernie in the bathroom brushing his teeth. Ernie mumbles with toothbrush in mouth.

"Hey," says Mackey. "Well how was it? What happened? You goin to tell me all about it?"

Ernie mumbles again and then spits into the sink. Mackey sees the blood.

"Hey, Ernie. I thought you were going to see the dentist about your gums. That's not healthy." Then he pulls his lips down over his teeth and says, as though he were gumming it, "You could loth alll of your teeth, ya know."

"You're right, Mac. I keep meaning to go, but I've been too busy. You know what my life has been like. Now it's only going to get worse."

"You wouldn't believe it," he continues. "They had this big banquet and everyone was there. Bob Hope actually sat near me and handed me the microphone once. Then the next day, there was this big press luncheon... but best of all, Mac... I shook hands with President Kennedy. Can you believe it? Me.. shaking hands with the President .. and he even knew my name, ... says he had seen me play a couple of times... That was really the big moment."

Chapter 27

Amidst all the clamor, confusion and demands Ernie tries to make as many practices as possible before the Liberty Bowl, but he is falling short on keeping up with it all. He needs to perform well in this final university game or they will wonder why he even won the trophy. It is more pressure than ever. And Ernie is more tired than he has ever been.

In subzero weather, the Philadelphia stadium is full and overflowing, the crowd is yelling for Ernie, wild to see him play. It is the last college game for Easterly, Sarette, Davis and Falon, but the game isn't going well during the first half. A bunch of things are going wrong for Ernie. Due to lack of practice and being targeted, he isn't being given the ball. The score is 14 to 0 when the team returns to the locker room. Ernie is not in good shape, he can barely straighten up.

"I got kicked near my kidneys," he groans and someone calls for a doctor. He had been injured early in the game when covering a fumble and then an opposing player coming down on him. As the band takes the halftime into an overtime, Ernie gets treated for his injury with an analgesic balm. The three others from the backfield Falon, Easterly and Sarette, gather in a corner and eye Ernie who is finishing his treatment.

Easterly opens the discussion. "You know, this has really been a tough year for Ernie. Every team has been out to injure him and put him out of the game. I don't like what's going on out there. They make him seem like he's not so great as he really is."

"I know what you mean..." agrees Sarette. "The fans are all out there to see the big Heisman Trophy winner and we can't even hand him the ball."

"Yeh," says Easterly. "I don't like them going away from his last college game thinking he's maybe not as great as we all know he is, do you?"

Falon is with them on this. "They'd be crazy not to see that Ernie's the best... the best in the country."

"Okay, so let's give him a chance to prove it. I say we give him the ball all the time. He's made us look good plenty of times when we haven't been on top of it," suggests Easterly.

Sarette and Falon agree and the three hit hands in solidarity.

Ernie is everywhere: down the middle, down the side, way up ahead catching a pass. He is like 10 guys instead of one. Ernie carries the ball 30 time for 140 rushing yards and completion of several passes from Sarette. They accomplish their goal and go out in a victory of 15 to 14, with some excellent plays. Dave Sarette helps Ernie off the field, arm in arm.

"Did you know you carried the ball 30 times?" asks a reporter of Ernie.

"Yeah? ... I would have sworn it was at least 20 more times than that," mutters the exhausted Ernie. It is Ernie's final big moment in college ball. He has lived up to the honors bestowed on him. But there is no rest for him yet.

Now he and other seniors are eligible for post season invitational games and this time they earn $100 plus expenses per game, a great deal more than the meager spending money their scholarships give them.

In spite of his fatigue, Ernie is excited about the All Star games. It's not just a chance to play some very exciting football, but also a chance to be with friends he's made along the way from other colleges. John Brown has been invited to the Hula Bowl Game too, but not Ernie's first game in San Francisco. Still he wrangles his way out there at the same time as Ernie, by using Ernie's name.

Ernie signing a contract with
Art Modell of the Cleveland
Browns

Meanwhile negotiations and speculations are going on full scale as to whom Ernie will sign with for his pro career. Ernie has three things going for him. He is a great running half back, a Heisman Trophy winner and the number one draft pick. He already knew he didn't want to go to Canada, so that left a battle over him between the AFL and the NFL, who were already in deep conflict. The Browns trade their halfback, Bobby Mitchell, to the Red Skins for the right to Ernie, and offer him a three year no cut contract for $80,000 while the Buffalo Bills of the AFL offer Ernie another $50,000 topping Cleveland with a total of $130,000 for the three years. Family Attorney DeFillippo from Elmira is running the negotiations on Ernie's side. The Browns refuse to go any higher. They have to worry about the morale of the other players, they say, who will resent Ernie getting too much more than them. Even Jim Brown, already the big name in pro football only made $31,000 the year before. Although Art Modell, owner of the Browns, is very anxious to get Ernie and play him in the strongest backfield ever seen with Jim Brown he admits that, "No player is important enough to merit wrecking the whole morale structure of the team."

The truth, however, known only many years later, is that both the Buffalo Bills and Cleveland Browns think that Ernie is that important and have in truth offered him a great deal more than ever acknowledged to the press. They offer Ernie two more contracts that end up making him the highest paid pro-rookie up to that time. They amount to a combined $120,000 extra over a period of three years; $60,000 for ancillary rights and $60,000 for off season employment. The total three year amount is $200,000 from the Cleveland offer. The total offer from Buffalo is $250,000. From Ernie's perspective, both amounts are impossible for him to imagine, and so, really wanting to play for Cleveland in the backfield with Jim Brown, Ernie chooses that. He isn't indifferent to the money, but it isn't his only priority. Ernie does have plans for that money, though, mostly having to do with Marie and Dad. First he plans to pay off Marie's mortgage, then he might even buy her a new and better home.

Ernie has the world on a string and can't believe that his every fantasy and more is becoming a reality.

John Brown and Ernie have a great time in San Francisco and then on to Hawaii with John and Ernie's childhood friend, Sandy Stephens, all expenses paid, something that he and Sandy in their wildest childhood fantasies lying in the fields near the river in Pennsylvania could never have imagined.

It is almost perfect to have this great Hula Bowl and holiday together, but not quite. The three already know what they may encounter. They have been warned about the extreme prejudice in Hawaii. And not just in Hawaii, but so many of the places they have already gone, it is accepted custom that they must look around when they arrive in a new place for a local Black man to find out where they can go, what they can do, where they can actually stay without a hassle. So when they deplane the first thing they do is single out a redcap to talk with.

"Where's it at?" Ernie asks him.

"If you didn't bring it with you, you better forget it," is the sardonic response. But fortunately the NAACP is having a party for the few Blacks on the island and so they go there. It actually turns out to be a great vacation for them and they are determined to enjoy it with only a half hour practice per day. They get into jeeps and ride all over the islands, surfing in Tiki boats, and, generally, having the wonderful time that only college kids know how to have, loose and carefree.

Back at Syracuse Ernie finally has time to get to work on his studies so he can graduate and spend time with the lovely and patient Helen. She is feminine, but assertive enough to fill a special need for Ernie, that of buffer between him and the world. He has come a long way since his stutter days of early childhood, but he is glad to have this love that fulfills that one area of his life.

Still Ernie is called to talk and appear at banquets all over the country. His presence at them greatly enhances the reputation of Syracuse University. And Ernie's presence also serves to recruit thousands of students who admire him and want to emulate him, both Black and White indiscriminately. Ernie takes these responsibilities seriously and rarely refuses to speak in spite of the growing fatigue. He feels that he has received and he needs to give back.

John Mackey, however, watches Ernie with increasing concern. Living in close quarters with him he can't help but notice a number of things that others are unaware of. For one thing, Ernie seems to always be tired. Now that's somewhat understandable, due to the terrible hours he is keeping. But this tiredness seems to go beyond anything he has seen before in anyone. He falls asleep on a dime in some weird places, like a friends living room floor. Sometimes he walks so slowly getting out of the car or going into a building that it leads Mackey's mom to ask. "How is it that Ernie can be so fast on the field and so slow off of it." At the time they both laugh.

Mackey also watches over and over as Ernie stuffs his nose with cotton. Ernie tries not to be obvious, but it is hard for Mac to miss.

"What's the matter?

"Oh, just a nose bleed."

Well, Mackey supposes that that is fairly normal for a football player on the field, but wonders why it is still happening.

Then there is the continual gum bleeding that Ernie still has not taken care of.

Still these are basically minor annoyances that are soon forgotten by Mackey and just accepted by Ernie.

Ernie doesn't complain about the extra pressures in the classroom, but one day, when he is passing through the Hall of Languages, Dean Faigle stops him and asks how things are going academically. Ernie admits that when he had asked one professor to give him a make-up test for one of the days he had to go out of town, the professor told him he had to be there to take the test or he would get an F. Ernie is truly afraid this might prevent his graduation. The Dean takes Ernie into his office and sits him down. Then with a face as red as a fire engine he telephones the professor and tells him in no uncertain terms what he thinks of him:

"Listen, you jerk," he storms into the phone. "What's this story with Ernie and an F when he is going out of town to recruit for the university?"

Ernie sits there horrified and terribly embarrassed. He never believed the Dean would do anything like this.

The Dean continues with his flowering words, sparing nothing. "This guy has done more for the university than you'll ever do. He's raised money to keep guys like you around here on salary. Etc., etc."

The Dean goes on and on with Ernie in agony, growing smaller and smaller in his chair.

When Ernie goes back to class on Monday, he apologizes to the professor, telling him that he understood he was just trying to do his job.

When he reports the outcome to Will, Will understands perfectly what is going on. It is Ernie, being magnanimous again, defending a guy for his poor behavior. He tells Ernie that he bets the guy was just looking to arrive at a cocktail party and brag that "he GOT Ernie Davis." Ernie denies that and continues to make excuses for the professor.

Ernie is still trying to carry on his life as it was before, but it has become more difficult. For the Spring Break he heads home with John Brown to go barnstorming with his old friends, the Coleman brothers and others. Roland Coleman has set up some basketball games for them in Harrisburg and Virginia.

The trip had to be planned ahead and everything set up, because it wasn't possible to stay in hotels. They would stay in Black homes as usual.

Right outside of Richmond, the group parks their cars in front of a restaurant and goes in to have a meal. As soon as they enter, the owner approaches them and tells them they will have to leave.

"What?" says Roland, "Do you realize that this is Ernie Davis who just won the Heisman Trophy?"

"I don't care who he is, you can't eat here."

"You mean that this gentleman who had coffee in New York City with President Kennedy can't get coffee in this raggedy ass joint?" They are getting really angry now. Was it possible that even getting the Heisman Trophy didn't make any difference when it came down to buying a cup of coffee?

John Brown and some of the others are ready for a fight. Enough is enough! But Ernie dissipates the situation as usual. "Nah, com'on. Let's get outta here!" and he heads for the door. Ernie doesn't want trouble and the others tend to follow him even though tempted not to give in this time.

What's the point, thinks Ernie, of making a battle out of a little podunk restaurant. The other patrons of the restaurant are getting upset and angry at the owner. He ignores them all and stands his ground, so the group leaves.

The Elmira Bombers continue and go on to play games in West Virginia, but somehow the incident has taken all the fun out of the excursion.

They had always hoped that there were things they could do to change their lives; accomplishments that would finally prove their worth and gain them the respect they deserved as human beings. But what could it all mean, if a little man, in a nothing coffee shop could treat a man of great character and accomplishment, such as Ernie so disrespectfully and so abhorrently just because of the color of his skin, then how could they ever expect anything to change. Some battles just can't be won overnight.

Chapter 28

Back in the saddle, Ernie works hard to catch up on his school work, still fitting in as many appearances as possible. Meanwhile, Elmira prepares a major celebration for Ernie and they call February 3, Ernie Davis Day. They set it up for Notre Dame High School and invite all kinds of dignitaries from all over the state. Ernie's hometown wants him to know they love, admire and respect him. And frankly there is no way he can doubt it.

The festivities begin on Saturday at 2:30 in the afternoon at the YMCA where Ernie Davis and Jim Brown sign autographs for 500 excited kids. Ernie is wearing Brian Howard's favorite three piece suit, that although it belongs to Ernie, Brian keeps telling him looks better on him. He stands among the children and for once does not show a bit of his fatigue, probably because kids are Ernie's favorite people and he is a favorite among them.

At 4:30 there is an informal press conference featuring Ernie, Jim, Ben Schwartzwalder and Arthur Modell, to eventually be joined at 5:30 by Governor Nelson A. Rockefeller.

Ernie has invited John Brown to join them for the dinner and it is here that John gets to meet Art Modell, which later leads to John also being recruited to the Cleveland Browns.

At 6PM the doors of the Notre Dame gym and cafeteria open for the huge banquet in Ernie's honor. More than 1400 people attend.

After dinner the gym is open to the public and in pour hundreds more people. Among the throngs is a little troop of EFA teachers, mostly in their 50s and 60s. They scramble up into the bleachers like little kids, sharing stories of Ernie in their classrooms, as though he belongs to each one of them individually. In fact, everyone wants a part of Ernie for themselves. And it's easy to know why they all claim to be his friend. Ernie makes every one of them feel at one time or another that they are special to him. And in some way they are, because Ernie has the ability and sensitivity to view every other person as someone meaningful and important.

Ernie is presented with numerous gifts, the most magnificent being the keys to a 1962 Thunderbird. Ernie's friends had tried to put the money together for this, but were disappointed to have run short, obliging Ernie to have to pay it off later. Still the thought is there and they want him to have it, knowing that cars haven't been easy for him, they want him to have a wonderful dependable one. And Ernie, being Ernie, is beside himself with the joy of the day and his gratefulness.

Some think the Thunderbird is a bit ostentatious. But his friends have thought to honor him with a prize and they consider this a gift of esteem to a great man and a great athlete.

Everyone makes a speech for Ernie and there are constant applause and cheers. It turns out to be more like a pep rally than a banquet. They tease Ernie about his hat size, saying his head is the only thing that hasn't gotten bigger. Coach Harrigan tells the story about Ernie's fearsome plunge into water over his head at the YMCA camp. The one sport Ernie does not excel in is swimming. In fact he not only can't swim he is quite frightened of water. Ernie still remembers a good friend of his in Pennsylvania drowning in a dirt pond while he and others watched and couldn't help. He also thinks of his friend from Small Fry days in Elmira, who drowned at Fitch's Bridge a few years later. So one of the many gifts given to Ernie at this time is a lifetime membership in the YMCA partly in humor and partly seriously in hopes that Ernie can overcome this fear. He hopes so too.

They spare no expense and no extravagance, wanting to show Ernie their feelings for him. And none of it is lost on him. He is elated beyond belief. Ernie sits on his throne this night and wears the crown of victory with a quiet but appreciative dignity. Tomorrow will be another day and maybe then he will have to face the real world, but for now, his real world is all a glitter and he loves every minute of it.

Ernie and John Mackey in front of Ernie's new Thunderbird

On they go again, Ernie attends a dinner in Pittsburgh and then on to New York City for three days of intensive testing. According to the Browns it will require 3 days of testing by 18 different psychologists to evaluate Ernie for his off-season employment. Apparently Ernie is a very expensive property that they plan to be only too careful with. Modell picked this psych career center personally for Ernie already beginning to have that special feeling for him that seems to dominate Ernie's world.

Spring Fever hits on Syracuse campus somewhat late, but all the more potent because of that. The students are all hanging out their dorm windows or climbing onto the porch roofs of their Greek houses and dorms, sunning themselves, playing music loud and yelling from porch to porch, window to window, and roof to roof.

Ernie knows just how he plans to spend this superb break in the weather. He is going to take his new Thunderbird down to Thornton Park and wash off all the winter salt and spring thaw. You get something this beautiful, you got to take care of it. Just as Ernie and Mackey, having dried the car are putting on the polish, a police car comes along. The two of them pretend they are just hanging out, but the evidence is there. The policeman reads an ordinance to Ernie about park regulations that specifically don't allow what they are doing and takes them to headquarters.

Ernie is totally mortified. He can't believe he has gotten himself into this spot. There he sits in the room while the shifts change, wanting to crawl into a hole and hide. Of course everyone there recognizes him. You can't live in Syracuse and not know who Ernie Davis is. Three or four of the other policemen coming on ask him what he's doing there. He tries to keep his explanation honest but simple. They give him a look of sympathy.

"Who brought you in" they ask him.

When he tells them the name they roll their eyes and comment: "Yeh, that figures."

Ernie calls Ben with a hundred apologies. Ben and Val Pinchbeck arrive shortly to bail Ernie out. But believe it or not, the news media has already gotten wind of it. Ernie grimaces as he sees the two enter in their trench coats in supposed incognito. He's frankly a little disappointed in them, though, that they are so embarrassed they are trying to hide out. By evening all the local news stations are reporting that the great star Ernie Davis has fallen and was put in jail for misbehaving in the park. Naturally the national press picks it up too and so the world has a heyday for a day or two at Ernie's expense.

Ernie is hanging in there, with just a little more school to go before graduation: some exams, some papers, graduation and the East-West All Star Game in Buffalo. Graduation finally arrives June 2, 1962 and it is a relief, Ernie has completed all his courses with above average grades, an undeniable challenge, especially under the circumstances of the last half year with all the additional attention and pressures.

His final college honor is to be chosen as a Class Marshall along with Betsy Evans, an Elmira classmate who is first female president of the student council at Syracuse. The Class Marshalls lead the graduating seniors down the aisle, a very big honor. Betsy has decided that she and Ernie should lead the class arm in arm. Her father hears about her plans and absolutely prohibits her from doing it, but headstrong, leader and brilliant young woman has her way and Ernie gives in to it too. The racial murmurings escape Ernie's ears and all he hears is the fading chorus of:

"We're the class of '62

We're the best at ole S.U....."

Ernie straightening the robe for fellow marshal, Betsey Evans, for Syracuse University graduation

As soon as graduation is over, Ernie heads to Cleveland for some Spring Practice, Then back for the East-West All Star game in Buffalo. There is a two sided whammy for Ernie in this game. The coach for his all star team, Woody Hayes, is from Ohio State and has been against Ernie for a long time. He was the coach for Bob Ferguson and was resentful that Ernie won the Heisman instead of Bob. So during practice it is clear that he intends to give all the good plays to Ferguson and leave Ernie hanging. Ben acting as

Assistant Coach is not in a position to come to Ernie's rescue. In addition, the Buffalo fans are even angrier at Ernie then Woody is, because he didn't sign with them, he took Cleveland's offer. So the minute Ernie appears the boos begin and they don't stop throughout the entire game. To add pain to the already dismal situation, Ernie does not feel well at all. Although at practice, the coach could see his tremendous skill and effort when it comes time for the game, Ernie is completely worn out and it shows.

Ernie doesn't play well and is primarily used as defense and a decoy. The game is a disaster and the press has another Hay Day with Ernie, questioning his winning of the Heisman Trophy. Ernie is so tired after this game he just keeps turning to John Brown saying, "I'm so tired! I didn't do well," like a broken record. John tries to reassure him. "Ernie, it was really hot out there and I'm tired too." But nothing could ease Ernie's disappointment in himself.

Now his spirit is down and he is frustrated. He's supposed to go back out to Wisconsin for the biggest of the All-Star games, the All-Star College team with the NFL champions, Green Bay Packards. He doesn't really want to go. He wants to go home to relax and then get out to Cleveland for more practice. But Ernie isn't about to let anyone down.

He goes to Elmira for the Fourth of July holiday and a short rest with every intent to play in the All Star game with Green Bay.

Chapter 29

"He took his illness on his own shoulders, carried it, lived normally, simply. It was a tremendous thing to watch."

Jim Brown

July 4, 1962 Ernie finds himself once again in the backyard of his dear high school coach, Marty Harrigan. He throws the football with Harrigan's five sons, while Marty and his wife prepare a wonderful barbecue.

"How do you like your hamburgers, Ernie? Well done, right?"

"That's right, Coach, but only fix me one."

"One? I already put five on for you."

As they sit down at the picnic table to eat, the boys fight to sit next to Ernie. When Mrs. Harrigan goes to pick up Ernie's plate, she sees he has hardly eaten anything.

"I'm sorry, Ernie. I thought you were done."

"I am done, thanks."

"Why, Ernie, what's wrong? You've hardly touched your hamburger or your potato salad.."

"You're kidding," Harrigan tells his wife. "Why, Ernie, you never eat less than four or five."

"Well, to tell the truth, my teeth have been bothering me for some time. But it's been such a busy year. I haven't had time to go to the dentist. I'm planning to see one when I'm in Evanston, Illinois preparing for the All Star game with the Packers in Green Bay."

"You better take care of it," admonishes Harrigan. "Those teeth problems can really get you down. Imagine how funny you'd look taking out your dentures when you go out onto the field, instead of putting a guard in."

Ernie grimaces.

"Yeh, I know you're right. Mackey's been trying to tell me the same thing for months."

"In fact, I really feel so worn out right now, if I had it to do over, I wouldn't even be going to Green Bay. I'd just stay home, rest up and see the dentist here. I hate to start practice with the Brown's so tired out."

"Why don't you do that, Ernie. You don't need this game anyway."

"Yeh, I know... but what would I tell them. I promised them I'd be there... so I will."

In Evanston, Illinois where they have begun practices for the All Star game, Ernie is finally in the dentist's office.

"You should be more comfortable without those wisdom teeth, but you waited a little too long. Your gums look swollen and bleed much too easily. I've given you a prescription for antibiotics. Be sure to take them all. Call me in about a week and let me know how you're feeling. If you don't stop bleeding within a reasonable time come right back and let me look at those gums again. Here are 4 aspirin with codeine. They should get you through the worst of the pain."

Ernie is relieved that he finally has taken care of this. He's sure he will begin to feel better now. If there is an infection, that might explain why he is feeling so low and that will get better in a few days with the antibiotics.

Ernie stands at the sink in the bathroom and looks at the blood in it. He put gauze in his mouth like the dentist had instructed him, but he'd already used up all they had given him.... and the bleeding is coming stronger than ever. He goes to the phone right away and calls the dentist's office.

Ernie's in the chair and the dentist is transferring a sample of the blood to his microscope as he commends Ernie for coming back right away:

"It looks like you've done a lot of bleeding, Ernie."

He bends over his microscope to study the slide. Suddenly his body stiffens. He takes another look. The expression on his face changes to one of undisguised horror, but he is turned away so that Ernie can't see him. He excuses himself without turning back to Ernie. His voice a bit shaky, as he says: "I'll be back in a minute."

He stumbles out the door and leans against the wall in the hallway for a moment. He holds his stomach, his eyes damp and tries to regain his composure.

When he does return, he has calmed himself enough that Ernie doesn't seem to notice the change.

"Well, it looks like you've lost a little more blood than you should with this. You may have a bit of anemia. I'd like you to check into the hospital for a couple of days to get you back on your feet. They can do some tests and check out your blood."

"Okay, if you think so," Ernie replies. He is not that surprised. He has been feeling so tired for so long. And it is not difficult for an athlete, who is used to being in top shape and used to noticing what goes on in his body, to realize when something isn't quite right.

Ernie sits up in the hospital bed, impatiently awaiting the okay from the doctors for him to play in the All Star game with the Green Bay Packers. He feels better with the bed rest and is determined to get going. If it hadn't been for that darn molar that wouldn't stop bleeding when it had been extracted, he wouldn't have lost all this practice time. It would be hard for him to be in the best possible condition for the game, but he would give it all he could.

He is confident that now that he is on antibiotics he'll get better quickly. All he needs now is the okay from the doctor so he can get back to practice. His gums are still sore so eating is difficult, but he hasn't missed a game yet and he doesn't want this last All Star game to be the first one, in spite of his continuing fatigue.

Art Modell arrives at the hospital door. Ernie is surprised to see him.

"Mr. Modell, what are you doing here in Evanston?" Ernie smiles and starts to rise out of the bed.

"How you feeling, Ernie?"

"Oh, a lot better. I think I just lost a little too much blood with that dental work. It's really a stupid thing. I should have taken care of it a lot sooner."

"Well, I'm glad you're feeling better, but we don't want you to play in the All Star game. We're planning to take you back to Cleveland to the Marymount Hospital there and do a few more tests. We want to make sure you're ready to play in the fall."

"Really, Mr. Modell. I'm just fine now. I'm sure I can handle the game and still be up to summer camp practice."

"I'm sure you'll be fine, but the doctors don't want you to play until they get you into shape... and we'd rather have you at one of our hospitals in Cleveland. We'll leave together tomorrow morning. Meanwhile get a good rest tonight."

As Ernie is being prepared to be moved to Marymount hospital, his mother, Marie, visiting her husband's relatives in Galston, Illinois receives a telegram. She and her husband Bud Fleming are planning to see Ernie play in the All Star game and then take him back home with them afterwards for a little R and R before practice in Cleveland begins. Although most telegrams that she has received contain only good news of good fortune and congratulations, this one is different. Marie has a foreboding as she opens the familiar yellow envelope. Why would anyone send a telegram to her in-laws house for her?

"Ernie's in the hospital she informs Bud, confused and suddenly worried. She gathers up her things quickly and leaves with her husband to go see Ernie and find out what's wrong. They go immediately to Ernie's empty room when they arrive at the hospital in Evanston. There they find a rumpled bed and a note. It appears they have just missed him.

"We've taken Ernie to Marymount Hospital in Cleveland," the note reads. "Please phone the doctor before you leave. Sorry we missed you." And it's signed, Art Modell.

"Well here we go again," says Marie, frustrated and worried. "What could be wrong with Ernie that they're keeping him in the hospital like this?"

Marie goes right to the nurses station and asks if they can help her call Ernie's doctor. She shows them the note that was left for her.

"I'm Ernie Davis' mother, the young man in room 612... It seems they already left for Cleveland before I got here. Mr. Modell, who left the note, says I should phone Ernie's doctor. The name and number are right here on this note. Would you please try this number for me."

"I'd be very happy to, Mrs. Davis," responds the nurse.

"The name is Fleming, thank you very much."

She tries the number; lets it ring quite a bit; then hangs up and dials again.

"I'm sorry. It seems there is no one there right now. Why don't you sit down and wait over there. We can try again in a half hour, if you would like."

"No thanks." Marie is a get it done type of person. "I'm going to go as quickly as I can and try to get to Cleveland tonight. I appreciate your help. Please thank the doctor for me.... for taking care of Ernie."

At Marymount the tests have begun on Ernie. Dr. Siegler is trying to put a needle into Ernie's breast bone and finding it quite difficult. He tries over and over, watching Ernie with concern. But Ernie smiles through the whole thing.

"I can't believe this," comments Dr. Siegler. "You must be made of steel. I've never had so much trouble getting one of these needles in. I'll have to get another football player in here to handle you."

Minutes later, Dr. Horvath is added to the group around Ernie's bed.

"Hi, I'm doctor Horvath. Did I hear that someone needs me? So this is THE Ernie Davis. I used to play a little college ball myself. Nothing like you, though, but I enjoyed it. We're sure glad you're going to be playing here in Cleveland. Dr. Siegler tells me you need a strong arm."

"Glad to meet you. Hope you have better luck. I guess I've done a few too many push ups."

Horvath gets the needle in first try. Ernie jumps a little, but forces a friendly smile and thanks the doctor for his efforts.

The sample goes immediately to the laboratory where a group of doctors stand around the microscope taking turns looking. They are all moved to tears. One shakes his head, another turns away and rubs his eyes on his cuff. Dr. Ippolito, the physician for the Cleveland Browns can't believe what he is seeing. He's examined Ernie in the past and says he has one of the most perfect physiques that he has ever seen and he's seen some really big strong healthy men. But he nods and agrees with the others that the facts are undeniable. Ernie has leukemia, and it is an acute form of leukemia. In the early 60s, leukemia is always deadly, but acute leukemia holds a prognosis of about one to three months from diagnosis. They are all horrified.

Meanwhile back in the hospital room, they are gearing up for the All Star game. A television set has been brought in for Ernie to watch the game and Modell has asked John Brown, Jim Brown and Jim's roommate, John Wooten to stay with Ernie throughout the game, and keep him company. They are actually pretty nervous. Outside the door of Ernie's room, John and Jim talk with each other before they enter.

"Do you think it's really as serious as Mr. Modell is hinting at?" John asks Jim.

"It's got to be pretty bad," says Jim, "or Ernie wouldn't be sitting in a hospital room. You can be sure they would have him out there getting all the publicity he can. They certainly want to get their bucks out of him."

"Do you think they'll let him be on the first team in the fall if he misses too many practices?"

"You can be sure they'll try to get him in from the beginning. But they're making this whole thing sound ominous."

"Ernie's in such great condition. He always has been," says John. "I can't imagine anything getting him down for long. It must be mono or something."

Ernie himself is thinking the same thing. He knows this is more than just a gum infection. First of all, all the exams they are doing don't seem to be just for an infection. And second, he has enough awareness of his body to realize that he has not been okay for some time. He knows that he burned the candle at both ends and it's not unusual to get mononucleosis in college. He should have done something about it sooner, or cut back his schedule. Now he has to miss the All Star game and maybe even practice or the beginning of the season. Well, he is determined now to do everything they tell him so he can finally get back into shape.

When his teammates enter the room, Ernie is sitting in a chair and hops up the minute he sees them. Coming to meet them like that, so full of his enthusiasm and usual energy, the three relax and exchange a look. It couldn't be all that bad after all, they think.

"How's practice going?" asks Ernie.

"The usual crap. They expect more from us than the honkeys ... and ... as far as that goes, we give them more," Jim is already a little jaded. He's been four years in NFL.

John is struggling as a rookie. "It's great ... I guess. But I'm having trouble getting used to it. They play defenses so much different than college ball.... I don't know."

"Aww... I'm sure you'll adapt quickly enough, John. Just keep working really hard. Sure wish I could be out there. So tell me about the other guys. Who's there and what are they doing?" Ernie is hungry for any connection and information he can get.

"So what about your Mom, Ernie?" Asks John.

"Great, she came all the way out here. Said she just missed me in Illinois. Geeze I hate to think of her having to traipse around to all these hospitals. I guess they scared her half to death, but when she saw I was fine she felt better. She had to go back to work."

"Hey, do you guys want to watch the All Star game with me. It's coming on right now?"

Although Ernie had shed a few tears to realize he had to miss the game, he is fine now. Ernie had felt a little like the kid back in Pennsylvania, watching the parade go on without him, all the other kids in their uniforms, but he knew soon he would be back in the fold of things.

The illness is quickly forgotten with Ernie appearing to be quite normal. When the game starts, they are already cheering and talking loudly and excitedly about the plays and the abilities of the guys on both teams. They kid about how the game will go without Ernie.

"You don't think they've got a chance without me ... do you?" Ernie eggs them on.

"Yeh, they've got a chance," counters John Brown. "They've got a chance to pass the ball around a little."

The NFL Packers score three touchdowns against the All Stars in the fourth quarter for a final score of 42 to 20. Bart Starr led the game and they all know that if Ernie had been there, he might have been able to even the score up.

"Geeze, 42 – 20. The Packers really slaughtered those guys. You're right, Ernie, they did need you."

Ernie laughs.

Ernie watching the all star game with Cleveland teammates at hospital

Jim gets up to turn the television off then stops.

A Packer appears on the screen with a football in his hand.

"We want to dedicate the game ball to Ernie Davis, who is in the hospital"

"Wow," Ernie tears up again for a moment. He can't believe they did that.

The other two get up to leave and exchange a look, remembering why they are all here.

The public too, hearing about this gesture, is wondering why, and speculating about the reason for Ernie being in the hospital.

So Art Modell decides to take the media issue into his own hands. He sets up a very secretive press conference, including as many of the interested and dependable media people as possible. The reporters and sportscasters pile into the room. They whisper among themselves. There is almost something funereal about it, not the usual kidding and boisterous speculating. They talk among themselves while they wait for Art to appear.

"It's obvious that it's about Ernie Davis."

"Yeh, they say he won't be starting in the fall; may not even play the whole season."

"I heard it's worse than that."

"Whaddya mean?"

"There are guys saying he'll never play again... or maybe..."

Modell enters the room and a morbid silence falls over the group as he steps up to the microphone..

"I appreciate your coming here like this under somewhat unusual circumstances. What I am going to ask of you, is even more unusual. But I think when you've heard me out, you'll understand... and even cooperate."

"I have something to tell you today that I wish I didn't have to say... ever. In fact, I'm going to ask you not to print a word of what is said in this room today. I'll explain in a moment. "

"You've heard that Ernie Davis is in the hospital for tests."

Murmurs rumble around the room:

"Right...."

"I knew it...."

"Ah ... oh...."

Modell allows for the low exclamations and then continues:

"The tests are conclusive and we've got the report. Ernie Davis has acute monocyclic leukemia. It is the worst possible form.., incurable, .. and very rapid."

Modell can't help himself, his eyes cloud up a moment and he pauses.

"He has.... perhaps two months to live... at the best."

Faces turn white; mouths drop open. Gasps come from others. They have all seen him play. Who hasn't? Some have even telecast it themselves. They've all grown to admire and love Ernie. He is truly the special athlete of all time. They expected something bad, but not this bad. Their murmurs turn to comments:

"Oh... no..."

"Not Ernie...."

"How could it be?"

"I can't believe it."

"But he looked just great only a few weeks ago."

Modell continues. "I know you're shocked and I know you're saddened as we all are. I'm sure that you've grown to respect and even love Ernie as I have in the very short time I've been acquainted with him."

"I need to ask you a favor. I don't want a word of this to go out of this room. You needed to know what is happening. We knew there'd be a lot of questions and a lot of rumors. But Ernie, himself, doesn't know the gravity of his illness, and until we tell him, we're asking you not to print or speak a word of this. We will, of course, let you know the minute Ernie is told, but we'd like to put that off as long as possible, to keep his spirits up."

Now the questions begin:

Reporter: "When did you find out about the disease?"

Modell: "Only a short time ago."

Reporter: "What are they doing for him?"

Modell: "They are treating him with the most progressive medicines they have. They are also beginning transfusions. They'll do everything possible to keep him alive and keep him comfortable."

Reporter: "Are they sure about the diagnosis?"

Modell: "Yes."

Reporter: "When do you plan to tell him?"

Modell: "When his questions become so specific we can't avoid it. We don't intend to lie to him about his condition."

Reporter: "Is a remission possible?"

Modell: "It's possible, but very unlikely in this form of leukemia."

Reporter: "What are you doing about your contract with him?"

Modell: "Nothing. We will continue to pay Ernie, just as though he were healthy, as long as he lives. Thank you for your patience. Is there anyone here who has a problem with what I'm asking you?"

Silence. "I appreciate your help."

Modell lowers his head and goes out. He leaves behind a room that slowly becomes alive with concern, regret and shared memories:

"I'll never forget that time he had two twisted ankles and the West Virginia tackle almost broke one of them off. But Ernie never said a word to the referee."

"Yeh, he sure is a nice kid."

"I remember the Liberty Bowl, when he was sweating up a storm and all worn out from running the ball over 30 times, but he still gave us all interviews before he even went in to the shower."

"Modest too."

"What an athlete! I never saw anyone run like that. You'd swear he'd had dancing lessons the way he wove in and out of those tackles."

" I can't believe we're never going to see him play again...."

Then there is a loll. A silence at the thought of what is coming. Each reporter falls into his own reminiscence. Some have tears in their eyes. They move out of the room quietly now and very subdued.

Rumors about Ernie are galore, but there is no news story about his illness.

Chapter 30

In spite of Ernie's efforts to portray his usual cheerful attitude, in reality he is very sick. Although for the moment he doesn't understand the total impact of what is happening to him, he does realize he is getting worse not better. He doesn't feel good at all. Ernie is beginning to put the pieces together and he finally wants some more information.

His blood count has dropped and his temperature risen. The disease has begun to progress. While Dr. Weisberger is on vacation in New England, Dr. Siegler, his current physician, has sought out the advice of the hematologist, Dr. James Hewlett, who agrees with the original diagnosis and recommends treatment. Ernie has already been placed on a regime of blood transfusions and chemotherapy, consisting of various drugs being used intermittently. Someone in Detroit where the specialist is located has leaked the news about Ernie and Leukemia to the press and they have printed a story about it. It's just a matter of time until the news gets to Ernie.

The concept of chemotherapy is a new and exciting approach to dealing with leukemia, but still in its infancy. It is somewhat like comparing operating with large tools versus microsurgery. Years later chemo will be greatly perfected, but in the 60s it is rudimentary. In addition, there is a difficulty in determining which of the many varieties of leukemia a patient has. The methods of diagnosis are limited and the drugs used for different kinds vary significantly. Leukemia is a cancer that attacks the blood creating tissues such as bone marrow, lymph nodes, and spleen. The result is aberrant white cells that don't function properly to prevent disease, and at the same time prevent the formation of red cells that carry oxygen to all parts of the body. One of the symptoms is also a lack of blood clotting that leads to nose and gum bleeds along with other parts of the body.

Ernie is alone, lying in bed. His neck and face are still slightly swollen. His eyes are open, but he is just staring at the ceiling. Dr. Coviello enters.

"Doc, I've had some phone calls." Ernie says, who has been receiving calls and letters from around the country with bits and pieces of information that are beginning to concern him, along with his deteriorating condition.

"That's great, Ernie."

"No, what I mean is ... people are saying things and asking things ... you know... about my illness. Is it true what they're saying?

"Well, Ernie. I told you before. What you have is refractory anemia. And we're treating it with everything we've got."

Dr. Coviello has never used the word leukemia with him and it appears that Ernie has not made the connection yet, that this type of anemia actually refers to leukemia. Ernie seems satisfied with the answer.

Ernie had read the entire play book for the Browns several times already and now, having reassured himself somewhat about his illness he's raring to go, in spite of feeling a bit low physically. He figures that is something exercise will take care of. He's just been lying around too long. "When can I go out and visit the Browns' summer camp? I don't want to get so far behind. I don't even know what they're doing or what they'll expect of me."

"Okay, Ernie," responds Dr. Coviello, being the Browns' physician he figures he's the one who ought to be there with Ernie if he goes out to Camp Hiram. He's a bit concerned about Ernie going out, but pressure is on him to respond to Ernie's desires. . He has seldom in his sports medicine dealt with anything of this sort. "I'll take you out there Friday."

He knows that Ernie is not really doing well, but he believes that perhaps some positive experiences and upbeat situations may help his condition temporarily.

The car arrives at training camp. Ernie gets out of one side and Dr. Coviello gets out of the other. Ernie walks across a long stretch of grass toward the playing field, savoring the familiar smell of the fields and the dirt and sweat of the practice area. A few players see him coming. They hesitate, start to move toward him and then back off, pretending they don't see him there. One of them walks over to John Brown and points toward Ernie. John runs over to the sideline and greets him enthusiastically.

"Hey, are you coming back to the apartment?"

The two had long ago planned to room together and during one of Ernie's trips out to Cleveland they had found a great apartment and moved their stuff in. John can't wait until Ernie gets back into the groove of things. He's really missed him.

"Naw. They just let me out for a visit this time. But I've been talking the boss here," he points to the doctor, "into sponsoring a little basketball pickup game on Sunday. You want to come?"

John looks surprised and relieved.

"You bet! I'll see if I can get a bunch of guys together." As they talk, the others relax a bit and several of them meander over and hit Ernie on the back or just nod at him:

"Hi, Ern..."

"How's it going, kid."

"Good to see you."

"Hey, glad you're back.

Ernie responds excitedly. "Hey, it's good to see you. You getting ready for the season? How's it going? We're going to have a great year, aren't we?"

Off to the side a few players exchange quiet words with each other:

"He doesn't look so sick, does he?"

"I don't know. It's hard to believe a guy as physically excellent as him could really be that sick."

"It sure is depressing...."

"Yeh, I like Ernie, but I really don't know what to say to him."

"Well, I don't think it's anything serious. I think they're exaggerating."

Ernie watches practice a while and cheers the players on. When he returns to the hospital he is very tired and happy to lie down on the bed. He realizes he's not in shape yet to undertake practice, but he really feels a lot happier and less isolated for having gone. He just guesses this is part of his road to recovery.

Coviello too decides that the visit to the Hiram camp was a success. That, together with his regular transfusions and chemo, seems to be stabilizing him a bit. He knows that with this virulent disease, though, it is just a matter of time and they won't be able to continue to fend it off. But as long as he is able to get out a bit, it's probably a good idea. Sitting alone in a hospital room is likely to just speed up the process. One thing is for sure, except for the need to keep him comfortable and his ongoing treatments, staying always in the hospital room isn't going to benefit him. After all, rest won't cure this problem.

There is one person, though, who is not too happy about visits from Ernie, Paul Brown. He has been briefed by Art Modell to include Ernie when possible, but he wonders exactly what Modell intends to do with Ernie at this point. Brown assumes that they will see very little of Ernie in the near future and he doesn't want appearances like this recent one to disrupt the focus of the team that needs to stay upbeat.

When Sunday arrives and Ernie is already dressed for basketball, Dr. Coviello decides that he's going to go through with it. It must mean Ernie feels pretty good anyway, he figures. So, bunch of big guys pile into Coviello's car to head out to the basketball court at Dr. Coviello's old university, John Carroll. Ernie is among them. It is reminiscent of the recent fad of squeezing a dozen guys in a telephone booth.

Coviello has already warned Ernie that he is to play on the outside, and only for half the game. "Just take it easy, Ernie. You're not ready for strenuous activity."

Coviello does not yet know the world as Ernie perceives it. He agrees profusely to the limitations set for him. Ernie in his most cooperative posture, agrees totally with Dr. Coviello and proceeds to play only half the time on the outside alright, but manages to make 19 points within the time allotted shooting only from the outside. As Coviello watches on while Ernie works up a sweat he becomes a little fearful that he has allowed him to go this far. He certainly doesn't want to exacerbate the illness. He doesn't want to step in and spoil the fun either, so he hopes that the benefits outweigh the risks.

At the end of the game, Ernie is happily tired. He is reassured that there is really nothing seriously wrong. Tired is good when it comes after good competitive fun. The group ends up at Coviello's house, whose admiration and affection for Ernie continues to grow. He has planned a barbecue for them. Ernie has worked up an appetite from all the activity, after having sat in a hospital room for days. He approaches the doctor with a plate ready for hamburgers.

"Great playing, Ernie," says Dr. Coviello. "How do you want your steak?"

"No blood," says Ernie, not an unusual request for him, but appearing clearly ironic to the doctor. Ernie takes over the cooking of his own burger and ends up happily with a burger more like a piece of old shoe leather. Ernie returns to the hospital feeling pretty upbeat and ready for the next surge of tests and treatments.

Ernie starts making regular appearances at the camp, cheering on the guys, sitting on the bench with them, wanting desperately to participate. He's chaffing at the bit.

Paul Brown, who is not happy about Ernie's more and more frequent appearances goes to Art Modell's office looking for some resolution to this situation. .

"I think Ernie is a great kid, but you've got to understand the problem he's creating with the morale," says Paul, trying to be diplomatic.

"What do you mean he's creating a problem? The kid is always cheerful. How could he create a problem?" Responds Art who has been out there regularly and observed Ernie's demeanor.

Paul is frustrated with the situation. "That's just it. Some of the guys have heard that he's got leukemia, although they're not sure about it. When they see him, though, he just walks around looking like he could take on the Green Bay Packers all by himself. It's got them spooked. They like him, of course, who wouldn't, but they're not comfortable around him. They're really upset for him."

Art is adamant. Ernie is going to be included wherever possible. Already he is emotionally attached to this young and brave kid and wants to do everything he can to make him happy. Art is still a young man himself and he can't imagine what it would be like to have the whole world on a string and then have it ending so quickly.

"Ernie wants to be there and I want him there. He may not be able to play, but he can sit on the bench with the other guys. I want him to be part of the opening game."

Paul can't hold back his anger now. The opening game is another point of controversy between the two. "That's another thing. The double-header. That's a crazy idea. We've never done that kind of thing before...."

They're hosting a pre-season game in which the Dallas Cowboys will play the Detroit Lions and the Browns will be pitted against the Pittsburgh Steelers.

Art knows what he wants and he won't budge. "The fans will love it. We already sold out over a week ago."

Paul leaves the room in a huff and bangs the door behind him. He just got nowhere. It hasn't been easy for him. He was the owner and coach. Now that Art Modell has bought the team, he realizes it's different coaching under these circumstances. He's not used to taking orders from others. And he doesn't like it.

Boredom is definitely the enemy of Ernie right now so he tries to keep up on writing. In particular he misses Helen and daily long distant phone calls weren't considered an option in the early 60s.In a letter dated Aug. 9, 1962, from Ernie Davis to Helen Gott, Ernie's girlfriend, his frustration is apparent, but as usual he focuses on being upbeat.

188

"Dear Helen,

How's everything with you? I hope and I pray that all is swell. As for me, I am feeling fine. I'm sitting here in my room with nothing to do, so I decided to write you and find out what's happening. (smile) As you know, I am here at Marymount Hospital recovering from my illness. I hope all that publicity that I received didn't scare you. The way they put it, it seems that I was about to die. (smile) I have yet to feel real sick, "Thank God," but I have a blood dis-order. That is, my red & white blood cells are not being manufactured 100%. This dis-order is something like mononucleosis. While I won't be able to start this season off with the Browns, I am hoping and praying that I can re-join them before this season is over. I am anxious to get started. (smile) I really don't have to be here at this hospital, but I am here so that the Doctors can keep a careful eye on me, so that I can have a speedy recovery. I am taking all kinds of little pills. Here at the hospital, I am an out-patient with the liberty of going and coming as I please, so long as I take my medicine and be back at bed time. I have my car here and I usually go to watch the Browns practice or go to my apartment and lounge around. So, I can't complain too much, even though I am a little bored. (smile) Now concerning you. What have you been doing? I take it that you are just taking life easy, writing poetry, catching up on your reading during the day and partying during the nite, as well as seeing the sites of New York. You have it made. (smile)

I guess I have rambled on long enough now, so I'll close for now wishing you the best. Write soon,

Love,

Ernie."

With the first doubleheader happening shortly, excitement and disappointment become bedfellows for Ernie.

Since mid afternoon, the crowds have been arriving at the Cleveland stadium for the big double-header, a historic moment in the NFL. The box office is closed, since the tickets have been sold out for several weeks. The air is filled with excitement for those lucky enough to get tickets.

All 80,000 seats are filled, when the teams come racing out. Ernie is among them, but not suited up. He looks more like one of the coaches dressed in a nice suit, joining them on the bench. He is very grateful to be there and be participating, but it is so difficult for him to have to watch it from the bench and not be out on the field. He barely notices the fatigue and weakness that has been tormenting him now for weeks. The game begins and Ernie can't contain himself. He is up and cheering, racing forward as various players come in from the field, patting them on the back and telling them how great they are doing. The first game ends in a victory for Cleveland and the crowd goes wild. They can't believe there's a whole new game coming. The players run off the field.

The crowd gets up to do the bathroom trek and the food thing. Once they've been given enough time the lights flicker and they come back to their seats. When most of them are seated again, the lights begin to dim and the rest rush to find their seats, expecting a major between game show. Then the lights dim again and continue until the stadium is in the dark. An expectant hush falls over the entire stadium as the stars above come into focus and the field below is dark and empty. They can't imagine what is going on. Then they see two figures emerge from the Cleveland bench area and walk out into the darkened field. They arrive at the very center. One of the two stays there while the other one returns to the sidelines. Suddenly the lights explode into a brilliance that is so great, at first no one can tell who it is out there in the center. The crowd holds its breath, only for a second, and then a murmur passes through the spectators:

"It's Ernie Davis."

"Ernie!"

Then rising rapidly like lightening into a deafening roar:

"Ernie Davis! Ernie Davis! Ernie Davis."

Electricity courses through them and the crowd rises as a unit, into a standing, bellowing, earth quaking ovation for Ernie.

Ernie stands with tears in his eyes, unable to comprehend, recognizing the love coming to him and surrounding him; and he is grateful.

Chapter 31

The doctors in Cleveland had talked with Marie. They assured her that everything possible was being done for Ernie, who had a rare blood disease, telling her what medicines were being used and explaining the possibility of a remission, but she didn't remember hearing the name of the disease mentioned, and no one had used the word terminal. They had thought that she had understood that Ernie had leukemia, but she had left Cleveland the last time, not understanding what was actually wrong with her son and not knowing the terrible prognosis of his disease.

Marie had visited again and still realized nothing more than she had gleaned from her other conversations. Now, Saturday morning, a week after her last visit she is once again on a plane to Cleveland. As she sits listening to the loud roar of the motors, her mind flies through what she already knows about Ernie's illness. For some time in the back of her mind she had the idea of sickle cell anemia. Then suddenly it came to her in a flash. These were not the symptoms nor the family history for that. And things weren't going well. "They"re not telling you everything, Marie..." her mind declares. Her whole motherhood rebels against the real verdict but now it is time to come to terms with it.

Marie sits on the airplane with an open book in her lap, but her eyes are gazing in front of her. She is unable to concentrate on anything. Why is Ernie still in the hospital? Why has no one told her what is wrong with him? Why isn't he back to playing with the Cleveland Browns? Something is terribly wrong and she intends to find out what it is.

Marie enters an empty hospital room at the Cleveland Marymount. She exits the room quickly and walks directly to the nurse's station. This time she's determined to find Ernie and the doctor.

"They've taken him downstairs for treatment. He should be back in an hour."

Marie makes up her mind quickly. She tries phoning Dr. Coviello first, but he is not there on weekends, so she calls Dr. Ippolito's office. He has been kind and helpful before, maybe he will see her this time. "Is there something wrong?" he asks.

Marie responds ironically with a "no", then continues, "I just want to talk to you."

He says he has time to meet between 11 and 11:30 and then directs her to his office, telling her what to say to the cab driver. Dr. Ippolito thinks she just wants an update on Ernie's condition.

Marie leaves the hospital. She is on a mission now and she won't leave Cleveland without finding out what is wrong with Ernie. She hails a taxi and arrives at a tall nondescript building, takes the elevator upstairs and enters the doctor's waiting room. Dr. Ippolito comes out to greet her and takes her into his office.

"You mean no one has told you what Ernie has? The doctors in Evanston were supposed to tell you. What happened?"

Marie explained that she couldn't find anyone to speak with and she had wanted to see Ernie before she went back to work. She had not thought at the time that it was anything serious, but now.... she wonders why the treatments and why still in the hospital.

"No one has said a word to me, " she adds. "This has gone on long enough. I want to know exactly what is wrong with my son. They keep saying it's a rare disease, they're doing this and they're doing that, the drugs they're using, but the truth is I haven't heard it named."

Dr. Ippolito is stunned. He doesn't hesitate. Obviously she needed to know a long time ago.

"Ernie has leukemia ... acute leukemia."

"Exactly what does that mean?" Marie wants the whole story now.

He doesn't know how to soften it and doesn't want to mislead her after all this time that's passed since Ernie's diagnosis. No one knows when things will begin to go bad for Ernie.

"It is a very severe and rare form of leukemia and there is no cure. It is terminal. It usually moves quite quickly and he has already been sick with it for a while. We are treating him with drugs and transfusions and although he isn't getting better, we are temporarily holding it at bay. That could change at any time."

Marie's face turns to stone. For a moment she is paralyzed. She never imagined... in her wildest dreams/nightmares .. or her greatest mother fears... that she would lose this dear... handsome ... strong ... gentle ... kind ... terribly talented son in this manner. No, no, no.... not possible.

"I thank you ... very much ... Doctor ... for your time...." she can barely get it out. "Good day."

She lets herself out of his office and he follows her to the door, wanting so much to say something.... something that might ease the pain. Something that could give her hope. But there is nothing he can say. So he says nothing. And she leaves quickly.

Out on the street she enters another taxi. By now she is overwhelmed with her grief. She can barely get the words out to tell the driver where to go.

"Marymount .... Hospital... pppplease," she manages to blurt out and then she breaks down and starts to sob uncontrollably. The driver turns and looks at her a moment, then pulls out into traffic. Marie can no longer stem the torrent and cries her heart out.

When she arrives at the hospital, she goes first to the ladies room and splashes water onto her face and dries it with a paper towel.

She approaches Ernie's hospital room but pauses at his door. Gathering herself together, and showing the kind of bravery and courage that Ernie has apparently inherited from her, she takes a deep breath, puts on a weak smile and enters the room. Ernie is sitting in a chair by his bed in his pajamas reading a book.

"Hey, what you doin here. How great! Now you can come out and see the Brown's practice field with me. It's enormous. I can't wait until they let me start practicing again."

Marie looks away for a moment so he won't see her eyes cloud up.

"So how they treatin you, Ernie?"

"Oh they're great here, but it gets awfully lonely and boring." He changes the subject quickly. "How's the family? I haven't heard anything from Chuck in a while. Is he still makin trouble?"

Marie laughs. "Of course he's makin trouble, but he doesn't do it so well without you there eggin him on like you do."

"Me...? why I was only a victim. I never would play a practical joke on anyone."

"You may be able to fool the rest of the world, boy, but you can't fool me...."

Marie starts to relax. It's hard to think that maybe this isn't the same old Ernie he's always been. Maybe it's all a mistake. Maybe we can pretend it's a mistake. Being there with Ernie, it just didn't seem so bad.

The news is spreading quickly now:

At the Green Pastures Bar, the Coleman brothers have just heard:

"No... not Ernie? No. I don't believe it."

Angie on the phone crying:

"Marie just told me. I know! I can't believe it either. There must be some mistake."

At EFA Harrigan stops Flynn in the hallway and pulls him aside. He speaks so softly, only one word jumps out... "Leukemia."

Flynn's face turns white. "Oh no!" is all he is able to say.

On Marshall Street as students pass their friends they stop them and spread the word:

"They say Ernie has Leukemia."

"I know, I heard. Do you think it's really true?"

"I overheard the coaches talking about it."

"Why Ernie? He's the last person that deserves to die."

And other students walking across the quad:

"Ernie Davis? Leukemia?" And the students start to cry.

At the hospital a group of doctors are standing around a microscope in the lab, taking turns looking into it. The doctors nod their heads in despair.

"He's definitely getting worse. The treatments are no longer holding it at bay."

"Isn't there anything else we can try?"

"We've thrown the whole bag at him."

The Syracuse University football coaches had developed the custom of coming to the Cleveland Brown's camp in Hiram for four or five days in August to observe the summer training, trying to pick up new ideas and pointers for their college boys. This year they were particularly excited about the prospect of three Syracuse graduates playing for Cleveland, the famed Jim Brown of course, and as rookies, their own John Brown and Ernie Davis. They are so proud that these superb athletes have come out of their training grounds. But now a cloud hangs over their enthusiasm and excitement. Ernie is sick and has been in the hospital for at least three weeks. The news of it being leukemia is now widely spread.

Meanwhile, Ernie has been lying in the hospital room watching the four walls, and thinking about his life. He contemplates all the wonders and joys he has experienced and that the future holds for him. Although no one has told him the entire story yet, deep inside he suspects he is dying. He can feel that he is becoming weaker and weaker and feeling so terribly tired all the time. Ernie has prayed a lot in these lonely long hospital days. It isn't the traditional prayer he is used too, though. Christ has walked beside him for a long time now, he feels his nearness and the words come naturally to him; like a conversation, a beseeching to help him understand what is happening and what it means; what sort of new challenge this is and how he is to deal with it.

Ernie has already prayed for life and a chance to go on with the wonderful future he thought he had. Now he is praying for the strength to face whatever he must face. And some of the time, when no one is around to see, he lies there despondent and depressed, sorry about all that he's missing.

It is this Ernie, weakened, confused, and very, very sick, struggling to find meaning in his life and in his illness, who is in the hospital room when the Syracuse University coaches get off the elevator and walk to the nurses station.

"We're here to see Ernie Davis," says Ben. "Can you tell us which room he is in?"

"It's down the hall, third door on the left. Room 315. The coaches start down the hall, but the nurse stops them in a halting voice...

"Uh.... sir."

Ben turns. "Yes?"

"You're his coach from Syracuse University aren't you? You've been here before."

"What is it?" he responds a little impatiently.

"This may be the last time you see him.... he...." She stops.

"Thank you... thank you...." He doesn't really want her to finish that sentence. He doesn't want to know. But he does know and it's breaking his heart.

Ben turns to walk down the hallway. His shoulders are slumped and his vitality seems gone. From the back he almost seems an old man, barely able to put one foot in front of the other. He hesitates a moment, wipes his eyes with his sleeve... turns to the other coaches and tells them Ernie isn't doing too well... then he moves slowly on down the hall. They all stand in front of door 315 for a few minutes, each one waiting for the other to make the first move. They're afraid of what they'll find in there.

Finally they nervously enter the room. Ernie is sitting up in a chair and the minute he sees them, he breaks into a huge smile and welcomes them. He starts to try to rise from the chair and Ben sees that it is requiring some effort.

He walks over quickly and gives Ernie his hand.

"Hey, Ern. How you doing?"

"Great, just great. Well. I am getting a little bored, though. I'm really anxious to get out of here and back to practice."

Nervous movements and awkward silence demonstrate the discomfort the coaches have at realizing that Ernie will never play football again.

Ernie covers their awkwardness by changing the subject.

"Well, I've heard you've been having a pretty good year so far."

"It's pretty hard to run the team without you out there lyin to all those guys." says Ben. "But we got Mackey now, who is really tellin them how it is."

Ernie laughs, "I'll bet he is."

Silence.

"You been watching the Browns?" asks Ernie.

"Yeh... sure." Several coaches respond.

"Hey, they're doing really great aren't they?" Ernie fills in the empty space as though there was nothing wrong. "Especially Jim. Isn't he wonderful? He's having a fantastic season...."

Sims responds this time. "Yeh... he's really maturing. He's a great player."

"Your Mom been up to see you?" asks Ben.

"Oh, yeh... She was here last week. She's coming back soon as she can get two days off work in a row. Yeh... it sure was good to see her."

"She's a great woman... your mom," says Ben

"Yeh... she is...."

Another silence makes everyone uncomfortable.

A coach breaks the silence. "The guys said to send their best to you... You know... Mackey and the others... He says he'll be coming out to see you after Christmas... when the season's over."

He ends nervously, talk about the future is difficult. It seems there is no safe ground for conversation. Ernie, on the other hand seems oblivious to it all, going on just as though nothing has changed. They wonder if he has any idea what's happening to him.

"Oh, that's great. Tell him he can stay at the apartment with John Brown and me. We've got plenty of room."

Another pause.

"John's doing just great. He says they make him play offense differently, though. I guess he likes Syracuse's way best."

"Yeh," says Ben. "That's what he says now... you should have seen him complain before he started playing with the big boys, though...."

The coaches laugh. Although they've all relaxed a bit. Ben can't handle the situation any longer. He is way too personally attached to Ernie to be able to stay there making small talk, knowing what he knows. He rises and heads toward the door. The others follow course.

"Well, Ernie. We just wanted to stop in and be sure you weren't picking on the nurses or anything... We know how irresistible you are. Don't want you to tire out... or anything... you know what I mean." He rambles a little.

Like a flash, Ernie is out of his chair. He seems to leap at the door and stands in front of it, his large frame blocking it. Then he lets the bombshell hit.

"Don't leave yet... please... you just got here. You can't go... I'll never see you again."

There it is said! The silence is broken. The coaches' faces go white. It's out in the open and everyone is confronted with the reality. They don't know what to say, but they certainly can't push past Ernie to leave when he's begging them to stay. Ernie has never asked for much from them except to let him play, even when he was injured. In a way, this is all he's asking again. "Please let me play. Let me play at life with you, just a little longer." It requires a force of will for all of them not to break down and cry in this moment, but they realize if Ernie can be so strong, they darn well better be strong too, so they return and sit down again, with every intent to talk with him and keep him happy.

So Ernie speaks... and now he's saying what he really feels. "It's terrible, you know... not being able to play... watching the others go on out there and to be stuck in here. I get so bored I can't stand it. I wanted so much to play in the backfield with Jim. Now I don't know if..." (drifts off for a moment). "I've missed so many practices now... I.. Well. I just wish it could be different..."

For just a moment Ernie indulges in his sadness and frustration, never really saying what he does know, but implying everything, then he wants to talk about Syracuse, to replay every play and talk about all the kids and the good things, about those years that they had spent together.

"Hey, how are the other guys doing. I haven't heard anything about Art. What's up with him?"

Sims relaxes a little now that it's out in the open. "Yeh. Sure. We don't really hear from him, but we do hear about him. It sounds like he's doing great. He went to Canada to play in their league."

"Hey, and what about Jimmie Wright? What a guy! If anybody could scare me, it was Jimmie Wright, cause he knows how to think. Can't believe him."

Ben takes this one. "Oh yeh... Jimmie's out there conning the world now... just like he conned you guys. I think he's gone into the military or something."

"I couldn't believe that guy," continued Ernie. "Captain of the greenies... How'd he always second guess us anyway... you set him up to it, didn't you, Coach."

"What? ... I wouldn't do that. He just watched you guys carefully and knew just what you were going to do next... For a little punny guy that didn't know nothing about football, he sure knew a lot about keeping the first team in line."

"Yeh... unbelievable. The best teams in the country couldn't beat us, but the fifth string led by Jimmie stopped us over and over," Ernie acknowledges.

"That's just cause you guys were so transparent," adds Sims.

The conversation continues in this vain. They've found a fun topic that diffuses the real deep issues that no one can change. Now they're on to Jim Brown.

"I always thought that Jim should've won the Heisman trophy," says Ernie. "Can't imagine why he didn't and then I did later."

"Well, Ernie, you know you broke a lot of his records. And then... there's the issue about character...."

The nurse sticks her head in the door and interrupts.

"I hope you don't intend to stay the night here. The room's a little small for all you big guys. Actually, you've been here a long time and Ernie needs to take some medication and rest for a while."

"Aw, com'on," says Ernie. "These guys came all the way from Syracuse to see me. You're not going to throw them out, are you?"

"I'm afraid so...."

They check their watches and realize they've been there a full six hours. Ben stands up, once again relieved. "Right. Well, we have to go anyway. We got to get out of here, let you eat, and find a chow place for us too. We'll be back, Ernie."

Ben looks straight into the eyes of Ernie when he says that. He wants with all his heart to believe that's true.

"Sure, sure..." Suddenly Ernie is feeling completely drained, almost unable to remain sitting up. "Gee... thanks for coming. I can't believe you flew out here and then took all this time to see me.... I really appreciate it."

"Well, don't let it go to your head, Ernie. Don't think we just came to see you. We're here to spy on the Browns and learn a thing or two."

"I'm sure you could teach them more than one thing too."

The coaches cdge out the door during this conversation. Ernie doesn't move this time. He probably couldn't even if he had wanted too. The goodbyes are quick and Ernie slumps when they are out of sight. The nurse hurries back into the room and only she, at this point, understands the huge toil the visit took on him.

Chapter 32

Over the next few days Ernie's condition worsens rapidly. He is no longer getting out of bed. He mostly lies on his bed, staring at the ceiling, the walls.... Ernie reads his Bible when he can, but becomes so sleepy it drops from his hands. He is looking much weaker, puffier, and sallower. But his expression is not angry or defiant or sad. It is just resigned.

Attorney Anthony DeFillippo and Gerald Schneider board a plane from Elmira to Cleveland.

"Tell me again," Gerald says to Tony, "what did the doctors say when they phoned you from Cleveland this morning."

Tony is the lawyer who got Ernie the outstanding deals from the various NFL teams only months before. Now he is seeing his protégé at death's door. How did this happen so fast? Tony is tough and determined and he's not going to let Ernie down.

"They just said that we ought to come and get him. That he should be transferred to a hospital in his hometown. They told me to bring his physician with me. I asked them what they were really saying, but they continued to hedge. They said they couldn't do any more for him there. Of course I know what they're really saying. They're saying, that's it! He's dying. Now take him home to die there."

"Maybe you're right. Maybe that's what they're saying. Certainly these acute leukemias can go very quickly and Ernie's already hung on pretty long. Lots of them don't even make it this long. One or two months is the most you can expect."

"Well, not me," says Tony. "I expect more for Ernie. This kid is tough. He's a real scraper. He's got one of the best physiques in the country. You can't tell me that it's time to take him home to die."

"Well, what do you want to do, then?

"I want you to tell me what our options are. If it were your kid, what would you do? Where would you send him? What's the best place in the world? Isn't that what you'd do with your own kid?"

"Well," responds Schneider, "I have examined the medical reports they sent us in the mail. Personally I have a somewhat limited knowledge about leukemia so I took them to Dr. Hobart Burch at St. Joseph's Hospital here in Elmira. He's considered one of the finest radiologists in the state and I understand he has been treating leukemia with radiation successfully for many years. It's true he can't save them, but he has prolonged many lives"

"Hobie confirms that the acute leukemia is very different and much more difficult. With the generic childhood leukemia sometimes he can give them many years before it finally takes its toll. He recommends that we get him to a top teaching hospital, and one of the best, he says is the Cancer Clinic at the National Institute of Health in Bethesda, Maryland. They are having some great successes with the new chemotherapy. He's not sure we can hope for a remission with this form of leukemia, but he thinks it is worth a try. He says if it were one of his five children, he'd definitely give it a shot. Let's look at the tests when we get to Cleveland and decide then."

"Well there's no question in my mind! We've got to try for a remission by getting him to a top cancer center as soon as possible."

While the plane takes off, they sit silently thinking about what is to come, worried about what condition they'll find Ernie in and whether or not it's too late to make this move.

In Cleveland a limousine picks them up and takes them to Art Modell's office in the stadium to meet with Art Modell, Dr. Ippolito, and Jim Brown (who insists on being there too, wanting to advocate for Ernie). There is an atmosphere of confusion about what should be done with the media. Should anyone be told what is happening to Ernie? It's clear the news has slipped out already and they think it is better to free up the media from the silence they had asked them for. But even before that can be decided they must determine what to tell Ernie. He will have to be told before the media has been given full leash.

Ippolito doesn't mince words. "Ernie is clearly dying. HE needs to be told now that he has leukemia, if he hasn't guessed it already, and he needs to be given his prognosis in case there is anything he wants to take care of first."

Tony votes against it. "Nah, you can't tell a kid like that that he's going to be dead within a couple of weeks, when he still thinks he's gonna play with the Browns. Why make him feel worse than he does."

"If it were me, I'd want to know." Jim feels he should speak on behalf of Ernie who isn't present. "I think you should give him all his money and let him go out and have a good time, while he still can. Besides, you're not fooling him. Any athlete in as good shape as Ernie has been can tell when things aren't right in their bodies. Even little things. Of course he already knows. He's probably just trying to protect the rest of you."

"I hate to tell him, but I guess it ought to be done." Modell has the final word. The decision is made.

Then Dr. Schneider and Attorney DeFillippo head for Ernie's room. It surprises Schneider how apprehensive he feels. After all, as a physician he has been dealing with disease and death for many years. When they arrive at the room, the sight of Ernie is as traumatic as his fearful expectations. He has been dozing. He only rouses himself slightly when he becomes aware of them. The doctor sees immediately all the symptoms which clearly define the dangerous point to which the disease has progressed. Ernie's mouth and nose have dried blood on them. His skin is pale with an almost gray tone. He is fatigued and bewildered and clearly terribly ill. Hope for remission appears to be fading if not gone. And Ernie, even in this state, manages the same pleasant, honest and polite demeanor that has always been his way.

He looks at the doctor through cloudy eyes, slightly recognizing him as one from Elmira. "Are you the guy that's going to take me back home?" And imbedded in the question and in his eyes is the clear knowledge that he is dying.

"Yeh, maybe," Schneider doesn't commit anything yet. "We'll see."

Almost before Schneider's words are out, Ernie has drifted off again. They tiptoe out of the room and head directly for the lab. They both have a sense of urgency, especially after seeing Ernie.

Then Dr. Schneider sees the most recent lab reports: no platelets at all, aplastic bone marrow, abnormal white cells. The reports are as bad as he could have imagined. He leaves the lab sweating and nauseous, needing to hold himself up for a moment against the wall.

He next meets with Dr. Weisberger, the world renowned hematologist who has just come from a visit with Ernie. The doctors sit down together and ask the question: "What's the best that can be done for Ernie?"

Maybe a more precise diagnosis could be made and maybe more recent effective drugs can be found. Dr. Weisberger feels that the only hope left is to try for a remission, but there will never be a hope for a cure for Ernie. When Schneider mentions Bethesda, he offers to contact his very close friend, Dr. Berlin, the director of the Cancer Clinic there, confirming that they have the medication and blood supplies that can help Ernie, plus a huge experience in dealing with a large quantity of leukemia patients, including those with rare forms like Ernie's. The decision is an easy one to bring back to the group. "We must try for the remission. We have to do everything we can."

On August 23, 1962, it is decided that Tony DeFillippo will accompany Ernie to Bethesda as soon as they can get on a plane. Art Modell gets his secretary to set up the tickets. It is clear now that Ernie must be told what he has today. When he arrives at Bethesda, it would become obvious to him anyway. Better not to send him there unprepared. So Ernie is brought in to Dr. Weisberger and Dr. Ippolito.

Ernie can barely sit up in the chair. He is listless and working at holding his head up.

"Leukemia!" The word rings out in Ernie's head. The word that means the end, no possible hope, no future, no more football, no more life itself. How he had already tormented himself over that very possibility during the previous month and even before; before anyone else had even suspected that Ernie was ill, something inside him had left him understanding that he was up against something big.

"Leukemia?"

Ernie weighs the word and plays with it, and somehow, now that it is finally spoken, with the very speaking of it, the fear has gone out of it. The long hours of the unknown weighing upon him, are finally lifted so that he is left with only the dull ache of acceptance, an acceptance that his long lonely hours over the last month has brought him to and the recent days that his worsened condition has forced upon him. Now he knows who the real enemy is. He knows the opponent and now no matter how difficult the battle, he can fight it. He knows he has managed to win impossible odds before on the field, on the basketball court in the baseball diamond, so why not here?

Ernie can accept the fact of the disease itself, but defeat? Never! He is ready for the newest challenge that God has placed before him, but the challenge is clear to Ernie – it is a challenge to life, not death. And live he will, for whatever time there might be. The time, however, is very short now.

"What can be done about it?" The pause is only brief. Now Ernie is ready for the game, a game with very high stakes. It is his life on the line.

The doctors watch in amazement. Rarely have they given such a verdict and witnessed such an unequivocally brave response.

They explain to Ernie that he can have a complete remission and during that time he will feel quite well. They do not explain how unlikely that would be in his current deteriorating condition, nor do they explain what happens after. And he does not ask.

"We want to take you to the Cancer Center in Bethesda, one of the best in the world. They deal with this disease often."

The others in the room exchange looks that acknowledge that they consider little hope for a real remission, but Ernie only hears the positive. He perks up. His posture improves and he seems to take on a new vitality.

"Hey, that's great. Well, what are we waiting for? Let's go." Ernie is not used to losing battles. All he was waiting for was something specific to fight and the tools to fight it with. He has already done the undoable, run the unrunable run, caught the uncatchable ball, made the unmakable touchdown, and won the unaccessible Heisman trophy. No one has conquered this foe before, these are impossible odds, but Ernie has understood a major truth of life, already in spite of his young years, it is not about winning, but about playing your best, right up to the last second of the game.... and that's just what he is going to do.

"Our plane leaves around noon," pipes up DeFillippo encouraged by Ernie's new enthusiasm. "I'll be going with you. We'll go straight to the hospital from the airport. They'll certainly be able to help you." And a part of him really believes that. He's never seen Ernie give up yet.

The doctors exchange a look again, but say nothing.

Art Modell notifies the press that they can report what Ernie is suffering from, but to do it in an upbeat manner and to focus on his upcoming treatments in Bethesda.

Within an hour Ernie is packed up and on his way to the airport. They transport him in a wheelchair and he is still too weak to protest. Once in his seat he struggles to fasten his safety belt so Attorney DeFillippo leans over and helps him with it. Now Ernie is looking terribly sick again, nauseous and sweating profusely so that Tony wonders if he might even lose him during the flight. DeFillippo moves down the aisle for a moment and speaks to the stewardess. She watches Ernie as Tony speaks to her and then nods. Back at the seat he reaches above and pulls down a blanket and pillow trying to make Ernie comfortable. Once he sits down and fastens in, he takes out some vials of pills and pulls out two pills. There is one kind to be taken once every hour and another to be taken every half hour. The doctors are still bombarding his system with deadly chemicals that will hopefully kill off the cancer cells before they can kill him. By this time the stewardess has arrived with a glass of water and leans very solicitously over Ernie while he takes his pills.

"Right after take off, you can put your seat all the way back," she tells him. "There's no one behind you."

"Thanks." Ernie murmurs. Then he turns to DeFillippo. "Did anyone let my Mom know where I'm going?"

"Dr. Schneider is flying right back to Elmira and will phone her and talk to her about it as soon as he gets there."

When the plane arrives DeFillippo makes sure there is a wheelchair waiting and a taxi right outside the gate. Ernie is such a big guy, he finds it hard to get him into the chair and then the car. Ernie puts all his effort into moving from the wheelchair to the taxi and together they succeed.

"Let us off at the back door," says DeFillippo, "as close as you can get." He wants to avoid anyone seeing them enter and the resulting publicity. Tony helps Ernie out and they enter the hospital. The driver gets out to shut the door and sees a book sitting on the seat. He picks it up. The title says "Funeral Masses". He looks after Ernie and Tony who have already entered the building and starts after them with the book in hand. Later one of the nurses produces his lost book for him.

Tony DeFillippo hands over to the doctor all of the slides that he has brought with him from Dr. Weisberger, then he and Ernie sit in the waiting room for what seems an endless time. Tony doesn't know how Ernie manages to hold up after the plane ride. Finally the doctor returns and pulls Tony aside.

"Look," he says, "he's been given everything medically known for leukemia. Some new drugs are coming out, though. We'll do whatever we can, but mostly it will be a matter of waiting and seeing if something new works. There's no sense in your being here, you might as well get back to Elmira and just hope the remission sets in. Tony sees Ernie to his room and leaves.

Chapter 33

"A guy who had problems like Ernie, was such an inspiration, because he always thought of others first. I have two pictures of him in my drawer, and when I get down in the dumps, I pull them out to look at."

Phil Davis, Asst. Secretary of Agriculture, VP of Avon

Now that Ernie knows the realities of his condition and he understands the treatment, his emotions and body begin to respond. The doctors at Bethesda have found a variation to the original diagnosis and therefore are able to alter the medication.

The doctors are all amazed; within days Ernie is transformed. He is dressed and sitting in a chair in his room, reading a book when the doctor enters. What a different picture he makes than less than a week ago when he arrived. The doctor can barely believe it. He looks perfectly normal. Ernie looks up and smiles.

"Hello, doc. What's the news today."

"Very good news indeed!" he pauses for just a moment. "Your tests all came back negative. The remission has set in. That means that for now there are no signs of the disease."

Ernie bounds toward the doctor, grabs him in a bear hug, and beams all over.

"Thank you.... thank you so much."

Ernie doesn't waste any time before he is begging the doctor to let him leave the hospital for a few hours for the first time since he arrived in Bethesda.

"If there is no sign of the disease... I don't understand what harm it would do to go visit my friend at the Capitol."

The doctor can't think of a good reason, except explaining to Ernie how very sick he was when he arrived and the need to take it easy for a bit. Mostly they just need to continue some treatments, build him back up a bit and watch him for a while. The doctor then approves that he can have visitors and come and go with excursions outside the hospital.

Ernie is all dressed up in an elegant suit that he requested sent from Cleveland. He leaves the hospital by the back door to avoid the reporters who have been lurking there for several days hoping for good news.

Ernie arrives at the Capitol around 11 in the morning and finds his friend Phil Davis standing right under the Dome where they agreed to meet. He races toward him, feeling his muscles stretch a little after so much inactivity. It's a gorgeous day at the end of August and Ernie feels double alive to have been given a second chance in this fabulous world. The two go out onto the lawn and sit down to talk.

"So... how the heck are you, Phil?" asks Ernie.

"Great. Washington is exciting. Working at the Capitol is really cool.

"I hear you left school before you finished." Ernie knew that Phil had wanted to get a law degree.

"Aw, you know," says Phil, " I just couldn't get enough money together."

It is not as easy for a Black youth who is bright, but not top in sports to finance a college career. Phil, like Ernie, had grown up on sandlot courts and knew how to handle a ball, but his small stature had held him back.

"Hey," says Ernie. That's a real waste. You gotta go back to school. Listen.... I've got plenty of money. You go back to school. I'll cover it."

"Naw, Ernie, I can't do that."

"Sure you can. I'm asking you too. Promise me you'll go back. I'll make sure you get a check in the mail."

Phil is too embarrassed and grateful to say anything but thank you. He doesn't want to take the money, but it does renew his determination. Here's Ernie, he thinks, as he watches him resting on the grass. He's got problems much bigger than I can picture. And instead of feeling sorry for himself, because I'll be here after he's gone, he's really concerned about my future and wellbeing. If he can do that; if he can come out of the hospital, sick, to see me; then I can somehow find a way to finish my education.

A page arrives out of breath.

"Are you Ernie Davis?" he asks.

"Yes."

"I just got lucky finding you out here. Speaker of the House McCormack has heard that you are visiting here today. He would like me to invite you to meet with him."

"Wow....," says Ernie. Then he sees Phil looking disappointed.

"Uh... tell him I am very grateful, but that I have a luncheon appointment. I would be very honored to meet with him afterward if that would be possible."

He grins at Phil. The page runs off. Ernie and Phil head off to the cafeteria to pick up some sandwiches and take them back out on the lawn to eat them in the sun. Ernie is loving the fresh air and sunshine.

By September 7, 1962 Ernie is finally moved into his apartment in Cleveland, happy to be part of what he dreamed of when he had thought the dream was already over. He and John Brown enjoy a new kind of social life, as young rich bachelors, while spending most of their time working hard at the practice field. With the exception of twice a week when Ernie goes religiously for his blood tests, Ernie is suited up every day for practice just like the others. He is now doing warm-ups, calisthenics and running. In the film room he views films of the previous game. In the briefing room he suggests plays. At the game itself, Ernie is on the bench or on the sidelines, slapping the guys on the butts as they go into the field to play. He wants so badly to participate. He's willing to do anything needed. He doesn't want to be a burden. Why, he would even clean toilets if they asked him to.

Jim Brown had gone frequently to visit Ernie in the hospital in Cleveland, and now that Ernie is back, he comes to see him right away. The two have become good friends and Jim, a rather private person, feels freer to confide his feelings and emotions with Ernie than anyone he knows. Ernie feels a special closeness to this great athlete and bigger than life person. He has undying admiration and appreciation for him and his friendship. Some people think that Jim is tough, and, of course, in many ways he is, but Ernie sees his very positive attributes and aspires to be like him in those ways.

Jim finds Ernie a job working for the Pepsi Cola Company. That job, together with his daily team workouts gives a regularity to Ernie's life that he needs.

When Ernie first entered the field, the other players looked up from their exercises in amazement. Most of them had not really expected to see him suited up and working out, but now he is a familiar sight. He is not allowed to scrimmage with them, but he is showing every bit as much strength and energy as they have. They are amazed, but also embarrassed around him. What do you say to a guy who is dying, who has a fatal disease?

"How's the weather?"

"Did you have fun in the hospital?"

"What's new?"

"How do you feel?"

But they needn't have worried about it. He took it out of their hands.

"How's it going?" Ernie asks all about their workouts, their games, their lives. He turns it around and focuses on them until they begin to forget there is anything at all more serious about Ernie's stay in the hospital than the common cold.

He makes them forget for a while, but then when they are out on the field and he is sitting on the bench, waiting for permission to scrimmage or play, then a cloud begins to form close over the playing field again as they realize this young guy, big and strong like them or more so, looking healthy and fit, is seriously ill and will never live to marry, have a family, have a career, probably never play in a pro game.

Ernie trying on the Cleveland Helmet and uniform
he never gets to wear in a game

Ernie wants to get in and play more than anything. He wants to do just what the others are doing. And he keeps asking for what he wants, but he doesn't complain when he is benched again. The media now has the whole story and when they interview Ernie, he just answers that he probably won't get to play this year, because he has missed too many practices, but he will keep working out with them and be in shape to play during the next season. Ernie treats it all as though he will go on living forever.

The doctors, also, are confused by the situation. It is so rare, especially this surprise remission, and really, nothing like it has ever happened before. Their differing opinions also contribute to the fallout between the owner and coach. Dr. Coviello and Dr. Hewlett feel that the physical activity for Ernie should be somewhat controlled, and both are concerned about heavy contact activity. Coach Brown sides with this opinion. Dr. Weisberger, on the other hand, gives Ernie a clean bill of health for the time being and says to go ahead and let him play. Art Modell agrees with him and wants to give Ernie anything Ernie wants.

The dilemma is very real, because, although Ernie is currently symptom free, the disease could reassert itself at any time and a kick to a kidney or spleen could prove fatal to him. But since just living is going to prove fatal to him very shortly anyway, what is the ethical thing to do? Should they just let Ernie live his life as though it would go on, for the time being, or protect him... for what, from what?

In Modell's office, expectably, there is a heated argument going on and Ernie appears to be the primary target of the battle between Art Modell and Paul Brown.

"I can't play him," states Paul.

"Why not?" responds Art with some antagonism.

"What do you mean, "why not?" The guys got leukemia."

"Yes, but he's in remission," insists Art. "Weisberger says it won't hurt him."

"You got to be kidding. The kid is going to die. A remission doesn't mean he hasn't got the disease."

"The doctors say for now, it's as though he doesn't have it. The kid is desperate to play. At any moment the leukemia could come back and he'll never have another chance. I'm telling you. Play him!" Art is getting vehement.

"No, I won't. I've checked with other doctors and they say he could get hit in the spleen and set the whole thing off again... or it could come back suddenly and he could die right there on the field." Now Paul is reprimanding Art with a low shot. "You put a lot of money into this kid... didn't you?

Art bites.... "Just WHAT are you insinuating?"

"I'm not insinuating anything. It's just hard to believe that anyone could think of putting a kid with leukemia on the field. Among other things it's not fair to our guys and most of all it's not fair to the other team. They're going to have to worry about how hard they hit him. And what if he were to get badly hurt, ... or if he does die out there.... they'll never get over it."

"I'm telling you he's got to have his chance. I want him to have his chance."

"And I'm telling you that as long as I'm in charge on the field, it's not going to happen. It's hard enough on everybody to have him there every day. The guys' morale is really down."

"Hey... Ernie's a great kid. He's working as hard as anyone out there and he's always upbeat."

"That's just it. It has nothing to do with the kind of kid Ernie is... in fact, it makes it much worse, that he's such a likable kid. These other kids... can't get over it. Every time they look at him, and how strong and good he is out there, they think, "why that could be me." These are kids who've always thought they were invincible, that they would live forever, and frankly, out there on that field, that counts. They've got to believe that. They look at Ernie, knowing what they know... and they get depressed.... I get depressed..."

And although Modell is mad. He does understand. But his desire to see Ernie play and to fulfill Ernie's lifelong dream, to keep the kid happy, for whatever months he does have.... that's important to him. And then there's another thing. It's not okay that Paul thinks he still runs the show... he's gone too far this time... telling him that he'll do what he wants on the field, disregarding Art's orders. Why, he must still think he owns the team. That's got to change... one way or another.

Ernie remains distanced from these arguments, either he doesn't know they're going on or he pretends he doesn't. He lets them both know how much he wants to play. That's it. Coming in from practice he finds John Brown already home.

"Hey, John Brown, is dinner ready?"

"Whaddya mean... it's your turn tonight. I got some chicks coming by. We got to treat them right."

"Hey, ... gimme a little warning will ya, so I can plan something special."

"Like what?" John won't let him off that easily. "Your Gramma's chicken and dumplings. I think you forgot something important last time you tried that... like the dumplins."

"Well, whaddya expect. One thing at a time...   last time it was the chicken, .. next time I'll add the dumplins."

"Right."

John starts picking up a bunch of stuff and throwing it upstairs, clothes, blankets, books....

"You just missed Jim..." John adds as he works.

"Yeh? Was he here, then?"

"Stopped by after practice. Where were you, by the way."

"Oh just watching some plays on film. I wanted to see if there might be a different way to do it."

"What do you think you are, man? Coach?"

"So wha'd Jim want?"

"I don't know why you even bother talking with that guy. He's so tough and unapproachable, he must eat nails for breakfast."

"Whaddya mean....," Ernie responds as he stuffs some food left on the counter into his mouth. "You just don't understand him. He's really a fine person."

"Sure, like leaving his wife for another woman."

"Well, yeh, ... that's not okay, and I've told him what I think of that, but there are also lots of good sides to him."

"So name one."

"For one thing... he really has some good ideas about Blacks going to school. He's got a sharp mind, you know ... and he has a way with speech... You got to admire that..."

"I'll only admit that you've really got him hypnotized," John interrupts, "He won't even give the time of day to most of us, but he spills out his guts with you almost every day."

"You should just give him a chance. You'll see there's another side to him."

"Hey," says John. "He's a great football player and he's fighting for Blacks' rights, plus he's a really smart guy, will that do?"

"For now..." Ernie grins.

The doorbell rings as John, momentarily distracted, balls up the rest of the clothes and blankets and stuff and throws them upstairs.

"Hey that must be the girls and nothing is ready."

He straightens the cushions and answers the door, as Ernie picks up stray dishes and heads for the kitchen. John Brown comes back in without the girls. Instead there is a stranger in a suit with him. He stops Ernie and says,

"This is Jim Smith. I told him to come back when you're here. He wants to talk to us about life insurance. I thought you might like to hear what he has to say...."

It seems John has completely forgotten Ernie's condition. Now that he is back, he just seems like "good ole Ernie".

"You kiddin me, brother?" There is an edge to Ernie's voice and John can tell that he's angry. "You know I can't get that stuff." And he slams into the kitchen. John gets rid of the insurance guy as quickly as possible, embarrassed and saddened.

Although Ernie mostly acts like there is a future, he is not making commitments toward it. When possible, Ernie invites Helen to come visit and she stays over with John's girlfriend. He wants to be with her, but Ernie won't talk about marriage anymore. He loves Helen deeply and sometimes being together is painful, knowing they can't plan a future together.

Back on the practice field, Ernie stops his own calisthenics and watches the others scrimmaging. He has been exercising alone for weeks now. He feels great and is in excellent shape. He has built his body back up incredibly well. No one would ever guess how close he was to death. He walks over to Coach Brown...

"Couldn't I just do a little scrimmaging with the team. I feel great. I think I'm in really good shape now.

The Coach is finding it difficult to refuse Ernie. "I know you're in good shape, Ernie, but I can't put you in for contact. It's still too dangerous for you. We'll wait a while longer." Yet Brown knows that a little longer means never and it makes him angry again at Modell to have put him in this position with Ernie, letting him be there every day and work so hard and watch the others and never be able to be part of it. Ernie, too, understands that if it isn't now, it may be never, because he is well aware that the remission is not expected to last forever, and next time... well... he's not going to think about it. That's bad mental activity. He knows better.

Ernie hangs his head for a moment and then picks up his pace as he walks a small ways away and decides to do some running.... to let off a little steam. Then he stops on the other side of the field and cheers the guys on as they scrimmage. He won't give up the ship. Not now, while he is doing so well.

As the days wear on, John comes in from practice more and more depressed each night. He is just a rookie and one with a difficult problem. He has a trick knee, which had put him out of games regularly all through college. It had held back his potential. Now he is finding that the stress and direction of pro ball makes him wonder whether, everything considered, he should be here at all. In college Schwartzwalder had run the ball a lot and since John was a tackle, blocking for a running play was what he had been taught to do. Now, in pro ball, it is generally a passing game and blocking for a passing game is a very different technique. One evening he can hold it in no longer and bursts forward with his anger and anguish at the difficulty of it.

"What's the matter?" Ernie, reading a newspaper nearby, asks John.

"I've had it!" exclaims John.

"What happened?" Ernie puts down the paper and gives his full attention to his friend.

"I can't do it. That's all.... I can't play this way. Man.... I don't want this mess. I've had enough of this. This isn't the way I learned to play offensively at Syracuse. If you get too aggressive than the defensive end will just push you aside and go on. You have to pop him, and set up again. You have to be strong enough and quick enough that you pop him to stop him, neutralize him and then set up again to keep him from getting to the quarterback. He's going forward and you're going backwards."

"I can't seem to do anything right. I don't think I'm even going to make the team. I just made the wrong decision. ... That's all." He slams his bag down on the floor.

"Hey, man. You shouldn't give up so easily," says Ernie. "I know it's rough, but you got to keep fighting..." Ernie pauses, then goes on. "Yeh... I know I may not make it... but that doesn't mean I'm going to give up trying."

John Brown

John turns to him in shock. It's so easy to forget Ernie's situation. He so seldom refers to it and never complains. It stops him in his tracks and makes him feel very small, that a little problem on the field has grown so big and important to him when Ernie's problem is huge and he's still trying. That's it. John knows what he has to do. He has the chance Ernie probably will never have again... he's going to work until it's right.

"Thanks, Ern." John says quietly and goes into the kitchen.

He lived such an open strong life, that he taught me, not how to die, but how to live."

John Brown, Cleveland Browns, Pittsburgh Steelers

Chapter 34

For the first time after those endless days in the hospital, Ernie drives up to the gray duplex on Lake Street and finally home. It will be good to sleep in his own bed, to see his Mom and his friends. He is so excited. It doesn't seem possible. There had been a moment, maybe more than a moment, when he had thought that he would never see his home again, but he is feeling really well now. He feels the optimism wash over him. Ernie is all grins when he greets his mother with a great hug.

All her sleepless nights seem to vanish when she sees him. He looks so fine. It is impossible to believe that he could really be sick, and incredible to think that he might not/ won't survive this.

Ernie spends the next few days enjoying his mother's cooking and visiting his friends. He looks perfectly normal. In fact, he looks wonderful and no one can imagine what he has just been through for the last month. His appetite has returned and he is keeping up his exercises. He knows how important it is to stay in perfect shape, not just for the game of football now, but for the game of life. He still believes that somehow if he puts everything into it, he can beat it. The doctors have explained to him about the new drugs they are using and he realizes that his strong body may make it more possible for him to tolerate the drugs that have killed the cancer cells. But can they keep doing it? Ernie's body has not failed him yet. So far it is reigning victorious against the invading army of cancerous cells. Why couldn't it win in the end? Where there is life, there is hope and Ernie feels the new hope of life surging through his strong young body. Now Ernie understands the value of every minute and takes every opportunity to share himself with everyone who might need his support.

Not long after his arrival, Mrs. Williams calls Marie. Her daughter Bev and Ernie went to high school together and she is a friend of Marie's.

"Bev is having some kind of trouble," she tells her friend. "The doctors want her to go to Rochester for some tests, but I don't know how I'll get her there."

Of course Ernie knows very well who Bev is, so when Marie mentions the problem to him, he immediately offers to drive her to Rochester. Ernie arrives to pick up Bev and her mother, looking marvelous in his short-sleeved dark blue shirt and white pants, his coffee brown skin glowing with good health and his grin wide as ever. She cannot resist feeling a little more upbeat.

Bev is very nervous about the blood tests she is supposed to have. They've told her she might have a blood disease. Ernie, seeing her worried face, reaches over and reassures her."

"Just don't worry about it. We all have a blood disease," he kids her and smiles. His lightness is reassuring even though she hasn't heard about Ernie's disease and doesn't understand the meaning of it.

"Maybe I shouldn't be so worried," she agrees, as they speed off into a beautiful sun sprinkled day.

Ernie drops them off at Strong Memorial Hospital, then parks the car to wait. It seems strange to be waiting for someone else's tests and not his own. Finally Bev appears from behind the door.

"Well, how'd it go?" He rises to let her in.

"It wasn't what they thought," she answers with relief.

"I told you so," Ernie grins at her.

The sun is radiating its own joy on this late fall day, as Bev, Mrs. Williams and Ernie pass through Geneva and start down the lake road with its exquisite view of the thirty five mile long Seneca Lake. The vineyards along either side of the road are already ripening with juicy purple grapes some have even been harvested, filling the air with their pungent perfumes where grapes have fallen and been trampled on by the workers in the fields. Ernie is bursting with his love of life as he looks over the tranquil scene. He is even enjoying the warmth of the sun beating down on his bare arm resting at the open window and the song of the birds as they carry on their fall preparations. He is so glad to be alive, nothing can shadow this moment of vitality. Ernie's off pitch voice breaks out in a loud and joyous song as Bev, sitting beside him giggles, catching his contagious delight in the world around him. Her relief at the reprieve from her worries bubbles out of her too.

Toward the end of the lake, as their car descends the hill into Watkins Glen, there is a strange noise competing with Ernie's song.

"Opps, I think we've got a flat tire," surmises Ernie, still grinning.

Bev giggles inappropriately, but nothing can spoil this superb day. Ernie pulls the car over, cheerful as can be.

"Now you two just sit there," he says. "I'll take care of this." He jumps out of the car and goes about pleasantly changing the tire, while humming to himself.

Once more life seems back to normal to Marie as she hears Ernie in the shower – singing away as usual. Then off he goes, without saying much about his endeavor. He's on his way to the Reformatory in Elmira where he plays basketball with the inmates, since his college days. They are all thrilled and some won't forget it for a lifetime. Many have heard of his condition and admire him even more for that. Their sentences don't seem so bad to them as Ernie's. The administration doesn't let a lot of outside volunteers in to work with the incarcerated young men, most of whom are under 20, African American, from New York City, but it seems to have such a positive effect on the inmates that Ernie is always welcome. The inmates write about him, letters to him and some even paint his picture.

To keep in shape, Ernie goes out on the EFA field near his house and runs around the track. All the kids in the neighborhood show up. It's as though someone rang a bell out in the streets to let them know that Ernie is home and where he is. They follow him around the track and can barely keep up, even though they are running forward and he is running backwards. Then Ernie goes up and down the bleachers and the kids follow. He encourages them and talks with them, trying to include them when possible and still keep up his daily exercises.

In the evening Ernie goes over to Green Pastures to see the Coleman brothers and other friends. The beers go around, but Ernie still orders coke. He doesn't want to drink alcohol when he is in training. And as far as Ernie is concerned he is always in training. When the waitress takes his order, she suddenly bursts into tears. He touches her arm. "Hey, don't believe everything you hear. They haven't got me in my grave yet."

Ernie has still not told Betty about Helen. He had gone home one weekend from Syracuse after he had met Helen, but just didn't get around to it. It seemed easier to let things drift, the way they had. Now he supposes it doesn't make any difference. At least he won't have to hurt her... he thinks. They visit and their friendship is still strong. He enjoys her family that is still family to him. He doesn't want to talk with them about his illness and they don't push.

Ernie goes up to Syracuse to visit. He has not spent much time with Helen since he got sick. He just doesn't know what to say to her. They were planning marriage, but he knows he won't do it now. He wants to leave her free. She tries to be strong, but it's hard. She would marry him anyway... no matter what.

Back in Cleveland Ernie is rarin' to go again. Jim Brown is sitting with him in his apartment.

"You know, Ernie, you are just a pawn for these guys."

"I don't believe that," responds Ernie.

"Why do you think that Coach won't play you?"

"I think he's afraid I might get hurt...."

"Don't kid yourself. It's not really about you. He just doesn't like it that Modell says you should play. They're just using you in their battle for power with each other..."

"I think they're both trying to do what they think is right." Ernie closes the discussion here.

Ernie is more interested in giving back than getting angry about things he can't change. When Ernie gets a chance, he visits children with leukemia in the hospital.

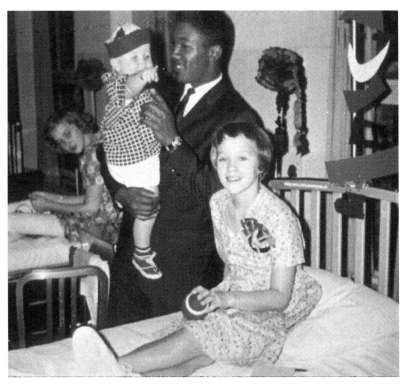

Ernie visiting children sick with leukemia

Ben asks Ernie to join him in December on a recruiting trip. Ernie, Ben and Bill Bell get out of the car into a terrible snowstorm and Ernie rings the doorbell of the house.

A woman answers the door and pulls Ernie in out of the blowing snow. The others follow... stamping their feet on the mat before they enter.

"Oh, you must be Ernie Davis," the woman is quite excited and almost ignores the others. "Floyd" she yells. "The people from Syracuse are here."

Three girls enter the room giggling and staring at Ernie.

"We're so glad to be here, Mrs. Little. Syracuse has heard some wonderful things about Floyd's abilities. Are these his sisters?"

Ernie puts out his hand to them. They move forward, one at a time and take it, both embarrassed and thrilled.

"Y'all take their coats for them, girls. You folks sit right down and I'll git you somethin to drink."

The men hand their coats over to the girls as Floyd enters. Ernie starts right away selling Syracuse.

"You know they need a good runner like you, Floyd... and Syracuse knows how to treat their players right... They want you to wear number 44. I'd be honored if you would."

Floyd is already seriously considering Notre Dame, but being offered Ernie's infamous number by Ernie Davis himself is very tempting. He still has time to give it some thought, though.

Ernie doesn't want to be away from Cleveland long. He feels a significant commitment both for the team and for the pay that he is receiving. Mackey is able to keep his promise and arrives in Cleveland while it is still winter to visit Ernie. The Syracuse football season is over and he's ready for some fun and relaxation. He had been apprehensive, hearing the rumors about Ernie's illness. But now, seeing him, he can hardly believe them. Ernie looks as strong and full of fun as ever. It must all be a mistake.

They head off to a movie and this time, Ernie assures Mackey that, not only does he have enough money to pay for his own movie, but he's treating Mackey too. Mac doesn't object, having already heard what kind of money Ernie is making.

"You know, Mac, if you come and play with the Browns next year, we'll be rookies together."

"Gee, Ern, I hadn't thought of that. We'll finally be able to see who's really best." They both laugh. Just then a man passes them on the street. He stares at them, turning around as they go by. Then he calls after them.

"Hey, are you Ernie Davis?"

"Naw... I just look a little like him."

The man starts to walk away, then stops and walks back to them.

"Yeh, well that's lucky," he says. You sure wouldn't want to be that guy, cause he's going to be dead within a year. Some say a lot sooner."

When Ernie and Mackey don't respond, he just keeps on talking with a little laugh and starts walking beside them. "Hey can you beat that." He figures he has a good audience now. "What a goddamn shame that this guy gets all that money and he isn't even going to play a stitch of ball for it."

Ernie ignores the man and speaks out of the side of his mouth to Mackey.

"Just keep walking... he'll get bored."

In the soda shop after the movie, Ernie and Mackey are indulging in some giant sized chocolate milk shakes.   Mackey   broaches   the awkward topic for the first time. "Ernie, ... you know what that man said, ... out there on the street before the movie... just suppose it was true..."

"Hey don't believe what they say...."

Yeh, but if it was true,... what would you do?" Mackey is determined to find out more about his friend's feelings."

"I wouldn't do anything different than I'm doing now. Just live my life as it is...as though it will go on forever."

Not long after Mackey goes back to Syracuse, Ernie gives an interview to a reporter that asks him a similar question. He asks how Ernie feels about what has happened to him.

"Some people say I'm unlucky," responds Ernie and it becomes an unforgettable headline. "I don't believe it... when I look back, I can't call myself unlucky. Many people haven't experienced as much in their long lives as I have in my short one."

Winter is long, but Ernie doesn't mind... every minute is for living. Now, the dreaded moment has come. Ernie looks into the sink one day in early Spring and he sees it coming to an end. This time he knows just what it means when he finds blood as he brushes his teeth; and the nose bleeds, he knows what they mean too.   He has just finished shaving when John Brown walks in on Ernie who is wiping the blood off the sink. His face is a mask. He tries to hide his horror from John. But John sees the signs and his heart aches. Half an hour later, Ernie is dressed up and packing his bag. He comes downstairs and speaks only briefly to John.

"I'm going to be gone for a few days. If anyone asks about me, tell them I'm on a trip...."

In the hospital Dr. Weisberger walks back into the examining room where Ernie is waiting for him. He keeps it brief. "I'm sorry, Ernie. The remission is over."

"Darn!" is all Ernie says.

They make a room available for Ernie and immediately hook him up to a bottle of blood for his transfusion. He is reading a book. "The God Who Failed." Dr. Weisberger, who walks back into the room to check on Ernie notices it, and wonders, but later finds out it is simply a political book. Apparently he had picked it up because of the title.

He explains to Ernie that the original diagnosis in August had not been exact and that Hopkins had found a more precise one and it was that, plus a new series of chemo that had given him the remission. He continues that, although it is not likely at this point to have another remission, the treatments may still help him for a while.

Ernie nods. He has reached a level of acceptance and is not surprised by the explanation. He is only happy for each day that remains... and happy too, when Weisberger informs him that he won't necessarily have to stay in the hospital all the time. In fact, he assures him. Much of the time, when he is doing well, he can be back at his apartment or visiting friends in Elmira or whatever.

"Do what you want now, Ernie, while you're feeling well enough to."

Ernie nods, thanks him and goes back to his book.

Chapter 35

A few crocuses break through the snow.

Daffodils are opening.

Robins are pulling worms out of the softened ground.

The sun is shinning through newly budded trees.

Ernie remembers how beautiful Syracuse can be this time of year, perhaps more so because of its cold bitter dark winters. Life opens up again and begins over. Ernie believes in the renewal. He is grateful for his church, his upbringing, his beliefs in eternal life. He hopes that he has done the best he possibly can. He has tried. He is ready if this is the way it has to be.

The Alumni team is suited up to play at the Spring Alumni game at the Syracuse Stadium. All his old buddies are there, those he played with and those from previous years. Ernie is with them, but he's wearing a suit with a trench coat over it. The team races out onto the field and Ernie bends down on one knee at the sideline with the Alumni coaches. He shouts encouragement to them.

At one point the refs take Sweeney out of the game for an infraction. Ernie races out onto the field and talks frantically with the referee.

"It's not fair to him," says Ernie. "Just have him sit out this play, but don't take him out of the whole game. He's been waiting all year for this game....."

"Okay, Ernie. If you say so...."

The ref signals something to the others and the loud speaker announces a change in the call. Ernie returns to the sidelines with a grin on his face and continues to shout advice to the players.

Several people come by, tap him on the shoulder and ask how he is...

"How's it going, Ernie?..."

"Oh, great... couldn't be better."

"How you feeling?" says another.

"Aw, I'm fine... Looking forward to being in next year's game."

But Ernie doesn't look fine and most of his friends can see it. His overcoat can't hide his swollen neck or how much thinner he has gotten. It hangs loosely on him. And the pallor is obvious. Brian comes in from a play and stops beside Ernie

"Hey, Ernie, you goin to be in town overnight?"

"Sure..."

"Stop by tomorrow and visit with me and my wife."

"Love to, Brian. Is 11AM okay? "

"Great!"

The next day Brian's doorbell rings, precisely at 11. He greets Ernie and takes his coat. Now he can see how loosely his clothes are hanging on him. He notices how gray his skin looks and his breath catches for a moment. Then he goes to hang up the coat.

They sit on the couch making small talk. They're all drinking sodas and laughing. Suddenly Ernie turns very serious.

"You know, Brian, I'm going to die."

Silence! Brian is shocked. Of course he knows the situation, but he never expected Ernie to say that.

"Oh no, you're going to be just fine. You'll lick this."

"No..." insists Ernie, "I'm really going to die. That's just the way it is."

"Oh, I don't think...." Brian tries again, but Ernie is determined to say it and get it out.

"I know it..."

"Well," Brian laughs nervously, "then you be sure to leave me your three piece suit. You know it looks a lot better on me than on you..."

Ernie lets go. He has said what he had to say, to someone. He had to hear himself say those ultimate words.

"You got it..." he says and breaks into the grin that is so Ernie, that is still Ernie even in the most dire of circumstances.

"Well," says Ernie, "how do you think the ole guys did out there yesterday, meaning you too, obviously...."

A week later, John returns home from playing basketball. He enters the kitchen and finds a note on the table: "I'm going into the hospital for a few days. Tell anyone who asks, I'm on a trip. See you around."

Ernie drops in Art Modell's office on his way to the hospital.

"Just wanted to stop by. I have to go into the hospital for a few days. I'm really sorry about it."

"It's no problem, Ernie. You know that we understand.

"It's just that I hate letting you down. You've been so good to me. I just wanted to thank you for everything... you know... Letting me work out with the guys, paying my hospital bills... everything you've done."

Modell is a bit taken back. He didn't expect this conversation and doesn't know what to say.

Several days later Ernie is lying on the hospital bed, perfectly still. His eyes are closed. He has an oxygen tent and there are tubes hooked up to him. A nurse and doctor stand by watching the machines in hushed silence. Ernie's body shakes as he coughs once. There is blood seeping from his mouth and he is still. Both the nurse and doctor begin to cry.

News travels fast:

Art Modell's home phone rings. He is in bed. He picks it up. He begins to cry as he sets it down, not saying a word, into the phone.

Art Radford is woken by the phone. Marie can barely talk. She is crying as she speaks. All she can manage to say to him is: "He's dead."

Chuck Davis picks up the phone and listens only. Then he puts his coat on and walks and walks through New York City. Finally he arrives at his brother's house. Both of them have tears in their eyes as minutes later they climb into a car and drive off.

John Brown is sitting in a bar and having a great time. He looks at the clock. It is two in the morning. He shivers. Later driving home with friends he wants to listen to the radio and they kept turning it off. Finally after he drops them off, he finds a station and settles on it:

"Ernie Davis, the greatly beloved football player, first Negro to win the Heisman trophy, died tonight at Marymount Hospital in Cleveland at approximately two in the morning. Ernie became renowned as a half back at Syracuse....."

John switches off the radio and keeps driving.... tears pouring down his face. As he pulls up at his house and climbs out of the car he is assaulted by reporters. He can barely face them.

Angie's phone rings. She turns on the light and looks at the clock that says 2 something. It's her sister Mary; they both start crying hysterically.

"Why Ernie," says Angie. "He was so good. He never did a bad thing to anyone. I can't stand it....."

Next day others find out the news:

Tony DeFillippo weeps at his desk.

Marty Harrigan throws himself crying into his wife's arms.

Ben Schwartzwalder lights a cigar, walks onto his porch and just holds it without puffing. Tears run down his face.

Phil Davis is handed a newspaper by his friend. He looks at it, sets it down and dry-eyed tells his friend: "Well, if he thought I should go back to school, I'll do it... If he could live with all his problems and still be thinking of me... I guess I can live with my little ones." Then tears well up in his eyes.

Another student finds Floyd Little in his college dorm room.

"Hey, you met Ernie Davis once didn't you?

"Yeh, he came to my house to recruit me for Syracuse."

"Well, I just heard the news over the radio. He died."

Floyd is stunned. Tears well up in his eyes. As soon as he gets it under control he calls Syracuse and asks for Ben Schwartzwalder.

"Mr. Schwartzwalder? This is Floyd Little. I heard about Ernie. I just want you to know that I've made up my mind. He wanted me to come to Syracuse. My answer is yes, I want to come, I want to play halfback and wear number 44."

He hangs up and begins to cry again.

Three days later at the Elmira airport a plane lands. It's pouring rain. The doors open and the whole Cleveland Brown's team, unsmiling, comes down the ramp. They head to the Neighborhood House. A line of people are standing in the rain. The line grows rapidly as over 10,000 people wait to give their last regards to their hero, Ernie Davis. The line winds around the streets for blocks and ends up entering and exiting the Neighborhood House where Ernie is lying. The streets are silent except for the incessant rain and the loud speaker, over which Rev. Latta Thomas's voice is being amplified. Familiar and unfamiliar faces pass by as those who played a part in Ernie's life pass by to pay their last respects. As the sound of Rev. Thomas's voice reverberates, the faces of every color and shade of color pass by and have their last look at Ernie.

Rev. Latta Thomas eulogizes Ernie:

"The greatest lives are those which have exhibited translucence and self-subordination. Translucence is like the electric light bulb, it shines, because it allows the light to come through it. It seeks never to claim to be the source of the light, nor to possess the light for its own ends alone. Great lives are like this in that they reach beyond themselves for their spiritual strength and moral guidance. They have become divested of the desire to pretend to be self-sufficient."

"The world often stands in questioning awe when it sees the wedding of greatness and humility in the human spirit without realizing that it is the humility which made the greatness genuine and beautiful. For, you see, when one allows himself to be placed in proper focus spiritually, there is removed from him paralyzing egotism and festering covetousness. Then he is able to live like a freely flowing stream which has both a living source and a free outlet, not as a stagnant pool which has neither of these."

When the visitation is finally finished people enter their cars and accompany Ernie to his resting place in Woodlawn Cemetery. They wind slowly through the streets of Elmira then into the cemetery and finally past a sign that denotes Mark Twain's grave. At every window along the way, curtains are pulled aside and huge, sad eyes peer through tear/rain soaked windowpanes.

At the gravesite, there are already people moving towards it. A little boy, holding his mother's hand looks around and says in awe. "I'll bet he's the best person buried in this cemetery."

Rev. Latta Thomas's voice rises again:

"During those primary and secondary school days Ernie demonstrated other concerns besides his athletic successes. It was not unusual to see a shy quiet, but affable lad sitting in church school, somewhere near the back of the room. Neither was it uncommon to observe this same young lad taking his seat at the Baptist Youth Fellowship meeting. That lad was Ernie Davis, and as the years faded, some of the shyness and much of the quietness gave way to a sincere inquisitiveness, and a profound respect for fact. He questioned... how should I go about determining my life's occupation? Is evil bound to lose and good bound to win? How will I know my duty in life?"

"His community was elated to learn of his decision to attend Syracuse University. It is well known that the history he etched into our memory there will survive many generations. However, it was the person there that commanded notice in its own right, aside from Ernie Davis, the great athlete, for he was possessed of a stabilizing quality too rare in some to whom fame has come, namely humility."

"For those of us who loved and admired the man and the athlete, and longed to see the full face and free smile of this Mr. Inspiration on television sets and from grandstands for a long time to come, the disappointment and pain is great."

"Yet heaven did not cheat us. For anytime we in this world are brought aspiration, inspiration and joy by a life, however short, we are not cheated, we are blessed. And the life of Ernie Davis brought us there."

The crowd begins to sing, "Amazing Grace" and Ernie is released, however reluctantly, by those who remain after him.

THE END

ACKNOWLEDGEMENTS

Thanks to the many wonderful people who shared their personal memories of Ernie Davis and their times spent with him.

John Brown, John Mackey, Art Baker, Jim Brown, Pete Brokaw, Dave Sarette, Floyd Little, Ger Schwedes, Dick Easterly, Bob Szombathy, Sims, Les Dye, Ted Daily, Ben Schwarzwalder, Art Modell, Val Pinchbeck, Brian Howard, Paul Paolisso.

Chuck Prettyman, Bill "Will" Fitzgerald, Leo Hughey, Coach and Mrs. Marty Harrigan, Coach and Mrs. Snowden, Betty Snowden, Coach Flynn, Coach Wipfler, Bev Williams, Margaret "Mugsie" Burch, Atty. Jack Moore, Rolley Coleman, Howie Coleman, Buzzy Sparks, Jack Moore, George Williams, Mrs. Celia Hutchinson, Jeannie Conklin, Al Mallette.

Chuck Davis, Angie Davis, Will Davis, Marie (Radford) Fleming, Sandy Stevens, Art Radford, Bud Fleming.

Dr. Hobart Burch, Dr. Schneider, Dr. Ippolito, Dr. Coviello. Dr. Siegler

Atty. Tony DeFillippo, Atty. Fred DeFillippo, Atty. Gerald DeFillippo

Special thanks to Robert Welton for proofing of the inaugural edition.

Many more of you told me stories, anecdotes and other information about Ernie and your experiences with him, that have found their way into this story. Thank you so much for your help.

For further stories and information please see our website: www.erniedavis.info.

A HALO FOR A HELMET

Complete Biography of Ernie Davis

First Black to Win the Heisman Trophy

by K. Coralee Burch, Ph. D.

Copyright September 10, 2008

SUMMARY

This is the life story of one of the greatest athletes to ever live. Ernie Davis was the first African American to win the Heisman Trophy, recruited to the Cleveland Browns at the highest package ever given in the NFL, and expected to be a running back playing in the backfield with another great African American athlete, Jim Brown. He died of acute leukemia before he could ever play a game in the NFL. In spite of his youth and his incomplete athletic history, Ernie remained an inspiration in the hearts of everyone who met him, knew him or had seen him play. It was not for Ernie's fabulous athletic performances or his exceptional abilities that he is remembered and venerated, but for his loving nature, humility, fairness, honesty and goodness that he took a place in the hearts of every race of his generation. This is a story long waiting to be told. How did Ernie become such a man, and touch the hearts of all in so few years? What brought this poor minority stuttering fatherless boy to the heights Ernie achieved in an environment that had great difficulty getting past the superficiality of his beautiful cocoa colored skin? What made a generation of Americans think twice about the ridiculousness of prejudice? This is a story also of the less obvious, but dramatically pervasive prejudice and discrimination in the North in the 50s.... so little talked about in White circles, so obviously felt among the Black population.

Made in the USA
Monee, IL
15 July 2020